AF361511

The War Comes with You

THE WAR COMES WITH YOU

Enduring War in Life, Fiction, and Fantasy

STACEY PEEBLES

Published by the University of South Carolina Press
Columbia, South Carolina 29208

uscpress.com

Printed in the United States of America

Library of Congress Cataloging-in-Publication Data
can be found at https://lccn.loc.gov/2024035437

ISBN: 978-1-64336-514-5 (hardcover)
ISBN: 978-1-64336-515-2 (paperback)
ISBN: 978-1-64336-516-9 (ebook)

Contents

List of Illustrations

Acknowledgments

Thanks to Aurora Bell, who deserves a place in the corps d'elite of editors. She encouraged this project from its inception and provided invaluable guidance along the way, always with good information, good support, and good humor.

Thanks to Aaron DeRosa, who conceived the idea for a special issue of *Modern Fiction Studies* devoted to representations of contemporary war and brought me into the project. Several of the authors whose work is featured in that issue—Brenda Sanfilippo, Patrick Deer, Roger Luckhurst, Alex Vernon, and Jennifer Haytock—are referenced in this book, and the special issue was a great way to think about the central concerns of this evolving field. Thanks also to Jennifer for including me in her *War and American Literature* collection, which allowed me to develop the argument that I make more fully in this book.

Thanks to Peter Molin, whose breadth of knowledge about contemporary war writing is unparalleled, and who has boundless enthusiasm for keeping this collective conversation going. I vividly remember telling him my idea for this project one afternoon at an American Literature Association conference. "Write that book," he responded unequivocally. Peter has a great gift for encouragement, and I'm certainly not the only one who has benefited from it.

Thanks to Mauricio Castro for reading chapter 5 and giving me significant guidance on Star Wars and Marvel, and thanks to Sami Sweis for reading chapter 4 and patiently (very patiently) coaching me into an understanding of the Arabic literary tradition and proper transliteration for Arabic names, terms, and titles. I'm lucky to work at a place like Centre College, where stars like these are just a few office doors away.

Thanks to Brian Williams, Ty Hawkins, Alex Vernon, Patrick Deer, and Hilary Lithgow for all the projects we have worked on together, and for their terrific collegiality and friendship.

Thanks to my friends at Centre who listen with support and often actual interest as I describe wrestling with arguments and fretting over deadlines: Tara Strauch, Sara Egge, Mary Daniels, Lee Jefferson, Robyn Cutright, Danielle LaLonde, Jenn Goetz, John Harney, Jamie Shenton, Kaelyn Wiles, Mei Li Inouye, and Eva Cadavid, among others.

Thanks to Tom Palaima, for his many years of mentoring and friendship, and for inspiring my interest in war and storytelling.

Thanks to Mom, Dad, and Willie, for their love and support. And thanks to Calliope, who is just the best. (And who suggested this wording.)

Sections of the introduction first appeared in a different form in the following:

Aaron DeRosa and Stacey Peebles. "Enduring Operations: Narratives of the Contemporary Wars." *Modern Fiction Studies* 63, no. 2 (2017): 203–24. Copyright © 2017 Purdue Research Foundation by Johns Hopkins University Press. Reprinted with permission of Johns Hopkins University Press.
Stacey Peebles. "The Forever Wars." In *War and American Literature*, edited by Jennifer Haytock, 254–70. Cambridge: Cambridge University Press, 2021. Copyright © Stacey Peebles. Reprinted by permission.

Sections of chapters 1, 2, and 3 were originally published in a different form in the following:

Stacey Peebles. "The War Comes with You: Twenty-First-Century War Memoir." In *The Many Faces of War*, edited by Lawrence Tritle, 107–24. Los Angeles: Marymount Institute Press, 2018.

Sections of chapter 5 were originally published in a different form in the following:

Stacey Peebles. "21st-Century Star Wars: Profiles in (Female) Courage." In *Contemporary American Science Fiction Film*, edited by Stuart Joy and Terence McSweeney, 128–41. London: Routledge, 2022. Copyright © 2022 by Routledge. Reprinted by permission of Taylor & Francis Group.

Excerpts from poems by Brian Turner:

Brian Turner, excerpts from "Historians," "Metal Fume Fever," "The Weight," "Central Park in the Spring," and "All Our Lazy Sundays" from *The Dead Peasant's Handbook*. New Gloucester, ME: Alice James Books, 2023. Copyright © 2023 by Brian Turner. Reprinted with the permission of The Permissions Company LLC on behalf of Alice James Books, alicejamesbooks.org.

Introduction

Harbingers of a New Era

The eighty-second Oscars were a hot race. The 2009 Academy Awards ceremony was the first to feature a slate of ten Best Picture nominees, as opposed to the five previously considered, a move by the Academy aimed at including more widely popular films. And a popular film was indeed one of the nominees—James Cameron's *Avatar* had become the highest-grossing film of all time while also earning widespread acclaim for its groundbreaking use of digital effects and immersive world-building. Cameron's film was up against smaller but notable competition—Quentin Tarantino's *Inglourious Basterds*, Joel and Ethan Coen's *A Serious Man*, Pete Docter and Bob Peterson's *Up*, and Lee Daniel's *Precious*, among several others. But the little movie that became *Avatar*'s biggest competition was *The Hurt Locker*, a war film about an Explosive Ordnance Disposal team working in Iraq. Starring Jeremy Renner, the film was directed by Kathryn Bigelow and was based on a screenplay by Mark Boal. The fact that Cameron had directed a visual effects extravaganza about fantasy war while Bigelow chose a contemporary, realistic war story based on real-life reporting by Boal—and that Cameron and Bigelow used to be married—was not lost on the media.

In the end, it was the little war movie, and not the big one, that prevailed, winning six Oscars, including ones for Best Picture and Best Director for Bigelow. In doing so, she became the first woman to win the latter award (something that didn't happen again until Chloé Zhao won for *Nomadland* in 2020/2021). *The Hurt Locker* itself claimed a somewhat more dubious distinction—it became the lowest-grossing film to ever win Best Picture, though it achieved that honor over the highest-grossing film of all time.

A decade and a half later, that dichotomy continues to define the field of contemporary war stories. *The Hurt Locker* appeared at a time when literature and films about contemporary war were still relatively sparse—by 2012, it had a lot more company. That year saw the beginning of a surge of acclaimed representations that included Ben Fountain's novel *Billy Lynn's Long Halftime Walk* and Kevin Powers's novel *The Yellow Birds*. Phil Klay's short story collection *Redeployment* won the National Book Award two years later, and the field continued to grow apace. And yet despite the variety of artistic representations dealing with the relevant and pressing issues related to the wars in Iraq and Afghanistan—a variety that has inspired its own rich critical conversation as well—this has not been a genre that has commanded a great deal of public attention. (A notable exception has been Clint Eastwood's film adaptation *American Sniper*, a narrative that traffics heavily in both clarity and satisfaction, as I will discuss in the Conclusion.)

Instead, for stories about war, audiences head to superhero movies, a genre bubble that rivals the 1950s- and 1960s-era Western for its popularity and ubiquity. As more realistic representations have explored the changing nature of conflict in their depictions of the military-civilian divide, physical and mental trauma, the increasing presence of female soldiers, and the globalization of contemporary war, science fiction and fantasy films have addressed comparable issues. These narratives are similar in implication if not in affect—both the ubiquitous superhero genre and recent Star Wars films are also portraying how one prepares for and engages in combat, how gender affects a soldier's identity, the political and moral implications of war, and how one understands the enemy. These fantasy films, then, deal with surprisingly challenging content, though they do so with plot developments and resolution that are often decidedly more comforting, and less provocative, than their realistic counterparts. There's a reason, after all, that the real money is in light sabers and super serum rather than IEDs.

But whether the context is historical or fantasy, the wars are ongoing—"forever wars" in every sense. The defining characteristic of these war stories is a lack of delineation, evident not just in the absent temporal boundaries of wars that seem to go on and on, but also blurred spatial, personal, and collective boundaries as well. Here, combat violence overtakes civilian spaces, crosses borders and other cultural demarcations, and even disrupts chronology. In consequence, many of these narratives feature fragmentation as a prominent trope—of language, of a character's identity, of bodies, and of the story itself—as typical scaffolding falls away. That fragmentation is taken to an even greater degree in Iraqi-authored works about the war, many of which have only recently been available in translation. But while some American works suggest the practice of renunciation as a possible response to the personal devastation that war can cause, Iraqi literature develops a different and complex engagement with storytelling and an emphasis on collective imagination. These characteristics are different in many senses from those defining the earliest works about the post-9/11 wars, the first wave of representations that I explored in my previous book *Welcome to the Suck*—more about that distinction below.

That an individual can be traumatized and experience a sense of psychological or temporal fragmentation as a result is nothing new to war narratives, but here I want to draw together the various kinds of fragmentation evident in these stories as symptoms of a larger-scale problem—an inability to contain war within traditional modes of delineation, which is a failure that takes place on personal, cultural, and national levels. Several scholars have identified the centrality of various kinds of fragmentation in contemporary American war literature. Roger Luckhurst describes "the temporal disadjustment of narrative" found in novels such as Atticus Lish's *Preparation for the Next Life* (2014), Michael Pitre's *Fives and Twenty-Fives* (2014), and Fountain's *Billy Lynn*. Luckhurst notes other modes of fragmentation or confusion in these works as well, observing, for example, how the proliferation of drones "disembodies the experience of the unfolding war" because it takes the pilot so completely out of the war zone. Thus "American bodies disappear but Middle Eastern ones are increasingly realized only as targets" ("Iraq War" 363). Patrick Deer has linked a sense of fragmentation to the conflation of wartime with everyday life as well as the lack of a broader, comprehensive history about the wars in Iraq and Afghanistan. Whereas earlier, imperial visions of warfare "rested on grand narratives of civilization and progress," more recent war stories "are fragmented and partial, boundaries between civilian and military are blurred, and a coherent historical narrative for the wars has yet to emerge" ("Mapping" 51). And Brian Williams has identified a kind of spatial confusion in contemporary war texts, what he calls anatopism: "the presence of items that seem spatially out of place, as foreign to their location as anachronisms are foreign to their times" ("The Desert" 360). Williams describes a scene in *The Hurt Locker*, when Sgt. First Class William James (Jeremy Renner) invades an Iraqi residence and finds it domestic and tastefully decorated, outfitted with appliances and electronics that he might have in his own home. "As the amorphous nature of the war on terror challenges traditional definitions of 'home' and 'enemy,'" Williams writes, "globalization produces traces of the familiar in an unknown environment, where participation in a global marketplace of ideas and technology re-creates the conditions of home—bringing traumatic anatopisms into a landscape the combatant has been led to view as 'uncivilized'" (361). Just as Williams describes those encounters as uncanny, the unsettling identification of elements oddly out of place, many of these second-wave narratives have that same effect. When things fall apart, after all, it can happen in a variety of ways, some that are familiar and some that are more surprising. In what follows, I will trace these various forms of fragmentation and link them to a lack of delineation evinced, among other ways, by a globalized culture thoroughly suffused by war and militarization.

Everywhere War, All the Time

In the years since 9/11, war has permeated society at many levels, although it is often not as immediately noticeable as it was when the nation underwent a full-scale mobilization in World War II, for instance, or when everyone was talking about the draft, the protests, and the war on the evening news during the Vietnam years. In the second decade of the Iraq War and the War in Afghanistan, it was often unclear exactly what was happening. How many troops are at war, and who are they? Are they still fighting? How long will this go on? After the 2007 surge, President George W. Bush announced plans for eventual troop withdrawal from Iraq, a plan codified in the 2008 Status of Forces Agreement. Remaining servicepeople were formally withdrawn on December 18, 2011, although President Barack Obama recommitted troops in 2014 as a result of the subsequent rise of the Islamic State. And although the Iraqi parliament voted to require foreign troops to leave in January 2020, US troops currently remain in Iraq to assist the Iraqi military. Brown University's Costs of War project tracks numbers of deaths directly related to war, and as of August 2021, reports that 4,598 US military personnel and between 185,831 and 208,964 civilians have died as a result of the Iraq War; their total, which also includes others such as journalists and humanitarian workers, comes to 275,000–306,000 (Watson Institute). Writing in the *Military Times* in 2020, Neta Crawford notes that "about 4.1 million post-9/11 war veterans are receiving medical care and disability and other compensation. Roughly half the spending for those veterans is Iraq related, with the total nearing $199 billion." She adds that the total bill for the Iraq War would be about $1.92 trillion in current dollars, an amount that includes funding for the war, State Department spending on Iraq, veterans' care, and interest on debt taken on to fund sixteen years of military involvement.

In Afghanistan, the United States announced plans to draw down troops after Osama bin Laden was killed by a US special operations team in 2011. The Taliban gained strength as troops prepared to depart, and in August 2021, they seized control as the United States made a chaotic exit at the end of the month, drawing sharp criticism, especially given the similarly large numbers of lives lost and money spent. "The costs of the war were immense," reported the *Washington Post*, "lasting through four administrations—more than 2,400 U.S. military deaths and tens of thousands of Afghans killed, and trillions of defense and development dollars spent. Yet at the end of the day, the final departure returned Afghanistan to the undisputed rule of the Taliban, the Islamic fundamentalist militants whom U.S. forces ousted from power in 2001 and battled for nearly two decades" (DeYoung et al.).

Given the length of these wars, it is not surprising that commentators would emphasize their seemingly unending nature. *The Forever War* was not a new term when Dexter Filkins used it as the title of his 2008 nonfiction book about Iraq and Afghanistan—James Pinkney Harrison and Trần Văn Đôn used the similar phrase "endless war" in the titles of their books about the Vietnam War—but it has become a common way to refer to America's twenty-first-century conflicts, as in *Newsweek*'s 2021 story "Why America Can't End Its 'Forever Wars'" (Arkin). That expanded temporal scale has been accompanied by an expanded sense of the spaces of war as well. The United States has carried out smaller-scale military operations in countries like Syria, Somalia, Libya, Yemen—the Costs of War project lists 85 countries where the United States undertook counterterrorism operations just in 2018–2020 (Watson Institute). Most recently, the United States has provided money, weapons, and military advising to Ukraine after Russia invaded in February 2022, and support during the Israel-Hamas conflict that began October 7, 2023. Even a truncated list of countries and cities where America has conducted operations, Derek Gregory writes, "suggest[s] the need to analyse not only 'forever war' but also what we might call 'the everywhere war'" (238–39). Gregory notes that the concept of the battlefield in US military doctrine has been replaced by the broader, multidimensional term "battlespace," and that distinctions between "our" wars and "their" wars, Green Zone and combat zone, and ground war and cyberwar have all become uncertain. "The boundaries are blurred and each bleeds into its other," he notes. As "military violence is loosed from its frames, the conventional ties between war and geography have come undone" (239).

It only follows, then, that the homeland itself is included in this increasingly globalized militarization. The protests following the deaths of George Floyd and Breonna Taylor that spread throughout the United States and the world in the summer of 2020 were an outpouring of outrage—not just about those two lives lost but also about the effects of systemic racism and the militarization of police. The police's tactics and gear have come under particularly scathing scrutiny, as Officer Derek Chauvin knelt on Floyd's neck for eight minutes and forty-six seconds, causing his death, and Taylor was shot in her home by Louisville police officers executing a no-knock search warrant. In some cities police used riot gear and tear gas to subdue protesters, and news flashed images of clashes in Minneapolis, Los Angeles, New York, Chicago, Atlanta, and many other cities. These resulted in widespread attention to overly violent methods and mindsets as well as demands for justice against officers and departments with histories of racist brutality. None of these are new messages—the alarm has been sounding for some time now, particularly with regard to these more extreme police tactics. In its 2014 report, "War Comes Home: The Excessive Militarization of American Policing," the ACLU identifies the problems evident in a police force that has become "unnecessarily and dangerously militarized, in large part through federal programs that have armed state and local law enforcement agencies with the weapons and tactics of war" (2). Police officers are trained to "adopt a 'warrior' mentality and think of the people they are supposed to serve as enemies," and pack flash-bang grenades, battering rams, and armored vehicles (3).

The story of Micah Xavier Johnson serves as an important exemplar of the broader effects of militarization, perhaps even more so than the deaths of Floyd and Taylor.[1] On July 7, 2016, demonstrators gathered in Dallas to protest the recent police shootings of African American men in Minnesota and Louisiana. They rallied to memorialize Philando Castile and Alton Sterling and, as in 2020, bring attention to systemic racism. But the rally went horribly wrong. Johnson, a twenty-five-year-old Army veteran who deployed to Afghanistan in 2013–14, shot twelve police officers at the event, killing five of them and also wounding two civilians. Apparently enraged by the shootings of Castile and Sterling, he responded with his own violence. Using an assault rifle and a handgun, Johnson engaged in a firefight with police until he was cornered in a parking garage and finally killed by a remote-controlled robot carrying a bomb. CNN reported that the killings "reignited the simmering national debate about police-community relations and fairness in the criminal justice system, as well as the larger questions about race and gun control" (Gaouette and Visser).

Notably, Johnson's actions were neither the first nor the last national flashpoint for all these issues. The event is also emblematic of the long shadow of America's contemporary wars. Here, a veteran used military weapons and tactics to do battle with a militarized police force and was killed by a remotely operated explosive—a drone—in a scene that prompted many to wonder about the tangled causes and effects of violence. Ongoing eruptions of violence such as these reveal that the wars haven't remained spatially or temporally contained—they are present in real and destructive ways in public servants' training grounds and in citizens' gun cabinets; for the veterans living with disabilities, emotional trauma, and traumatic brain injury; and in debates about foreign policy, immigration, the use of drones, and presidential elections.

How do war stories reflect this endless, diffused, and destructive violence? In *Welcome to the Suck*, I explored the first wave of representations of the Iraq War, when that conflict still had the shock of the new, and artists were working out how these twenty-first-century wars would compare to ones of their parents' and grandparents' generations.[2] In works including Colby Buzzell's blog-turned-book *My War* (2005), Kayla Williams's memoir *Love My Rifle More Than You* (2005), the film *In the Valley of Elah* (2007), and Brian Turner's collection of poetry *Here, Bullet* (2005), I was struck by the portrayal of soldiers' desire to transcend categorization—to be their own person, challenge societal restrictions, and embrace technology as a means of doing so. Individual soldiers reflected broader cultural interest in identities that are cyborg, hybrid, avatar. But in their stories, that desire is thwarted. The works suggest that war, and particularly the war in Iraq, reinforced categorization and hard boundaries, even as it forced soldiers to confront ruptures of nation, the body, gender, and technology.

However, war narratives appearing in 2011–2012 and beyond—what I call a second wave—appear to tell a different story. In American literature, the novels, short stories, and memoirs demonstrate a stronger focus on the veteran and his or her attempts to frame the war experience within the larger narrative of life both before and after the war. In addition, these later works approach that framing differently from many previous war stories. Samuel Hynes, writing in his influential study of war memoirs in particular, notes that in twentieth-century iterations of the genre, war changes the man (and it is mostly men in the memoirs he examines) but it doesn't stay with him in his civilian life: "a war narrative concerns a separate life that, however vividly it remains in the memory, is not continuous with the life the teller lives as he writes . . . military service is a kind of exile from one's own real life" (8). Elaborating on these ideas, Alex Vernon explains that because being a soldier so often entails a loss of control, of experiencing violent events that "happen to you" rather than as a result of your own agency, veteran memoirists "divorce the period from their larger sense of themselves" in order to "separate or textually enclose that brief moment when the war wrote their lives from the majority of their lives for which they have control, for which they are the 'manly' authors. They must lock the madwoman—the shell-shocked, 'hysterical' self— in the attic" ("Introduction" 20–21).

In this second wave of contemporary war narratives, soldiers are portrayed attempting to accomplish that framing, an enforcing of the boundaries between war and home, soldier-self and civilian-self. But in an ironic reversal of the failed attempts at transcendence that I described in my first book, here the attempts at separation and distinction fail. The war comes with you—not just into life after war, into which memories, behaviors, and sensory associations intrude, but into the lives of those around the soldier and the broader culture as well. That sense of invasion is much more literal in Iraqi-authored works about the war, but is also taken to more extreme narrative heights as stories are retold, nested within one another, and taken up as acts of collective envisioning. And surprisingly, something of that psychological and narrative complexity can also be found in the fantastical storyworlds of the Marvel Cinematic Universe (MCU) and Star Wars, whose very bedrock is—and has always been—war.

Vietnam and Legacy

The narrative patterns and characteristics that I trace here have a number of similarities to representations of the Vietnam War, particularly the confusion and nonlinearity often associated with narratives of trauma. Our understanding of trauma is very much historically and culturally linked to Vietnam—the American Psychiatric Association first included post-traumatic stress disorder in its official diagnostic manual in 1980, and veterans' experiences were no small part of the public's growing awareness of the symptoms of the condition. Luckhurst has noted, in fact, that literature about Vietnam such as that by Tim O'Brien and Michael Herr "helped shape not just any putative trauma aesthetic but the formation of PTSD itself" (*Trauma Question*, 87–88). Pointing out that the term "flashback" can refer to both a symptom of trauma and a cinematic device, Luckhurst further argues that films about the war—in addition to the 1976 made-for-television movie *Sybil*, about a woman with dissociative identity disorder as a result of the abuse she suffered as a child—gave the public an aesthetic and a clinical vocabulary for the consequences of traumatic experience. Late twentieth- and early twenty-first-century cinema often used the flashback as "an intrusive, anachronic image that throws off the linear temporality of the story," a "brutal splicing" that is meant to signal traumatic disturbance (180). If the use of this device is "uncannily mimetic" of how trauma works psychologically, "then it is probably because films like *Sybil* were instrumental in helping formulate the psychological symptoms of mental illnesses linked with traumatic origins" (181). This affected not only stories about the Vietnam War but also understanding of the veterans themselves: "Some ten years before psychiatric papers began to emerge on flashbacks in the Vietnam veteran, the cinema of the conflict was central in shifting the cultural representation of the veteran from violent misfit to traumatized, re-experiencing victim" (184).

The connection between the Vietnam War and trauma is so ingrained that some argue representations of the war are more properly understood as trauma stories, not war stories. Mark Heberle's *A Trauma Artist: Tim O'Brien and the Fiction of Vietnam* (2001) makes this claim, for instance. Heberle writes that "although Vietnam was both a site of traumatization and the origin of O'Brien's subsequent career, his resistance to being characterized as a war writer suggests that 'trauma writer' is a more pertinent label" (xix). In this book-length argument, Heberle traces how O'Brien's writing "mimics the phenomena of constriction, intrusion, hyperarousal, and the like that are characteristic of traumatized survivors and the experiences they have lived through" (xxi). Indeed, O'Brien himself has spoken about Vietnam as just one way out of many to talk about trauma, about the ways that suffering can stay with us. "Nam lived on inside me," he said in a 1994 interview, "and I just called it by another name. Nam, divorce, your father's death—such things live on even though you think you're over them. They come bubbling out" (Mort 1990).

Vietnam as metonym for trauma—for a disrupted story, for something that has gone off the rails and can't immediately be righted again—is also explicable because of the conflict's historical development. Compared to America's twenty-first-century wars, the Vietnam War was something of a slow burn. President John F. Kennedy sent in military advisers in 1959, and President Lyndon Johnson increased the military's presence there after the Gulf of Tonkin incident in 1964. Although there was no formal declaration of war, American troop numbers crept up, from 16,300 in 1963 to 184,300 in 1965 to 536,100 in 1968 (The Gilder-Lehrman Institute). In 1968, the public watched on the nightly news as casualty numbers increased as well, the Tet Offensive was sudden and devastating, and Walter Cronkite famously declared his opinion that the war had become unwinnable. After Richard Nixon was elected in 1969, US forces began to withdraw, and the war ended with the Fall of Saigon in 1975. The war's lengthy buildup was matched by its long cultural drag. Other than *The Green Berets* in 1968, a movie that had all the trappings of a World War II film—including John Wayne in a starring role—Hollywood didn't take up the subject in earnest until 1978 with Michael Cimino's *The Deer Hunter* and Hal Ashby's *Coming Home*. Those opened the floodgates, however, and a multitude of films, memoirs, and novels followed, with Spike Lee's *Da 5 Bloods* (2020) a prominent and more recent example.

Because of that history, most of the most well-known literary and cinematic narratives about the Vietnam War—Philip Caputo's *A Rumor of War* (1977), *Apocalypse Now* (1979), Tim O'Brien's *Going After Cacciato* (1978) and *The Things They Carried* (1990), *First Blood* (1982), and *Platoon* (1986), to name a few—are as much about the war's legacy, its larger meaning, and America's attempts to grapple with it as they are about the experience of fighting the war itself. The most influential articulation of this argument is John Hellmann's *American Myth and the Legacy of Vietnam* (1986), in which he traces the mythic understandings that soldiers took to war and the stories that attempt to revise and reinscribe that myth in the war's devastating aftermath. Hellmann writes of novels and memoirs by O'Brien, Caputo, Ron Kovic, William Turner Huggett, and James Webb that "Vietnam resonates against the American mythic landscape carried in the consciousness of the protagonist" (109). Of Robert Stone's *Dog Soldiers* (1974), Michael Herr's *Dispatches* (1977), and O'Brien's *Cacciato*, he further notes that "[in] contrast to the veterans' realistic narratives, these works focus not on the journey into Southeast Asia but rather on its legacy, on what it means to be an American after Vietnam. Their protagonists seek new symbolic landscapes where they can attempt to reassert the ideal American identity in the aftermath of Vietnam" (139). The war ends definitively in 1975—literature and film, then, grapple with the conflict after the fact, and how to fold the war and its outcome into the broader national narrative. "With the war over," Hellmann writes, "the enduring problem of Vietnam for America is its legacy for the story by which Americans have shaped their understanding of their place in geography and history. Thus the three Vietnam works [by Stone, Herr, and O'Brien] that have been most widely received as important literature have been less interested in a sustained portrait of the war than in an exploration of its implications for American myth" (167).

In American narrative, then, the Vietnam War is a story that is often really about something else. That "something else" might be trauma, for example, or the loss of exceptionalism, the loss of masculinity. (Or, in the case of the Rambo sequels, the revitalization of that exceptionalism and masculinity.) This makes sense, given the lag between the war's historical window and the bulk of representations. That thematic refraction is often made explicit in the stories themselves: when the narrator in "How to Tell a True War Story," one of the stories in O'Brien's collection *The Things They Carried*, insists that "It *wasn't* a war story. It was a *love* story" (85); when the narrator of Larry Heinemann's *Paco's Story* begins the novel with "This ain't no war story" (3); or when Herr ends *Dispatches* by saying, "Vietnam Vietnam Vietnam, we've all been there" (260). Or as O'Brien himself puts it in a different interview, "I've used it [Vietnam] in the way Conrad writes about the sea. . . . But Conrad is no more writing about the sea than I am about war" (Bourne 76).

When popular narratives about the Vietnam War finally began to emerge in the late 1970s, they grappled with a traumatic experience that both individuals and the nation were struggling to assimilate. But the war was definitively over, and the veterans were back home. This is a fine-grained difference with the second wave of twenty-first-century war stories, but a significant one. At least in realistic depictions of combat, these more recent works are less likely to be about "something else"—more so, they are enmeshed in the details of *this* war, *this* experience. (As I will discuss, the fantasy narratives are necessarily less direct.) This may also explain why so many of the recent realistic portrayals have been either lauded or criticized for being apolitical, as they are less likely to be overtly tackling broader issues like historical legacy or national identity. It is hard to trace the shape of legacy when you are still embroiled in conflict, after all, and when the weapons, rhetoric, and technology of war aren't confined to the combat zone. In what follows, I will consider *The Hurt Locker* and *Avatar* as two films that appear right on the cusp of this second wave of twenty-first-century war stories and are representative both of the divide between realistic and fantastic narratives and of stories that portray perpetual, cyclic, all-encompassing warfare—war that is far from over but rather is everywhere, all the time.

The Hurt Locker: A Pro-War Hero in an Anti-War Film

The Hurt Locker and *Avatar* are both transitional works, released after nearly a decade of war and inspiring one of the first broader public conversations about what this new war story would look like as a high-profile, fictionalized representation. Critics like Michiko Kakutani of the *New York Times*, George Packer of the *New Yorker*, and *Washington Post* reporter Jeff Turrentine wrote pieces about the new "Golden Age" of war stories (all of which appeared in 2014), but these films presaged some of that interest as well as some of the notable features of this next wave of narratives. *The Hurt Locker* makes use of an intentionally episodic, fragmented narrative, and both films feature an ambiguity about how thoroughly war should be embedded within a person and a society, though that ambiguity serves *The Hurt Locker* better than it does *Avatar*. And finally, both are couched within context of endless, repetitive, ongoing conflict. For these protagonists, the war is never over.

In the years since its release, *The Hurt Locker* remains the most acclaimed and one of the most well-known films about the Iraq War despite its relatively low profits at the time of its release. Critics have differed, however, in their understandings of what the film is saying about war and the people who fight it. Some called it pro-war, some anti-war, and some either approvingly or disapprovingly found it to be apolitical, avoiding a clear stance either way. Terence McSweeney notes that it was sometimes held up as an anti-war film *because* it was more neutral in tone than overtly patriotic—and simplistic— films like *Act of Valor* (2012). McSweeney himself finds that beneath the film's "detailed and intimate narrative is a rather reactionary treatise that emphasizes the humanitarian role of the American military in Iraq and detaches itself from any sense of political and historical context." He points to the charisma and heroics of protagonist Sergeant James and the film's presentation of James's job in a bomb disposal unit as primarily concerned with "preventing insurgents from killing Iraqi civilians and destroying Iraqi buildings" rather than facing off with the enemy ("*War on Terror*" 67–68).

Deftly played by Renner, James's magnetism is evident upon his introduction to the story. After an opening scene in which Staff Sergeant Matthew Thompson (Guy Pearce) is killed trying to safely detonate an IED, Sergeant J.T. Sanborn (Anthony Mackie) somberly acknowledges that loss as he contemplates Thompson's personal effects. Then he goes to meet James, his new team leader. James is framed in shadow, his hands flexing as he smokes a cigarette and listens to loud heavy metal music. He greets Sanborn, asks that he call him Will rather than sergeant, and then enlists Sanborn's help in moving a heavy sheet of plywood away from his window. "Maybe you shouldn't take this down," cautions Sanborn, noting that the wood helps shield the room from fragments from the mortars that come in at night. "Well, it's not going to stop the mortar rounds from coming in the roof," James notes. "Besides, I like the sunshine." A quick shot of Sanborn's half smile indicates that he's not sure what to think about James's wild-man style.

Their first time together investigating a possible bomb, Sanborn's nerves are palpable, as are the third team member's, Specialist Owen Eldridge (Brian Geraghty). James, however, is cool and collected, almost flippant, smoking another cigarette and refusing to use the bomb-disposal robot in favor of putting on the bomb suit and taking a look himself. "All right, let's rock and roll, man," he says as he walks away. "He's a rowdy boy," comments Eldridge, but Sanborn has made up his mind: "He's reckless." James pops a smoke grenade that inhibits visibility for any onlookers, but also for Sanborn and Eldridge. Sanborn is enraged, yelling at James through their audio connection and demanding to know how close he is to the IED. "I don't know, I'll tell you when I'm standing over it, cowboy," James responds. Suddenly a car speeds through the other soldiers and up to James—he pulls a sidearm and points it at the car, which stops immediately in front of him. As the others continue yelling, James gestures and tells the driver to back the car up, firing several warning shots at the ground and through the windshield. Finally he presses the gun to the driver's forehead, who then reverses, retreating back to where the other soldiers are waiting. They swarm him and push him to the ground, restraining him. "Well if he wasn't an insurgent he sure the hell is now," James comments wryly.

James continues his walk in the bomb suit, eventually uncovering a metal canister hidden beneath what, to the untrained eye, looks like just another pile of trash. He kneels before it and we watch his hands carefully extract wires and cut them. "Got it," he exhales, but then zeroes in on something else—another wire. "Secondary," he tells the others, and follows the wire to five other canisters, all connected. (The overhead shot of him pulling all of them up from the loosely packed gravel they were buried under was used for the film's poster.) James disarms them all as an Iraqi man watching nearby leaves a building, exchanges a mysterious but loaded look with James, and flees the area, dropping a small device of some kind as he does. Is this the bomber? We never find out. James, for his part, is unshaken, and looks happily spent when he returns to the other soldiers. After listening to Sanborn berate him for his lack of communication during the mission, he gives Sanborn a brotherly pat and says—by way of correcting his attitude—"It's combat, buddy."

Sanborn's right, of course. James is reckless, but his charisma and skill are undeniable. As Alex Vernon and others have noted, his character nods to the Western hero in his laconic nature, isolation, grace under pressure, and facility with violence. Those connections are reinforced by *The Hurt Locker*'s visual cues: "shots of empty vistas, the mise-en-scene detail of a Washington Redskins poster, a circle-the-wagons desert ambush by natives, whirling dust devils marking elapsed time, and the maverick protagonist's striding toward a final confrontation down a dusty, deserted town street at high noon" (Vernon, "Spectator-Citizen-Soldier" 378). Vernon adds that a note in Mark Boal's script refers to James as the Marlboro Man, an iconic cowboy.

In a classic essay, Robert Warshow describes the traits of what he calls "the Westerner" set against those of the gangster, another man with a gun, the two characters constituting "the two most successful creations of American movies" (703). While the gangster pursues wealth at any cost, the Western hero has no use for the trappings of success. "Where could he want to 'get ahead' to?" Warshow asks. "By the time we see him, he is already 'there': he can ride a horse faultlessly, keep his countenance in the face of death, and draw his gun a little faster and shoot it a little straighter than anyone he is likely to meet" (705). The gangster is surrounded by partners or henchmen and maybe a string of girlfriends, but the Westerner is an isolated figure. Coupled with his skills, that independence lends to the figure of the hero "an apparent moral clarity which corresponds to the clarity of his physical image against his bare landscape" (705). And finally, Warshow argues, when the gangster succeeds, he does so because he shoots first. "'Do it first,' says Scarface expounding his mode of operation, 'and keep doing it!'" (706). But the Westerner waits for the villain to make his play, thus reinforcing that sense of moral clarity and violence that is enacted for justice rather than selfishness or greed.

In many ways, James fits this Western hero profile. He is not motivated by desires for fame or monetary success—he only reluctantly answers Colonel Reed (David Morse) who compliments his abilities and asks how many bombs he has disarmed. First he claims not to know, but when pressed, he answers "eight hundred and seventy three," to the clear admiration of Reed. But he doesn't need the attention. James may have a team, but he essentially works alone—he prefers to walk out solo in the bomb suit instead of hanging back with other soldiers and sending in the robot. He keeps his cool even under extreme pressure. He also displays high-level skill with the tools of violence but doesn't jump to use that violence himself—he doesn't shoot the man in the car and, of course, he disarms bombs rather than setting them, or even detonating them from a safe distance. He operates with assurance and clarity, certainly compared to Sanborn and Eldridge. Eldridge is wracked with guilt over the death of Thompson, the first team leader, because he didn't shoot a man with a cell phone who might easily have been an innocent bystander but, it turns out, was using the phone to detonate the bomb that killed Thompson. He tells a military physician that he replays that moment in his mind over and over, and as a result his mental condition deteriorates. For his part, Sanborn is so disturbed and frustrated by James's refusal to play by the book that he punches him, and even considers detonating a bomb when James is within range. But lacking that assurance, he doesn't do it. Later we watch James support both Sanborn and Eldridge through a brutal ambush and standoff in the desert. James calms Eldridge's emotional panic and then encourages him to make the decision to shoot one of the snipers— thus providing some sort of closure for his grief over Thompson—and he gives Sanborn the tactical support and hydration he needs to make the long and difficult shots that eliminate the enemy.

Like a cowboy hero, James is unsuited for domestic life. When his tour ends and he goes back home to his wife and infant son, his discomfort and dissatisfaction are palpable. He is more agitated while grocery shopping with his wife than he ever appears to be in a war zone, and the looming aisle filled with too many cereal choices undoes him—he pauses, stares, grabs a box and throws it in the cart, smacking a small display in frustration as he walks away. (For James, this is much, much worse than uncovering a live IED.) He mucks wet leaves out of a gutter, and the next shot shows him staring blankly as a television set plays nothing but static. He talks to his wife and son, but there is no connection—the home front just isn't his home anymore. The film ends with James back in Iraq, back in the bomb suit, beginning a new tour. He strides confidently down an empty street, alert and ready for the danger ahead.

If you focus on James's character and these Western cues, then the film does celebrate him as a figure of clarity, even righteousness. Certainly James himself is pro-war, going so far as to tell his infant son that there is only one thing he really loves. He doesn't say it, but he doesn't have to—his return to war tells us all we need to know. The broader film, however, is more com-plicated, as that moment with his son suggests. This is a man, after all, who loves war, and loves it more than his family or any other aspect of his life. Even the classic Western hero, as discussed by Warshow, Richard Slotkin, Jane Tomkins, or any number of critics, would *like* to be able to settle down, and has an air of melancholy about him because of the isolation his righ-teous use of violence engenders. But there is nothing melancholy about

Figure 1. In *The Hurt Locker*, Staff Sergeant William James (Jeremy Renner) ill at ease back home in the States. (Summit Entertainment, 2009)

James when he is in the field, solving deadly puzzles, taking the risks that light him up with excitement and focus.

Joyce Wexler has argued that James loves war *as* war—he displays "exceptional courage and skill, but these virtues serve individual goals rather than strategic objectives" (2). As Yuval Harari has pointed out, patriotic and religious reasons for fighting have faded post-Enlightenment, and now soldiers are more often motivated by personal goals. Be all *you* can be. In that sense the film feels apolitical because James is—he simply doesn't care about the broader reasons he's in Iraq, because what he's after is the next adrenaline rush. *The Hurt Locker* makes this explicit with its opening epigraph from the journalist Chris Hedges: "The rush of battle is often a potent and lethal addiction, for war is a drug."

James's response to the intense pressures of combat is the sublime pleasure of experiencing and then overcoming them, though Sanborn and Eldridge react differently. For Eldridge, in particular, those pressures, and the speed at which deadly decisions have to be made, are almost too much. This makes sense, Florentina Andreescu explains, because "war is depicted as producing an acceleration of speed that interrupts the life rhythm necessary to create a sense of flow and continuity essential for routinized human life" (212). After the bomb team fails to save an innocent Iraqi with a bomb strapped to his chest, and barely survives themselves, Sanborn is distraught by that speed, that proximity of death, saying, "I fucking hate this place," and "I don't even have a son . . . I'm done. I want a son. I want a little boy,

Will." James, they agree, is fundamentally different—his whole temporal rhythm has changed, and he has left routinized human life behind. James has a son, but doesn't think about him. As Andreescu puts it, he's been "'rewired' in terms of [his] capabilities of enjoyment" (219).

Bigelow's direction, and the film's editing, call attention to James's rewiring and the changing pace of war more generally. Even given the broader cinematic context of Renner's performance as a flinty-eyed Marlboro Man, the tone of the film, and its real emphasis, is the jittery, fragmented, accelerated experience of the war—*this* war, at this moment—and the toll it takes on that would-be hero. Tight close-ups, quick cuts, and frequent point of view shots reflect that speed and tension, and the narrative is structured as a series of episodes or vignettes rather than an ongoing, continuous story. Rachel Fox has noted the film's use of what she calls "fragmentary focalizations," or the film's portrayal of viewing or recording devices: cameras, rifle scopes, computer screens. At one level, this reveals one aspect of war's changing nature: "Fragmentary focalizations—embedded, palimpsestic and *mise en abyme*—implicate a 'bigger picture' and call direct attention to how the face of war is changing in terms of mechanical and digital visualizing apparatuses not just being used to represent the Iraq War on screen, but also to facilitate that war" (472). But further, this device emphasizes how James is a broken person rather than a hero. War has no boundaries for him anymore, and the result is his personal fragmentation: "the failure to see the end of war in *The Hurt Locker* is marked by the film beginning in media res, and in the fragmentary sections, marked by each intertitle, in which the war comes to represent something of a disassociated and repetitive performance. In some respects, the short segment in which James does return home comes across as even more illusory than the scenes from the 'war front'" (474). War, in *The Hurt Locker*, creates excitement, terror, or death, and is cyclic, endless—a horizon that you just keep walking toward, alone.

The Hurt Locker, then, is both a prescient film and an influential one, depicting as it does soldiers' continued grappling with the changing technologies of war as well as a sense of blurred boundaries and the fragmentation that results. As Fox and others note, individual scenes of the film can feel like a collection of jagged, trembling shots, and those scenes are arranged to be both episodic and cyclic. Unlike Sanborn and Eldridge, however, James loves that fragmentation as the very essence of war. Not only does the war follow him home, but he can't wait to get back to it. Is that ultimately a celebration or a critique? The film is productively ambiguous on that and other questions. Should Eldridge indeed have shot the man with the cell phone? Was the mysterious man that James encountered the same one that planted the IED he discovered? The film's title refers to a soldier's practice of putting

Figure 2. At the end of *The Hurt Locker*, James (Jeremy Renner) is back in Iraq, walking alone toward the horizon at the beginning of another tour (Summit Entertainment, 2009). Text reads, "Days Left in Delta Company's Rotation: 365."

the thoughts or memories about bad experiences in a hurt locker, a compartmentalized mental space that is closed off from one's daily life, locked up and hidden. But, as the film as a whole suggests, you never really know when any kind of bomb, hidden or otherwise, is going to go off.

Avatar: An Iraq War Allegory, but to What End?

Avatar evinces some similar ambiguities, though in this case they read less as a narrative and thematic asset than as contradictions. As a film that completely took over the cultural zeitgeist, *Avatar* is an interesting case. It currently remains the highest-grossing film of all time, with four sequels planned for release beginning in 2022 with *Avatar: The Way of Water*. And yet it has proved less enduring as a pop cultural touchstone, leading Nathan Rabin to call it a "Forgotbuster." "It came, it crushed all long-term box office records, and it vanished almost without a trace," writes Scott Mendelson. While the visuals were amazing, must-see cinema for 2009, admittedly the dialogue is leaden and the story of the disabled Marine Jake Sully (Sam Worthington) turning against his military command structure in favor of joining forces with the oppressed Na'vi, the indigenous inhabitants of the planet Pandora—and, while in his Na'vi avatar body, falling in love with one of them, Neytiri (Zoe Saldaña)—has prompted unenthusiastic comparisons to *Dances with Wolves* (1990) and *Pocahontas* (1995). It is also true that the year before saw the release of *Iron Man*, the inaugural film of the ridiculously popular and prolific MCU, and that story of a man in a superpower-bestowing prosthesis captured the public's imagination in a much more long-standing way.

Avatar has, however, prompted a good deal of scholarly consideration from writers interested in its engagement with environmentalist, religious, and colonialist and postcolonialist themes. Cameron himself pushed the environmentalist angle in interviews, arguing that it was his primary motivation for writing the story. In *Avatar*, he said, when the Na'vi and the creatures of Pandora rise up against the militarized forces that would displace or exterminate them in order to mine more of the valuable mineral unobtanium, "Nature gets to fight back. It's 'Death Wish' for environmentalists. When did nature ever get to fight back in a movie?" Going on, he noted "that was my purpose in making the film. I wanted to make an environmentally conscious mainstream movie.... [20th Century] Fox ended up being enormously supportive and wrote this huge check. But they would have been much more comfortable if I had eliminated what they called the 'tree-hugging' elements" (Whipp). Fox did buy in with both resources and messaging. The DVD release on April 22, 2010, coincided with the fortieth anniversary of Earth Day, and Fox partnered with the Earth Day Network to announce the Home Tree Initiative, in which *Avatar* fans were encouraged to join in an effort to plant a total of one million trees worldwide (Erb 7).

Despite Fox executives' initial reluctance, the environmentalist angle was probably the least controversial that Cameron and the later marketing campaigns could have pursued. Sabine Meyer analyzes *Avatar* as a remake of *Dances with Wolves*, noting how the Na'vi of *Avatar* are aliens, but they closely resemble indigenous tribes of the Great Plains, as they "have long hair, wear feathers, are portrayed as extremely slender and muscular, and ride on equine-like Direhorses. Moreover, they live in clan structures similar to those of the Plains tribes. Their actions are often accompanied by the sound of drums—an instrument also well-known from Plains tribes' culture" (156). Both the Na'vi and the Sioux of *Dances with Wolves* are unabashedly positive portrayals, but the films resort to stereotypes for both the indigenous characters and the white protagonists that have led to criticism. As Meyer writes, both *Avatar* and *Dances* use versions of the "going native" and "white savior" myths: both characters are "transformed from alienated, white Americans into members of the respective tribes, shedding their former identities." And in addition, "Not only do Dunbar [the protagonist of *Dances*] and Sully go Native, but they also turn into super-Natives who soon excel over all the other members of the tribe" (157, 159). Thus *Avatar* in particular "reinscribes the very colonialist assumptions that it attempts to criticize" (Cettl 226). Despite that, as Meyer notes, "hardly anyone has dismissed the film entirely," and Cameron's full-throated environmentalism offered one way for groups to leverage the film's politics toward their own ends. "[*Avatar*'s] ability to elicit indigenous support despite its conservative racial politics," Meyer argues, "is achieved through its emphases on resource exploitation and environmental justice and, more significantly, on pantribal collaboration and indigenous rights, which inextricably link it to contemporary indigenous identity politics" (165).

None of these issues, however, proved as hot button as the film's echoes of the Iraq War. "That *Avatar* is really about the Iraq War was not lost on anyone," wrote Alec Barrett, and many conservative critics panned the film for being anti-war and anti-American. Certainly the film's depiction of a militarized foreign power invading another territory in order to mine its valuable natural resource, the mineral unobtanium (read "oil"), was a narrative familiar to those with anti-war sentiments. *Avatar*'s dialogue often makes those connections clear, as when Parker Selfridge (Giovanni Ribisi), an administrator for the mining operation, cynically explains their counter-insurgency tactics to Dr. Grace Augustine (Sigourney Weaver): "Look, look, we're supposed to be winning the hearts and the minds of the natives, isn't that the whole point of your little puppet show? You look like them and you talk like them and they'll start trusting us. We build them a school, we teach them English, but after—what, how many years?—relationships with the indigenous are only getting worse." It is not hard to draw a line to the postsurge situation in Iraq. It is clear Selfridge thinks little to nothing of those relationships, as profit is his only real purpose: "This is why we're here," he says, pointing to a chunk of the mineral. "Unobtanium. Because this little gray rock sells for twenty million a kilo. That's the only reason. It's what pays for the whole party. . . . Now those savages are threatening our whole operation."

Contemporary film audiences are well familiar with the broad strokes Cameron is painting with here—a healthy respect for the Horatio Alger story aside, unchecked greed is the sure mark of a bad guy, especially one who refers to an indigenous tribe as "savages." (Not to mention that his name, Selfridge, sounds suspiciously like "selfish.") In a later scene, he asks Jake to "find out what the blue monkeys want," since "killing indigenous looks bad," but Selfridge is nonetheless very willing to do it to get what they want. Jake eyes him with some suspicion but signs on when tapped by Colonel Miles Quaritch (Stephen Lang), a hypermasculine commanding officer. Quaritch speaks in terms that Jake understands and respects his military service, as opposed to the scientists, who repeatedly bemoan his ignorance, and the Na'vi, who call him a moron. Quaritch also promises Jake access to the medical care that would restore the use of his legs if he can find out more about the Na'vi.

Jake takes that opportunity, reveling in the buoyant physicality of his Na'vi avatar and eventually learning everything he can about the Na'vi community—their skills, tools, and weapons; their understanding of and relationship with the environment; their language; and their spiritual practices. He learns how to fight with them and then does, by which time Quaritch and the Company have been revealed to be truly despicable. Impatient to mine the huge deposits of unobtanium that lie beneath the Na'vi's habitat, Hometree, the military plans to drive the Na'vi out with gas and then bomb the area. "This is how it's done," Jake explains urgently to Grace and the other scientists. "When people are sitting on shit that you want, you make them your enemy. Then you justify taking it." The soldier knows how this kind of politics works, and the violent force needed to back it up.

The assault begins, the military approaching in helicopter-like vehicles that echo the famous "Ride of the Valkyries" attack on a village of Vietnamese women and children in *Apocalypse Now*—a connection that is emphasized when we find out during a later assault that the main bomber's call sign is Valkyrie 1–6. Quaritch's casual cruelty is a clear nod to Lieutenant Colonel Kilgore (Robert Duvall), as he watches the assault while holding a coffee cup and signals his approval of the devastation: "And that's how you scatter the roaches."

The bombing of Hometree echoes the cinematic memory of the Vietnam War, but when the Na'vi partner with other Pandoran tribes in order to mount a resistance, the references to the Iraq War come with increasing frequency. Quaritch fires up his troops with a speech:

> Everyone on this base, every one of you, is fighting for survival, and that's a fact. There's an aboriginal horde out there massing for an attack. These orbital images tell me that the hostile numbers have gone from a few hundred to well over two thousand in one day. And more are pouring in. In a week's time, there could be 200,000 of them. At that point they will overrun our perimeter. That's not gonna happen. Our only security lies in preemptive attack. We will fight terror with terror. The hostiles believe that this mountain stronghold of theirs is protected by their deity. [The troops laugh derisively.] And when we destroy it, we will blast a crater in their racial memory so deep that they won't come within a thousand klicks of this place ever again. And that, too, is a fact. [The troops cheer.]

Fighting terror with preemptive attack are the buzzwords of justification for the Iraq War, and Max Patel (Dileep Rao) utters another familiar phrase when he warns Jake about the impending attack on this sacred place, the

Figure 3. As *Avatar*'s hypermasculine Colonel Miles Quaritch, Stephen Lang channels Robert Duvall as Lieutenant Colonel Kilgore in *Apocalypse Now*. (20th Century Fox, 2009)

Tree of Souls: "Jake, it's crazy here. It's full mobilization. They're rigging the shuttle as a bomber. . . . It's for some kind of shock-and awe-campaign." But as in Iraq, the use of overwhelming force as a technique for rapid dominance is not successful. Here, the tribes expel their invaders in the resulting battle, a triumphant victory for the Na'vi despite the lives that are lost.

In interviews, Cameron soft-pedaled these connections. "I probably shouldn't have put in the direct references to the language used with the Iraq war, the 'shock and awe' line, because it takes you too much there," Cameron told Glenn Whipp of the *LA Times*. "But what I really was saying was, 'Listen to what your leaders are saying. Open your eyes. And understand what the run-up to war is like, so the next time it happens, you can question it.'" He laughed, and added, "If 'Star Wars' had been made after the Iraq war, people would have called it anti-American. I mean, it was a story of a small, ragtag band of insurgents fighting a major imperial power. George Lucas would be running for his life." In fact, Cameron might be more right than he knows here. At least according to Walter Murch, the legendary editor and sound designer who worked with Francis Ford Coppola on *Apocalypse Now*, George Lucas was originally going to direct that Vietnam War film, but the project was delayed and was also still too "politically hot" in 1973. His interest was really in telling a story about "the ability of a small group of people to defeat a gigantic power simply by the force of their convictions." So, Murch relates, Lucas decided to "put the essence of the story in outer space and make it happen in a galaxy long ago and far away. The rebel group were the North Vietnamese and the Empire was the United States. . . . *Star Wars* is George's transubstantiated version of *Apocalypse Now*" (Ondaatje 70). *Star Wars* and *Apocalypse Now* are both war stories, though the former makes that subject matter satisfying rather than unsettling by veiling those grimmer realities and striving for greater thematic clarity, maneuvers that are evident in more contemporary fantasy films as well, as I will discuss in chapter 5.

Despite Cameron's attempts to shift audiences' reading of *Avatar* from war story to environmentalist fable, its status as Iraq War allegory and anti-war manifesto is clear, with Quaritch emerging in the film's final scenes as hyperbolic bad guy par excellence, donning a motorized suit to fight Jake's avatar and kill his human body. He hits obviously racist notes once again when he asks Jake, "How does it feel to betray your own race?"—referring to Jake fighting with the Na'vi but also his relationship with Neytiri, a character played by the non-white actress Saldaña. Quaritch and his weapons, his preemptive strikes and his shock-and-awe—this is clearly not a nuanced presentation of the military.

And yet like *The Hurt Locker*, there are complications here as well, though they ultimately detract from rather than add to the story's overall effect. Quaritch and his team are veterans, but they are not on Pandora as representatives of the Armed Forces. They are contractors, a bit more like Blackwater than the Army, even if that distinction is not an obvious one. (That's a way for Cameron to sidestep directly criticizing the military, though it does reflect the confusion that can arise when private military contractors are working alongside regular soldiers in war zones, as when Blackwater employees killed seventeen Iraqi civilians at Nisour Square in 2007.) And although Jake eventually divorces himself from all that those militarized forces stand for—quite literally, as he releases his frail human body to totally inhabit his Na'vi self at the film's end—he is still celebrated for being a warrior. When he meets Neytiri's clan for the first time, and they ask him who he is, he answers, amusingly, "I'm a Marine. Of the jarhead clan." They want to know who he belongs to, and at this point, it's still the military. They see him, however, as a warrior, and that subtle difference is important. "This is the first warrior dreamwalker that we have seen," Eytukan (Wes Studi) says approvingly. Soldiers, in *Avatar*, fight with mechanized weaponry toward the eradication of indigenous populations, all for the goal of corporate profit. Warriors, however, fight for a higher cause. "I was a warrior who dreamed he could bring peace," as Jake puts it late in the film. Jake makes this statement in a straightforward fashion, but it highlights the irony of a film that criticizes the military (through the guise of contract forces) but celebrates the warrior, that portrays one hypermasculine fighter as the bad guy and another super-achieving male fighter as the good guy. Bron Taylor has noted a number of other tensions in the film, evident in viewers' responses: "The filmmaker and the film have been labelled pro-civilization and anti-civilization, pro-science and anti-science, un-American and too American, anti-Marine and pro-Marine, racist and anti-racist, anti-indigenous and pro-indigenous, woman-respecting and misogynistic, leftist and neo-conservative, progressive and reactionary, activist and self-absorbed" (6).

Franciska Cettl argues that the undermining of specific binaries in the film, between "technological and organic, Western science and indigenous animism, Western technology and shamanic practice . . . functions as a decolonizing gesture, putting into question the colonizing hierarchy between what has been legitimized as proper science and what dismissed as indigenous superstition" (226). While I agree with Cettl about the film's engagement with science, religion, and colonialism, I would argue that the broader ambiguities of the film are not a strength in the way that those characterizing *The Hurt Locker* are. James's clarity of vision is intentionally critiqued by the larger film, while *Avatar* strives for a satisfying simplicity of good guys and bad guys that doesn't fully take into account some of its broader contexts. Ultimately, too, if this is a war story that lifts up the indigenous against their invaders, it is probably a story that would best be told more fully from the perspective of an indigenous person rather than a man like Jake.

Like *The Hurt Locker*, however, *Avatar* sets the stage for much of what is to come in the following years, particularly its fantasy-based depiction of soldiers and war. When Jake fights Quaritch in *Avatar's* climactic scene, Quaritch in his mechanized suit and Jake in his avatar body, it is like the showdown at the end of a superhero movie, rather resembling the fight between Tony Stark (Robert Downey Jr.) and Obadiah Stane (Jeff Bridges) at the end of *Iron Man*, released the previous year, when hero and villain face off in their superpowered exosuits. And Jake's physical trauma, which he poignantly describes in voice-over at the film's opening, is also alleviated in superhero fashion. "When I was lying there in the VA hospital," he says, "with a big hole blown through the middle of my life, I started having these dreams of flying. I was free. Sooner or later though, you always have to wake up." He indicates that recovery is possible, but not for a low-level grunt like him: "They can fix a spine, if you've got the money. But not on vet benefits, not in this economy." But soon, he *is* fixed, and he *can* fly, using a prosthesis that works perfectly—save for a few initial stumbles—an experience that echoes superhero fighters like James Rhodes (Don Cheadle), who loses the use of his legs in *Captain America: Civil War* (2016), or Thor (Chris Hemsworth), who loses an eye in *Thor: Ragnarok* (2017), only to end up with well-functioning prostheses and more abilities than they had before.

(In the case of Bucky Barnes [Sebastian Stan], however, disability is treated in a more nuanced way, which I will discuss in chapter 5.) Thus *Avatar* is a war movie that elides some of the grimmer realities of combat and its consequences. But as with all of these war stories, whether realistic or fantastical, war is presented as endless, despite the Na'vi triumph at film's end. Four sequels are planned, and the first, *Avatar: The Way of Water*, continues the same militarized conflict as the 2009 film, thirteen years later. Oddly enough, although *The Hurt Locker* is a far more realistic film, it also presages the rise of the MCU, in that it stars Jeremy Renner, who goes on to play Hawkeye, Evangeline Lilly, who plays the Wasp, and Anthony Mackie, who plays the Falcon and then Captain America.

How the War Comes with You

In the following chapters, I will discuss these more recent war stories and their distinguishing features, drawing from memoir, poetry, and fiction from both American and Iraqi authors, as well as contemporary fantasy films that engage with themes of war, combat, and military service. Some aspects of war are universal, but who fights, and how, are aspects of the war experience that change from conflict to conflict, and certainly within the two-decade span of the "forever wars." These works all cover familiar topics like gender, technology, tactics, and trauma—topics that are as much part of the war story as when Achilles hefted his spear in the *Iliad*. It is the shape of these topics that changes, as in *Missionaries* (2020), a novel that Phil Klay published after *Redeployment*. Late in the book, the daughter of a lieutenant colonel in the Colombian Special Forces tweets out an image in connection with the kidnapping of an American war correspondent, an impulsive and righteous action that has unintended and lethal consequences. War is always rife with contingencies, Klay would argue, but in more recent years those vectors can operate quite differently.

In chapters 1 and 2, I focus on two milestone trinities of second-wave American war writing: works by Ben Fountain, Chris Kyle, and Phil Klay, and works by Siobhan Fallon, Helen Benedict, and Kayla Williams. Chapter 1 covers the characteristics of this new era of contemporary American war writing, best exemplified by Fountain's novel, *Billy Lynn's Long Halftime Walk*, which follows the protagonist Billy Lynn's feelings of loss and dislocation as he returns to Texas from Iraq with a group of his fellow soldiers. They have become famous because of a viral video a journalist captured of a firefight and are now to be celebrated at halftime of the Thanksgiving Day Dallas Cowboys football game. (After their brief "Victory Tour," they'll be taken back to Iraq.) The men are out of the war zone, but back home, war is everywhere—on the lips of the public who eagerly wish them well, in the militarized spectacle of the halftime show, and in the vision of a Hollywood producer who wants to make a war movie about Billy and his friends. It all makes Billy feel like he is coming apart, a fragmentation that is most evident in the broken word clouds of dialogue that Fountain uses to render Billy's conversations with passionate, awestruck civilians. The public adores Billy— for reasons that he quite literally can't put together.

In addition to its emphasis on the blurring of boundaries between war and domestic life and the fragmentation that can result, *Billy Lynn* is exemplary of these second-wave narratives for two other reasons. First, it is a popular and critically acclaimed war novel that was written by a civilian rather than a veteran. As David Eisler has noted, that Fountain's authority to write a story like this has remained largely unchallenged constitutes a major shift in assumptions about authorship and authority when it comes to representations of war, particularly twentieth- and twenty-first-century war. And second, *Billy Lynn* inspired a film adaptation of the same name, but it was one that garnered nothing like the audience or the accolades of the novel— something that is true of several of the works I will cover in this study.

I begin with *Billy Lynn* because it sets the terms for this project so well, and it reads productively with two quite different texts from the same period—Kyle's *American Sniper*, a gung-ho military memoir, and Klay's *Redeployment*, a veteran-authored collection of short stories. For all their differences in literary format, authorship, tone, and perspectives on combat, each text reflects that same lack of delineation and resulting sense of fragmentation, as well as the endlessness of war that always seems to find new ways to renew itself.

Billy Lynn, American Sniper, and *Redeployment* were the books that made critics sit up and take notice, to publish think-pieces and assessments of the new wealth of material about contemporary war. Fountain, Kyle, and Klay became flash points for the field—though in fact they were preceded by three other authors who were also working in the novel, memoir, and short story formats. These authors, however, were more inclusive and more pioneering in their constitution of the new war story. Siobhan Fallon's short story collection *You Know When the Men Are Gone* (2011), Helen Benedict's novel *Sand Queen* (2011), and Kayla Williams's memoir *Plenty of Time When We Get Home* (2014) tell stories about female soldiers, military spouses, and soldiers with disabilities, groups that historically have often figured as auxiliary to the "real" war story or were not considered part of it at all. Fallon, Benedict, and Williams were writing before public attention to contemporary war stories began to cohere, and thus their depictions of women's relationships to the military and the particular contours that boundary-blurring and fragmentation can take given those various perspectives should now be considered doubly groundbreaking, as I argue in chapter 2.

What happens after everything falls apart, as it does in so many of these stories? There are any number of possible responses, from the resolve reflected in Williams's *Plenty of Time When We Get Home* and Fallon's second book, *The Confusion of Languages* (2017), to the despair of Benedict's *Sand Queen*, or the emotional emptiness that ends *Redeployment*. In chapter 3, I argue that some works suggest a more radical response—a kind of renunciation or giving over, an acceptance of the war that one lives with. Here, I trace that response in Kevin Powers's novel *The Yellow Birds*, Brian Castner's memoir *The Long Walk* (2012), and Brian Turner's memoir *My Life as a Foreign Country* (2014). That renunciation is also evident in Turner's newer poetry collection *The Dead Peasant's Handbook*, though there he also hints at a different emphasis, one that I find in several Iraqi-authored works about contemporary war.

When Ikram Masmoudi published *War and Occupation in Iraqi Fiction* in 2015, many of the books she covered had not yet been translated into English. But since that time, a number of new and newly translated works have appeared to much acclaim, particularly Hassan Blasim's short story collection *The Corpse Exhibition* (2014), Ahmed Saadawi's *Frankenstein in Baghdad* (2013, trans. 2018), and Sinan Antoon's *The Book of Collateral Damage* (2019). In chapter 4, I argue that Iraqi literature reveals a different response to fragmentation—which in the Iraqi works is often much more extreme, as suggested by their titles. Instead of resolve, despair, or individual renunciation, these stories emphasize an acknowledgment of loss and devastation coupled with collective imagination, a communal storytelling. What these authors describe is not a literal recovery, and certainly not a re-covering, but neither is it a renunciation nor a giving over.

Fantasy films rarely earn the label of "war film," but many of them give us surprisingly complex portraits of conflict and combat that reflect some of these same emphases. *Iron Man* begins in Afghanistan and the character later struggles with trauma; Captain America is the quintessential WWII soldier who must later reckon with changing practices of war and politics; and Captain Marvel begins as a crack Air Force pilot who pushes against gender-based restrictions on flying combat missions. Likewise, recent Star Wars films feature lessons in female military leadership in the character arcs of princess-turned-general Leia Organa, rogue-turned-Resistance leader Jyn Erso, and the eponymous *Last Jedi*, Rey Skywalker. In chapter 5, I explore how these fantastical stories' ubiquity belies their status as mere fantasy, and as the major studios expand their storylines and character arcs over many,

many films, these narratives address more complicated questions of trauma and collateral damage, privacy and security, political control and oversight, conflicting values, and understandings of race and gender. Finally, the MCU's recent emphasis on the idea of the multiverse leads to a loss of boundaries between realities and ensuing narrative fragmentation that echoes that of more realistic war literature—although ultimately, these films do tend to put the pieces back together, to the end of leaving their audiences more satisfied than unsettled.

With the chaotic withdrawal of American forces from Afghanistan on August 30, 2021, headlines variously proclaimed that the "forever wars" were over—or that they clearly weren't. Drone warfare has come to epitomize all the blurred boundaries of contemporary conflict—pilots who strike targets thousands of miles away and then make the short drive home, video feeds in which combatants and civilians lose their distinction, and globalized missions that take little account of national borders. The drone as modern weapon and potent symbol has been taken up in films such as *Good Kill* and *Eye in the Sky*, both from 2015, as well as George Brant's play *Grounded* (2013), which I discuss in the Conclusion. All these stories finally emphasize that coherence and clarity of vision may be desirable in both war and narrative—but because war is never black and white, stories about it shouldn't be either.

CHAPTER 1

The Second Wave of War Stories

2011 and Beyond

In 2011, Matt Gallagher published an article in *The Atlantic* with the title, "Where's the Great Novel about the War on Terror?" In it, he noted how much writing there had been in the previous decade about the wars in Iraq and Afghanistan—but that that writing was largely nonfiction, either journalism, personal testimonies, or memoirs like those by Colby Buzzell and Kayla Williams that I wrote about in *Welcome to the Suck*. "There has been such a proliferation of non-fiction war writing over the last ten years," he noted, "that it's nearly impossible to talk to anyone in the publishing industry without hearing phrases like 'war fatigue' and 'market saturation.'" While he acknowledges that many great war novels don't appear until well after the conflict in question is over—for example, Erich Maria Remarque's *All Quiet on the Western Front* in 1929, Joseph Heller's *Catch-22* in 1961, or O'Brien's *The Things They Carried* in 1990—he also mentions the difficulty that his friend and fellow author Roy Scranton had in getting literary agents to read the manuscript for the novel he would eventually publish in 2016 as *War Porn*.

Gallagher's *Atlantic* piece set the stage for the short story collection that he edited with Scranton, *Fire and Forget*, which appeared in 2013. In the Foreword to the collection, Colum McCann makes the same point: "The stories of the wars that defined the first decade of the twenty-first century are only just beginning to be told. Television programs, newspaper columns, Internet blogs. We've even had a couple of average Hollywood movies, but we don't yet have all the stories, the kind of reinterpretive truth-telling that fiction and poetry can offer" (viii). Gallagher and Scranton had met Jake Siegel, Perry O'Brien, and Phil Klay at an NYU Veterans Writing Workshop and hatched the idea for the collection—some of them aiming, too, to attempt to fill the gap that Gallagher and McCann had diagnosed.

Several big war books were indeed on the way, some popular and some acclaimed. Chris Kyle's memoir *American Sniper* had already been on the *New York Times* bestseller list for seventeen weeks when Ben Fountain published his novel *Billy Lynn's Long Halftime Walk* on May 1, 2012. Kyle's book would stay on that bestseller list for twenty more weeks, selling even more copies after Clint Eastwood adapted it for film in 2014. *Billy Lynn* won the National Book Critics Circle Award for Fiction, was a finalist for the National Book Award, and was also adapted for film by Ang Lee in 2016.

Another finalist for the National Book Award that year was Kevin Powers's novel *The Yellow Birds*, which won the Guardian First Book Award and the Hemingway Foundation/PEN Award. Finally, Phil Klay's short story collection *Redeployment* came out in 2014 and won both the National Book Critics Circle Award and the National Book Award—he had previously published the title story in *Fire and Forget*.

That said, it's really 2011 when contemporary war fiction "became a thing," as Peter Molin put it, just as Gallagher was posing the question in his *Atlantic* article ("2011"). Siobhan Fallon's short story collection *You Know When the Men Are Gone* came out that year, as well as Helen Benedict's novel *Sand Queen*. Although they received less attention and fewer accolades, "Let's give credit to Fallon and Benedict for initiating the contemporary war lit surge," writes Molin. "Benedict, an academic and activist writing as a critic-from-outside unimpressed by the military effort, and Fallon, an Army spouse writing as a military insider full of knowing sympathy, established twin poles of literary possibility that virtually every other writer since has followed one-way-or-the-other." And, he adds, "That *You Know When the Men Are Gone* and *Sand Queen* were authored by women and featured women protagonists is also important." When you also consider Kayla Williams's second memoir *Plenty of Time When We Get Home* from 2014, these three constitute a milestone trinity of short story collection, novel, and memoir that would then be echoed and critically amplified by Fountain, Powers, Kyle, and Klay—I will cover Fallon, Benedict, and Williams's quite different, and more expansive, approaches to the war story in chapter 2.

Here, I begin with *Billy Lynn* as the exemplar of several of the characteristics of this second wave of contemporary American war writing: the ways that the military-civilian divide is simultaneously absolute and strangely blurred, the sense that war is everywhere and nowhere at the same time, the pressures war exerts on gender and identity, and the fragmentation of both narrative and character that results from all these factors. *Billy Lynn* has some surprising connections with *American Sniper* and *Redeployment*, given how different the three are in form, approach, and affect, and I'll explore those as well, leaving a consideration of *The Yellow Birds* for chapter 3.

Billy Lynn's Long Halftime Walk: The Everyman Soldier

Although *American Sniper*'s immense popularity far outpaced *Billy Lynn* and *Redeployment*, Fountain and Klay's books were greeted with acclaim and the acknowledgment that they might constitute a new era of storytelling. Geoff Dyer's review of *Billy Lynn* in the *New York Times* begins by noting that "the Iraq war has been covered to such high literary effect by reporters like David Finkel and Dexter Filkins that news of an imminent war *novel* is likely to be greeted with a shrug," but ends by calling the book "grand, intimate and joyous." Of *Redeployment*, Filkins himself said that "it's the best thing written so far on what the war did to people's souls." By the end of his reading, "I felt I had learned more about Iraq than in any documentary or factual account," thus implicitly making the case for literary approaches in addition to nonfiction work like his own—which, as Dyer notes, did largely dominate discussions of war writing in the first decade of the twenty-first century.

Billy Lynn demonstrates both a unique premise and a number of features that define the second wave of Iraq War stories. Billy Lynn is a nineteen-year-old soldier in Bravo squad (as they are known in the media, though in fact they are Bravo Company, second platoon, first squad, teams alpha and bravo). In Iraq, they engage in a firefight at the fictional Al-Ansakar Canal, during which Billy both returns fire and renders aid to one of his commanding officers, Sergeant Breem, known in the squad as Shroom. Shroom sustains lethal injuries and dies; a soldier named Lake is also hit and grievously injured. The incident is filmed by a Fox News journalist and the video later goes viral, making the soldiers famous, hailed as precisely the kind of heroes the American public has been craving in the early years of the Iraq War.

That alone is a great deal for a young kid from a small Texas town to process, and he revisits the memory often, trying to sort it all out. "Billy was doing about ten different things at once, unpacking his medical kit, jamming a fresh magazine into his rifle, talking to Shroom, slapping his face, yelling at him to stay awake, trying to track the direction of the incoming rounds and crouching low with absolute fuck-all for cover" (61). He has seen the video, but it doesn't quite track with his own experience: "The Fox footage shows him firing with one hand and working on Shroom with the other, but he doesn't remember that. . . . Is this what they mean by courage? Simply doing all the things you were trained to do, albeit everything at once and very fast" (62). Billy's struggles to understand are exponentially amplified by the military's decision to send Bravo squad on a "heroes' tour" of the United States, culminating with their appearance in the halftime show at a Dallas Cowboys' Thanksgiving Day football game. Once there, everyone wants a piece of them: the well-wishers who press in to greet them and shake their hands; a Hollywood film producer who is trying to leverage a deal to make a movie about the firefight; and Norm Oglesby, the Cowboys' owner (a thinly veiled version of Jerry Jones), who uses the Bravos as fodder for his smooth-as-silk statements about patriotism, heroes, and America. It all swirls around Billy as he tries to settle his own understandings of his military service, his family, and his sense of himself as a soldier and a young man. He wants some truth, a solid foundation to stand on, but it is in short supply. Billy wonders, as he listens to Norm address the media, if Norm will someday run for office:

> He has the presence, the *werds*, plus he's mastered the wounded, vaguely petulant tone that is the style of political speech these days. If there's a grating artificiality in the performance—Norm's awareness of himself as a performer, sneaking peeks at a mental mirror off to the side—it's no worse than any other fixture of the public realm. Billy has noticed that audiences don't seem to mind anyway. All the fakeness just rolls right off them, maybe because the nonstop sales job of American life has instilled in them exceptionally high thresholds for sham, puff, spin, bullshit, and outright lies, in other words advertising in all its forms. (131)

In describing all these reactions to the Bravos, Fountain achieves a tone that Brian Williams calls "both hyperbolically satirical and painfully earnest" ("Soldier-Celebrity" 526). The soldiers are treated like celebrities, fawned over and feted with all the force of twenty-first-century, media-saturated, consumerist excess—an excess that is nonetheless realistically rendered, as are Billy's touching attempts to reckon with it all. In some ways, the story of Billy and his fellow soldiers echoes that of James Bradley, Rene Gagnon, and Ira Hayes, the three survivors of Iwo Jima who became iconically associated with the flag-raising that symbolized America's victory there. Like Billy, Bradley, Gagnon, and Hayes were treated as celebrity-heroes, though that attention was at best uncomfortable for them and at worst devastating—particularly for Hayes, who struggled with and then succumbed to alcoholism when he was only thirty-two. More recent versions of this story—the nonfiction book *Flags of Our Fathers* (2000), by James Bradley, Bradley's son, and Clint Eastwood's 2006 fictionalized film adaptation of the same name—strike a somber, tragic tone. These tellings implicate the military and the media's manipulation of these men through straightforward journalism and cinematic drama rather than Fountain's breathless, almost hallucinogenic descriptions of what it is like to be in the glare of all these spotlights, on all these screens. But although Billy may never be real for the crowds that surround him, he is very real to the reader, a fully fleshed-out character in contrast with the simulacra around him.

The halftime show itself is the epitome of this American simulacra, as Destiny's Child sings their song "Soldier" amid an overwhelming deluge of light, sound, and sensation. Fountain titles this chapter "Raped by Angels," and Billy describes the experience as being at the behest of a malevolent divinity, "whatever in us that's so supreme and terrifying that we have to call it divine" (235). It's too much for him: "It's a bad place to be. They talk up God and country but it's the devil they propose, all those busy little biochemical devils of sex and death and war that simmer at the base of the skull, punch up the heat a few degrees and they rise to a boil, spill over the sides. Do they even know? he wonders" (235).

Billy still tries, though, to figure out the world and his place in it. He talks to his sister Kathryn, who wants him to go AWOL rather than return to Iraq. He talks to a pastor. He talks to his other commanding officer, Sergeant Dime, who has more years and experience than he does. He talks to a wealthy Cowboys patron and tries to figure out how people make lots of money. And he talks to Faison, a rookie cheerleader with whom he forges a sudden, intense connection. Billy wants to find someone "who can explain his experience, or at least break it down and properly frame the issue" (47). His struggles are poignant, not least because of the enormity of what he is up against—the devastating memory of his friend's death coupled with the world's celebration and commodification of that same event. His grief would be enough, but the pressure of the public's fascination with war is too much. Fountain's novel, then, dramatizes the military-civilian divide in a way that makes that divide both interpersonally tremendous—Billy and the civilians talking to him do not understand each other, even when it is someone like his sister, who loves him dearly—and culturally nonexistent, as the halftime show revels in militarized display and Hollywood flirts with their story, "a tale of heroism ennobled by tragedy" (6). Mark Bresnan has argued that the civilians who call after Billy, who approach him smiling and grateful, eager to shower him and the other soldiers with praise, "are best understood as fans—passionate and engaged, yes, but also fickle, arbitrary, and rigid in their expectations of what a soldier or football player or pop star should be" (171). What Billy, as a soldier, is really thinking is as unimportant to them as what a winning quarterback really wants out of life.

The pressure of that cultural militarization coupled with the interpersonal divide results in what appears on the page as the novel's most notable stylistic feature—the fragmentation of language. When the well-wishers press in on Billy at the stadium, eager to get up close to real, live soldier-heroes, they frame their praise in the moral touchstones of the war effort: reprisal for 9/11, the need to protect freedom, ideals of courage and sacrifice, the guiding hand of God. But for Billy, it just rains down as a hail of verbiage, and so appears as a kind of word cloud on the page:

                                   terrRist

                                                              freedom

evil

                                         nina leven

                                 nina leven

                                           nina leven

troops

                               currj

                        support

                                                        sacrifice

                                     Bush

values

God (2)

    This happens throughout the novel, "their words sloshing around Billy's brain like soft ice cubes," blips about pride and honor and "Kicking Ass!" that even break into his conversations with Faison, who feverishly talks to him about "bearing witness" and "deeds" and "*acks of sack-rih-fice*" (289–90, 148). In the end, Billy just can't put it all together. "Take us someplace safe," his fellow soldier Koch, known as Crack, says as they speed away from the stadium at novel's end. "Take us back to the war" (307). He's kidding, but not really—everything is a battlespace now. And like James at the end of *The Hurt Locker*, they are indeed going back to Iraq.

    Billy Lynn reflects the blurred boundaries between war and home, past and present, reality and unreality, the sense of endlessness, and the trope of fragmentation that I want to highlight in this study, but in addition it shows how the second decade of the war made for different war stories than the first. The novel is itself set around 2004, when soldiers writing blogs and capturing video that could be instantly seen by people back home were big news, and a stark departure from the radio silence that often necessarily accompanied soldiers fighting in previous wars. Fountain, however, is writing in awareness of the exponential proliferation of that media culture that happened over the next decade. In a talk he gave about the novel at the Air Force Academy in 2013, he described the broader culture as "the 24-7 force-feed of movies, music, television, Internet, youtubes, youporns, cell phones, iPods, iPads, sports of all kinds at all hours, right-wing news, left-wing news, celebrity news, texts, tweets, emails, and all the rest of it, and that's even before we get into the numbing effects of the huge array of pharmaceuticals available to us, legal or otherwise" (3). All of this he termed the "Fantasy Industrial Complex." Although Billy's inadvertent star-making by a viral video predates YouTube's founding in 2005 and thus the kind of overwhelming media saturation that Fountain details, the vortex that Billy stands at the center of is clearly reflective of both his experience and a harbinger of more to come, "the general insanity of American life in the early years of the 21st century," as Fountain put it, and which he satirizes in *Billy Lynn* with hyperbole that is also quite realistic (1).

Adam Kaiserman, writing in 2021, has similarly noted how *Billy Lynn* reflects concerns about "the agnostic relationship to the truth so dear to the George W. Bush administration during the Iraq War" that are only exacerbated by the 2016 presidential election and the era of Donald Trump's dominance in politics. Given the rise of what he calls a "post-truth" era and a "current political and epistemological crisis," Kaiserman argues that literature like Fountain's novel not only can help by providing a portrait of a character attempting to navigate the pressures of competing and often baseless rhetoric, but also that the practice of reading literature itself might be a way out of that morass. Fountain describes the project of literature that way in his talk: "To see things as they truly are, and to find the language that describes those things as accurately and fully as possible, without sentimentality, or a political agenda, or a wish to please the reader" (11). Kaiserman agrees, and adds that "*Halftime Walk* teaches us that calling bullshit is easy. The real struggle that we all must face is how to make the truth more persuasive to our fellow citizens" (583).

Billy Lynn, then, presents a 2004 story in ways that a more contemporary readership would recognize and frames that story around both the war zone and the home front, showing how they bleed together. That Fountain is not a veteran himself and is not telling a version of his own story perhaps allows the focus of the book to become not just the searing truth of Billy's combat experience but also the American public's understanding of that experience—or rather their lack of understanding, their enthusiastic consumption of its representation and proliferation. Regardless, Fountain's status as civilian rather than veteran hasn't hurt the book's reception at all, as David F. Eisler has noted it would have in earlier eras. Whereas John Dos Passos and Willa Cather—both lauded, canonical authors—each wrote novels about World War I, "*Three Soldiers* [from Dos Passos in 1921] still stands as one of the genre's most influential early texts, while *One of Ours* [from Cather in 1922] has never fully recovered from its initial negative reception despite later attempts to rehabilitate its image as a war novel" (29). This is because the veteran's experience and authority—to know and convey the "real truth" of war—was long considered inviolable.

But after the United States transitioned from conscription to an all-volunteer military, Eisler argues, something changed in the artistic community. "If only those who have experienced war can understand it," he writes, "only those who choose to serve are condemned to bear the burden of that experience while the rest of the country carries on" (83). And that burden isn't just experiential but communicative as well—those who volunteer are then the only ones who can tell that story. That realization "has led to a pattern of veteran-authors ceding their authority by deemphasizing the need for personal experience as a source of narrative authenticity; it is a way for them to share the experiential burden of their memory with the rest of society" (85). Eisler describes an interview, for example, with Fountain and Kevin Powers that took place in 2012, after both *Billy Lynn* and *The Yellow Birds* had been nominated for the National Book Award. The subject of war and authorship comes up, and while Fountain expresses some reservations about his "right" to write about war, Powers is having none of it. Instead, Powers says, conscientiousness about what Fountain is representing and "good, true art" is "far more useful as a metric than whether or not experience equals any kind of authority in artistic expression, which for the record I'm pretty sure it doesn't" (John Williams). As Eisler puts it, instead of asserting his own authority of experience, Powers "reframes the aesthetic criteria for artistic expression in terms of the author's attitude toward the subject of war" (105). Thus a suspicion, or at the very least an uncertainty, about writerly authority that might have accrued to Fountain as recently as the Vietnam War has not been in evidence, and hasn't stopped *Billy Lynn* from becoming one of contemporary war literature's touchstones.

The novel was enough of a success that Ang Lee adapted it for film in 2016, but despite a fair amount of hype, the film did poorly at the box office, grossing only about $31 million over a $40 million budget ("Billy Lynn's"). Conversations about the movie's content were somewhat overshadowed by

Lee's decision to shoot the film in 3D and at 120 frames per second, which is five times the normal frame rate of 24 frames per second. That meant that the film captures an astonishing level of clarity and detail, but also that it could only be shown that way in a handful of theaters—most theaters had to project it at the standard frame rate. Discussions among film connoisseurs mimicked the questions asked about *Avatar* before its release—will this change the way we see movies, the way we think about realism in film?

With regard to *Billy Lynn*, the answer was no—neither the narrative nor the lure of enhanced visuals proved enticing enough to make the film a zeitgeist, and some reported that the heightened clarity was off-putting or distracting. Ironically, however, the destabilizing effect of a hyperreal viewing experience is perfectly befitting for the story of *Billy Lynn*. Reviewer Godfrey Cheshire, for example, wondered if his feeling of vague nausea came from the visuals or the film's depiction of "the football stadium's garish grotesquerie and bizarre artificiality, complete with Jumbotron—an environment that oddly compounds the photography's dizzying impact." Despite that congruity, *Billy Lynn's Long Halftime Walk* remains a milestone for war fiction but not for war films—an outcome that is reversed in the case of the next work covered in this chapter.

American Sniper: The Soldier of Exception

In many ways, Chris Kyle's *American Sniper* would seem to be the polar opposite of *Billy Lynn*—it is a memoir (written with Scott McEwen and Jim DeFelice) rather than a novel, and it largely serves as an underscoring rather than a dilution of the values and moral assertions that Billy experiences as a kind of conversational deluge. In addition, Kyle is not only a veteran, but a celebrated one whose claim to authority is indeed the book's raison d'être. The cover of the mass market paperback features the SEAL Trident, and much of the book's popularity is likely due to its narrative of clarity and success—the subtitle is, after all, "The Autobiography of the Most Lethal Sniper in U.S. Military History." In some ways Kyle positions himself as an everyman like Billy Lynn—he talks about his typical upbringing in north-central Texas, his family's traditional values, their Christian faith. They would often go to church, Kyle relates, on Sunday morning, Sunday evening, and Wednesday as well. Still, there was nothing too surprising about that: "We didn't consider ourselves overly religious, just good people who believed in God and were involved in the church." Kyle demurs even further: "Truth is, back then I didn't like going a lot of the time" (11). Kyle says he wasn't terribly patient when he was younger, wasn't terribly good at ranch work, and was even rejected by the Navy the first time he attempted to enlist. The book's title reflects that sense of normality—he's an *American* sniper, after all. But Kyle wants to show how that traditional foundation allowed him to grow into someone exceptional. And as a sniper, his war experience is indeed quite different from the average soldier's. Although his SEAL training is intensely physically and mentally challenging, he loves it, and doubt about his choice to enlist never enters his mind. Neither does he doubt any of the battlefield choices that he later has to make.

Kyle exhibits none of the hesitation or uncertainty of Billy Lynn—he claims to have an innate understanding of his role as a soldier, his work in the war, and how it should all be understood. But Kyle's story of mastery and control is undermined, interestingly, by its structure, which interpolates segments of commentary from Kyle's wife Taya throughout the book. Those segments sometimes reinforce Kyle's own understanding of and feelings about the events in his life, but more often they provide an alternate account that serves to emphasize the inability to separate war and home life that Kyle experiences after serving four tours of duty. Kyle was killed in 2013—not at war, but at a gun range in Texas, where he was shot six times by a troubled veteran struggling with trauma.

In the opening pages of *American Sniper*, Chris Kyle gets right to the point. He describes looking through the scope of his sniper rifle while in Nasiriya, Iraq, in 2003, and seeing an Iraqi woman with her child. Suddenly, the woman pulls out an object and yanks at it. Kyle's platoon chief identifies it as a Chinese grenade and orders Kyle to shoot to protect the ten Marines approaching her on foot patrol. He hesitates, then fires. "It was the first time I'd killed anyone while I was on the sniper rifle," Kyle says. "And the first time in Iraq—and the only time—I killed anyone other than a male combatant" (4). The moment has the potential to be a troubling one at the very least. Kyle doesn't mention what happened to the child, and I've written in *Welcome to the Suck* about how the unintentional killing of a child haunts many Iraq War stories, precisely the kind of traumatic intersection of culpability and lack of agency that has the potential to rupture soldiers' postwar lives and sense of identity.

But Kyle follows the story with assertions of great certainty. "It was my duty to shoot, and I don't regret it," he says. The woman was too "blinded by evil" to give appropriate consideration to noncombatants who might have been killed by the grenade, including her own child. Kyle's shot saves the American soldiers, "whose lives were clearly worth more than that woman's twisted soul. But I truly, deeply hated the evil that woman possessed. I hate it to this day" (4). Kyle insists that he feels no regret whatsoever about killing as many "savages" as he did, because one does that to protect one's countrymen, and "that's what war is" (4, 7). In fact, Kyle "loved what I did . . . [and] had the time of my life being a SEAL" (7). Ultimately, however, he characterizes his memoir as "about more than just killing people or even fighting for my country. It's about being a man. And it's about love as well as hate" (7).

Thus Kyle frames his combat experience emphatically. The enemy are inhuman savages to be killed at every opportunity, and the excitement of that combat is deeply pleasurable. According to Kyle, the wrenching dread that many soldiers feel when confronted with the necessity of killing other humans is simply not part of his experience. As he says when he begins telling the story of his upbringing, "I have a strong sense of justice. It's pretty much black-and-white. I don't see too much gray" (8). Writing retrospectively, Kyle isn't merely reasserting control over a personal narrative that was subjected to the chaos of modern war—he asserts that his control was never lost in the first place.

It is all the more striking, then, when Kyle's narrative is interrupted and often undermined by his wife Taya's own recollections, which are set off from his own and italicized. In her account of their first meeting, she tells him that SEALs are *arrogant, self-centered, and glory-seeking*" (49), and although she is swayed by Kyle's rebuttal—and eventually marries him— her later descriptions of their married life revisit those accusations, especially as reflected in her objection that Kyle always puts the concerns of war above those of his family. And despite Kyle's unwavering sense of righteousness about the killings he does, Taya is quick to note the problems his combat experience causes at home. Kyle is blasé about much of that experience. "People say you have to distance yourself from your enemy to kill him," he writes. "If that's true, in Iraq, the insurgents made it really easy" (98). But when he returns home for the first time, Taya writes that his adjustment *"was hard. He'd wake up punching. . . . One time I woke up to him grabbing my arm with both of his hands. One hand was on the forearm and one just slightly above my elbow. He was sound asleep and appeared to be ready to snap my arm in half"* (106). He eventually wakes up, but it is an unsettling intrusion of the war into their marriage.

That sense of intrusion grows sharper after Taya gives birth to their first child and Kyle then returns to Iraq for a second deployment. Seven months later, she strongly opposes his desire to re-enlist, and when he does anyway, she realizes that *"being a SEAL is more important to him than being a father or a husband"* (243). Their relationship becomes tense and distant, despite having another child. He tells Taya that he won't re-enlist again, but then signs up for a fourth deployment. The two begin marriage counseling and Kyle gets into a number of fights during his training period. Finally, Kyle acknowledges the toll that four deployments can take—he describes experiencing high blood pressure, a racing heart, ringing ears, vision problems, and an inability to feel at ease (404). "The more I tried to relax, the worse things got. It was as if my body had started to vibrate, and thinking about it only made it buzz more" (405). He decides not to re-enlist yet again, but it's a tough decision for him. "I still resented my wife for presenting me with what felt like an ultimatum," he says, and he drinks too much, totaling his truck in a serious accident that he miraculously walks away from (421). Eventually he sets himself straight and comes to grips with the challenges of family rather than war. He recommits to his wife and children, and ends his memoir restating his opening assertions, confident in the righteousness of his wartime actions. "But in that backroom or whatever it is when God confronts me with my sins, I do not believe any of the kills I had during the war will be among them. Everyone I shot was evil. I had good cause on every shot. They all deserved to die" (430). His only regrets, he says in closing, are the people he couldn't save: "Marines, soldiers, my buddies" (430). Kyle's sense of righteousness is so absolute it borders on farcical, but even so his memoir as a whole is surprisingly frank about the difficulties even a celebrated paragon of military masculinity like Kyle experiences in his marriage and during his transition into civilian life. The war comes home in profound ways for both Kyle and Taya, and the book's very structure—as well as the circumstances of Kyle's death—attests to that tension and the impossibility of distinguishing one world from the other.

Clint Eastwood's 2014 film adaptation of the book was so popular—it is the highest-grossing film that Eastwood has ever made—in part because it hits many of the same beats as Kyle's memoir but ultimately emphasizes Kyle's moral clarity rather than his marital struggles or traumatic reactions to combat. Like *The Hurt Locker*, the film makes use of elements of the Western, with early shots of Bradley Cooper as Kyle in full cowboy attire while riding in a rodeo. A flashback to a moment in Kyle's childhood (which is fictionalized and not included in the memoir) features his father telling his sons that there are three types of people in the world: sheep, wolves, and sheepdogs. Sheep "prefer to believe that evil doesn't exist in the world," and thus cannot protect themselves. Wolves are "predators who use violence to prey on the weak," or the sheep. And sheepdogs are those "blessed with the gift of aggression, an overpowering need to protect the flock. These men are the rare breed who live to confront the wolf." The message is clear—evil exists, and violence must be used righteously in order to defeat it.

In the film, that evil is epitomized by Mustafa (Sammy Sheik), Kyle's nemesis, an enemy sniper who competed in the Olympics as a marksman. After Mustafa—the epitome of black-clad, dark-skinned maliciousness— wreaks havoc on the American troops, Kyle finally does him in with a successful, ultra-long-distance shot. Mustafa is in fact a conflation of several Iraqi soldiers that Kyle engaged; in his memoir, Kyle writes that he "never saw him, but other snipers later killed an Iraqi sniper we think was him" (158). Eastwood, then, uses Mustafa as the classic cinematic villain, the black hat to Kyle's white hat. That Kyle is ultimately killed not by enemies abroad but by a fellow soldier struggling with PTSD makes for an abrupt ending of the film, which concludes with real footage of Kyle's funeral procession through the streets of Dallas that ends, appropriately enough, at Cowboys Stadium (which replaced Texas Stadium in 2009). Kyle's own struggles, suggested by Sienna Miller's nuanced performance as Taya and later scenes when Kyle is at home and either overreacts to stimuli or seems to zone out, are subsumed by the tragic narrative arc of a Western-style hero. As I will discuss in the Conclusion, the film's portrayal of a protagonist who can see with clarity and know with certainty that he is doing the right thing makes for an unrealistic war film, but nonetheless a popular one. Clarity, after all, can be deeply satisfying.

Redeployment: The Endlessness for Everyone

Phil Klay's *Redeployment* is the third book in this milestone grouping, combining the literary ambitions of *Billy Lynn* with the authorial veteran status of *American Sniper*, and uses the short story cycle to present a multivalent portrait of modern military engagement. In addition to stories focusing on soldiers in combat, Klay includes first-person stories from the perspective of a military chaplain, someone working in Mortuary Affairs, a specialist in Psychological Operations, a foreign service officer heading an embedded Provincial Reconstruction Team, and an adjutant who works in administration and helps write citations for medals. That range serves to underscore the variety of roles one can inhabit in the military—Klay himself was a public affairs officer—and further how difficult it can be for people dealing with war in any capacity to make coherent sense of their own identity and the purpose of their service. The title story, which also opens the collection, exemplifies many of these characteristics. It begins with the memorable sentence, "We shot dogs." Sergeant Price is back at home after his tour, and as he's trying to put it all together, those dogs just won't compute. "Not by accident," he says about the dogs. "We did it on purpose, and we called it Operation Scooby. I'm a dog person, so I thought about that a lot." It sounds sadistic, although Price offers a halfhearted explanation: The dogs were drinking the blood of bodies in the streets, and "that's the last straw, I guess, and then it's open season on dogs" (1).

It stays with him, this upsetting memory, one of many that he can't figure out how to place, and he tries to explain that. Simple delineation just doesn't work: "See, it's not a straight shot back, from war to the Jacksonville mall. . . . The problem is, your thoughts don't come out in any kind of straight order.

You don't think, Oh, I did A, then B, then C, then D. You try to think about home, then you're in the torture house" (1, 2). His war self and home self are all blurred together, and when he is physically at home with his wife Cheryl and his old, ailing dog Vicar, the scrambled memories are as present as the other details of his home life. Like James in *The Hurt Locker*, innocuous shopping trips with his wife feel more threatening than Iraq, because "you don't have a squad, you don't have a battle buddy, you don't even have a weapon" (12). Ultimately, Price fails to understand himself at home: "And glad as I was to be in the States, and even though I hated the past seven months and the only thing that kept me going was the Marines I served with and the thought of coming home, I started feeling like I wanted to go back. Because fuck all this" (11).

"Fuck all this" is the only explanation for his feelings that he can conjure, and the story ends as Price insists on ending the life of Vicar himself, rather than Cheryl taking him to the vet to be euthanized. He takes Vicar and his AR-15 out to an empty dirt road, gets Vicar in his sights, and fires three rounds, precisely as he was trained to do in combat. Price then freezes, his sense of self in pieces. As the evening light fades, he realizes "I couldn't remember what I was going to do with the body" (16). Linguistically, a vicar is a representative or substitute, someone who stands in for someone else—does Price see Vicar as one of the Iraqis he killed in the war, or perhaps as himself? Either way, shooting his dog strongly suggests that the war isn't leaving him anytime soon—an idea reinforced by the story's title, suggesting further that Price will indeed redeploy, and like Sergeant James, Billy Lynn, and Chris Kyle, go back to the war.

The title of the second story, "FRAGO," refers to a fragmentary order that provides changes to an existing order. (In it, Klay uses a fair amount of military acronyms or jargon, though not quite as much as he does in a later story, "OIF," or Operation Iraqi Freedom.) The speaker of "FRAGO" is a combat soldier as well, one who sees extreme violence when he raids houses, exchanges fire, and encounters prisoners who have been tortured, though his tone is seemingly blasé. When a lieutenant asks him if he's ever seen anything like those torture victims before, he shrugs. "Sometimes I forget it's his first deployment. . . . Not this, exactly, I say, but there's not much that'd surprise me. . . . Sir, I say, don't let yourself think about it until we're back in the States" (22). Of course the speaker himself isn't back in the States—in his dialogue with the lieutenant, he implies he's a veteran of multiple deployments. And we've seen how well "think about it later" worked for Sergeant Price in the opening story. Compartmentalization—the hurt locker—always has a faulty latch.

Military personnel in the other stories have similar reactions despite having different jobs or different positions. The Mortuary Affairs worker in "Bodies" likes to tell stories about his experiences—that aren't really his experiences—using varying emphases depending on whether his audience is men or women. Eventually, though, he wants to tell his old high school girlfriend Rachel a story that actually means something to him. He seeks her out while on leave, but he can't do it, or say much of anything, really. So she moves on, as does he. "I never saw Rachel again, but we're Facebook friends. She got married while I was on my third deployment. She had her first kid while I was on my fourth" (71). He's trying to make his narrative make sense—and to connect to people he cares about—but it's such a difficult process that he defaults back to war. War may not make sense, but at least everyone around you knows that story well. Similarly, the NCO in the story "OIF" loses a soldier to an IED, and then makes the decision to move from OIF, Operation Iraqi Freedom, to OEF, Operation Enduring Freedom—Afghanistan.

In *Redeployment*, the only coherent narrative that comes together has more to do with spin than truth. In the darkly funny "Money as a Weapons System," the foreign service officer who joins a Provincial Reconstruction Team accepts the fact that supporting the locals can be an effective counterinsurgency tactic, but he struggles to understand his colleagues when they tell him he would be better off teaching widows to raise bees than trying to get a water treatment plant operational. While the water plant stagnates under absent leadership, lack of maintenance, and the inconvenient fact that the US military built pipes for it that don't support the correct water pressure—meaning that turning on the water could make a lot of Iraqis' toilets explode—beekeeping is an achievable goal. As his colleague Bob explains, "Give someone a job. That's economic improvement. Give women a job. That's women's empowerment. Give a widow a job. That's aiding disenfranchised populations. Three LOEs [Lines of Effort] in one project. Widow projects are gold. With the council supporting it, we can say it's an Iraqi-led project. And it'll cost under twenty-five thousand dollars, so the funding will sail through" (82). As the speaker butts his head up against the difficulty of dealing with the water plant and a wealthy civilian's zealous plan to send baseball uniforms to Iraqi children as a kind of "sports diplomacy," he finally parrots the beekeeping idea to his boss. "Yeah," his boss responds, "A lot of ePRTs [embedded Provincial Reconstruction Teams] are doing that one." The speaker pauses, confused. "Do you . . . do you know this is bullshit?" (99). Finally, however, the speaker figures out how to use the language that the higher-ups want to hear in order to achieve the goals that he sees are actually valuable—keeping a women's clinic open, for instance. "There is a direct link," he later tells his boss, "between the oppression of women and extremism." His boss tells him not to "give me that bullshit," but he responds, "This is real"—meaning, his language may be just parroted phrases, but the results would actually help people (116). Everything is a souped-up mess, but the speaker thinks he has found a way to ride that lack of clarity rather than push fruitlessly against it.

Many of Klay's stories have this emphasis—how do you navigate the mess of a violent, bureaucratic, politically complex war and find a way to communicate effectively, to tell the story that you want to tell? The priest in "Prayer in the Furnace" struggles to talk to soldiers about their experiences, and later, to properly reflect those experiences when he writes a memorial service for the sixteen soldiers in Charlie Company who had died. "How could I express what those deaths meant?" he wonders. "In the end, yielding to exhaustion, I wrote an inoffensive little nothing, full of platitudes. The perfect speech for the occasion, actually. The ceremony wasn't about me. Better to serve my function and pass unnoticed" (161). Real meaning, real coherence, seems no longer possible. In "Psychological Operations," a veteran enrolled in Amherst plays with several ways of describing his war and postwar experience—and a sharply honed awareness of how to use that storytelling to achieve the ends he wants, all based on his time as a specialist in PsyOps, as he calls it. He finally tries to tell his story honestly to a fellow student named Zara, but he's frustrated: "Now that I'd told the story, I didn't feel I'd actually told her anything at all. I think she knew it, too, that the story hadn't been enough, that something was missing and neither of us knew how to find it" (189). He keeps trying, because "if you're going to be understood, you have to keep talking" (197). It can get old, though, as the speaker of "War Stories" begins the chapter: "I'm tired of telling war stories" (213). He sits at a bar with his friend Jenks, who was severely injured and disfigured by an IED. Jenks has tried to write down a narrative of what happened to him, through many attempts and multiple drafts. This time, he's reading parts of it to a pretty woman named Sarah, an actress working with a group of writers from the Iraq Veterans Against the War. She's writing a play, "a collaboration with the New York veterans community," as she puts it, and she wants the details of Jenks's experience—of the explosion itself and its long aftermath in his life (222). Neither soldier particularly enjoys the interaction—"She's got a sliver of ice in her," the speaker thinks—but Jenks plugs away as best he can, giving the details that might be used for a performance that he's not to be a part of (231). As for the speaker's own story, he doubts the whole enterprise. "I don't trust my memories," he says. "I trust the vehicle, burnt and twisted and torn. Like Jenks. No stories. Things. Bodies. People lie. Memories lie" (226).

As Klay's collection demonstrates, as the twenty-first-century wars have gone on and on, there are more and more stories to tell about them, but it's no easier to do that than it ever has been, especially given the lack of distance from the wars themselves. As Ryan Hediger writes about *Redeployment*, Klay suggests that the "challenge of reintegration is due not just to the horrors and the intensity of war experience, but to its unsorted and unprocessed character. Klay insists on the difficulty of making sense of events" (162). And just as Billy Lynn feels the pressure of everyone else's understanding of his experiences, so do the characters here. Lucas Thompson writes that Klay's book "chronicles the contemporary soldier's experience of being entirely at the mercy of broader political machinations, along with its compelling account of the ways in which various forms of large-scale political manipulation have metastasized throughout the broader culture" (192). Everything is PsyOps—recruitment, medal narratives, ceremonies, language that compresses experience into acronyms, "bullshit" or ambitious artistic representations, money as a weapons system. And all this is hardly confined to the war zone.

In the introduction to Klay's most recent work, a collection of his essays titled *Uncertain Ground: Citizenship in an Age of Endless, Invisible War*, which includes nonfiction that he published from 2010 to 2021, Klay reflects on how his own understanding of his military service and the character of contemporary war has affected his life and work. As an author writing about war, "I envisioned my task primarily as making sense of the past," he says. "But the Global War on Terror, begun in Afghanistan and Iraq but soon expanding to Syria and Somalia and Pakistan and the Philippines, wouldn't stay behind me. Unlike [the first Gulf War], which ended with the declaration of a cease-fire and the liberation of Kuwait on February 28, 1991, and [World War II], which ended on September 2, 1945, my war just kept going" (xii). Klay makes the point—as I argue so many authors do in this period— that war has expanded beyond traditional temporal or spatial boundaries, with broad implications for the state as well as the individual. Thus, "even though in America we're swaddled from the consequences, we're still at war. Wherever we're regularly killing, we're at war." But it can be hard to find out exactly where we *are* killing people. Yemen, Libya—what about Niger, Mali, Nigeria? As his friend Brian Castner, whom I cover in chapter 3, notes of those countries, "We don't know when the U.S. kills people in Niger" (xv). It occurs to Klay that Americans pay the most attention to combat when it happens on our own ground, as in the violence at the US Capitol on January 6, 2020. "Tragically and farcically, the wars have come home," writes Klay. "Unable to find an overseas enemy who'll allow us to definitively vanquish him, our greatest fears have become each other" (xviii).

Resistance and Renunciation

At the end of *Billy Lynn's Long Halftime Walk*, Billy is with Bravo squad, gliding away from Texas Stadium in a limo, headed back to war. He has survived the great crush of attention and spectacle, said goodbye to his erstwhile love Faison, watched the Hollywood deal that was supposed to make them rich get diminished and finally fall apart. After trying and failing to find someone who can explain it all to him—Shroom's death, his own grief, the war, life in general—Billy finally just gives in and takes the ride:

> He knows he will never see Faison again, but how can he know? How does anyone ever know anything—the past is a fog that breathes out ghost after ghost, the present a freeway thunder run at 90 mph, which makes the future the ultimate black hole of futile speculation. And yet he knows, at least he thinks he knows, he feels it seeded in the purest certainty of his grief as he finds his seat belt and snaps it shut, that *snick* like the final lock of a vast and complex system. He's in. Bound for the war. Good-bye, good-bye, good night, I love you all. He sits back, closes his eyes, and tries to think about nothing as the limo takes them away. (307)

In response to all the confusion and losses of his own war experience and all the ways it has been reflected back to him, Billy just gives in. He'll live with the ghosts, the grief, and the love—he'll live with the war. In Billy's case, he's quite literally returning to combat, though that sense of renunciation is one that resonates with other American works about contemporary war, as I explore in chapter 3.

CHAPTER 2

Running Point

Women Writing War

Writing about *Billy Lynn's Long Halftime Walk*, Carrie Johnston argues that although the novel is primarily focused on the all-male Bravo squad, Ben Fountain does offer a more potentially fluid representation of gender than many war novels. The female characters are complex where they could easily be stereotypical. Billy's sister Kathryn, for instance, is passionately anti-war at least in part because Billy is serving in the military because of her: When her fiancé left her after she was in a traumatic and disfiguring car accident, Billy avenges her by destroying the man's expensive sports car with a crowbar, and afterward he chooses to join the Army rather than do time in jail. Faison, Billy's unlikely love interest, is young and naïve, but it's a realistic portrayal, much like Billy himself. She is both impetuously and cautiously sexual, is both sincere and prosaic in her religiosity, and understands her job with the Dallas Cowboys cheerleaders as a profession even as she is as much on display as Billy is during the Thanksgiving Day football game. Only women, Billy thinks, seem to vaguely understand the weight of his war experience, and he realizes that "only his mother, his sisters, and now Faison, only they have ever shown real grief for his sake" (156). Billy takes these women seriously, and as young as he is, he's also surprisingly open-minded on matters of gender and sexuality. The novel presents the idea that Hilary Swank could play Billy in a movie about their experiences mostly as satire—taking aim at a media culture that loves to profit off a gimmick— but Billy doesn't dismiss it outright or in vulgar terms. "It seems sort of weird," he tells Sergeant Dime, "having a girl play a guy. . . . She wants to play you too, Sergeant. Would you do it?" (14).

Dime is rather flippant, as he is about most things during this Thanksgiving Day hero show, but he is a complicated person, too. He has a Purple Heart and Bronze Star from service in Afghanistan but has absolutely no love lost for Vice President Dick Cheney, whom he savagely heckles during Cheney's visit to the troops. One of Billy's more searing memories of the firefight that made Bravo squad famous is an encounter with Dime that happened afterward, when the grievously wounded Lake was convulsing on an operating table, "howling and flailing and slinging blood." Billy understands this as "the breaking point, the bend in his personal arc that day" (67). He might have lost it completely, but Dime pushes him into a pantry, both of them weeping, and intensely whispers into his ear, "*I knew it would be you*"—referring to Billy's actions during the firefight and his attempt to save Shroom. Then, "he grabbed Billy's face in both his hands and kissed him full on the lips like a stomp, a whack with a rubber mallet" (67). Billy is more or less able to take the moment as another intense mystery of combat, except that he worries the Hollywood people wouldn't tell this part of the story right. "You couldn't put this in a movie and have people understand, not based on any movie Billy's ever seen," he thinks (67). That complexity and fluidity is in part what makes *Billy Lynn* less traditional as a war novel, and less beholden to established tropes of gender and sexuality. As Carries Johnston writes, "The women in *Billy Lynn* provide glimpses of hope for Billy and offer possibilities of finding a way out of this 'sterile and unproductive' hero narrative" (409). In the end, however, that potential isn't realized: "the novel precludes these possibilities when it does not allow female characters to speak for themselves" (409). For Johnston, then, "The sterility of *Billy Lynn* is a reflection and critique of the unproductive masculine narratives of American heroism" (411).

Johnston's point leads us to another trifecta of significant works in this second wave of contemporary war stories, this one by female authors and featuring female-centered narratives. Two of these, *You Know When the Men Are Gone*, by Siobhan Fallon, and *Sand Queen*, by Helen Benedict, appeared in 2011 and were overshadowed upon their release by *Billy Lynn*, *The Yellow Birds*, and *American Sniper* the next year, but they constitute the first entries in what Peter Molin has called the "coming of age of the contemporary war novel" and have justly risen in prominence ever since ("No Thank You for Your Service"). The third author, Kayla Williams, is continuing an already established career as a veteran writer and memoirist, following 2005's *Love My Rifle More Than You* with a second memoir, *Plenty of Time When We Get Home: Love and Recovery in the Aftermath of War*, in 2014. I track failures of delineation and ensuing physical, psychological, temporal, and spatial fragmentation in these works as well, but in addition to evincing the characteristics of this new wave of war stories, Fallon, Benedict, and Williams challenge both the vantage point and the constitution of the traditional war story itself—and not just on the basis of gender but also disability. That expansiveness is likely at least part of the reason why attention has been more drawn to their higher-profile, male counterparts.

What is a war story? Most people generally assume that it is a story of men wielding weapons, and historically that is indeed what most war stories have been about. Fallon, Benedict, and Williams are testament to not just the changing gender dynamics of the military and the increasing presence of female soldiers—about which more in chapter 5—but a more inclusive consideration of what counts as a war story, and who counts within that story. As Molin has written, warriors have always been lauded for risking injury and death, but the "red badge of courage" that marks a "true soldier" in many historical contexts was rarely a permanent disability like amputation, disfigurement, or blindness. Instead, "the non-disabling wound functions positively in the life of veterans and society as a sign of sacrifice, service, and hard-earned authority" ("Phrase Too Cute" 4). He notes that the Napoleonic Wars were a turning point for representations of veterans with disabilities, although they often served as objects of pity or handy symbols for anti-war sentiment. Vietnam War portrayals became more positive and fully drawn, in films like *Coming Home* (1978), *Born on the Fourth of July* (1989), and *Forrest Gump* (1994). These characters' "physical wounds tend to enhance, not diminish, other aspects of their personality" (4).

Vietnam War stories brought more physically disabled soldiers to the forefront of the war story, and twenty-first-century wars have broadened that focus to disabilities that aren't as visible, such as mental trauma or traumatic brain injury. Furthermore, writers such as Fallon, Benedict, and Williams have shown that not only men fight in wars or suffer from war's effects, whether those effects are obvious or hidden. Brenda Sanfilippo argues that representations like Benedict's *Sand Queen* as well as Beverly Gologorsky's *Stop Here* (2013), Katey Schultz's short story "Amputee" (2013), and Michael Pitre's *Fives and Twenty Fives* (2014) focus on female troops in order to show how they are sidelined in the ongoing narrative of war in general and treated like prosthetics, "as unnatural and unwanted supports even as they make the military numerically and functionally whole and relocate anxieties [about injuries] onto female bodies" (230). Sanfilippo highlights Annie Proulx's short story "Tits Up in a Ditch," first published in 2008—before any of the works covered in this book—about Dakotah Lister, a young woman from a poverty-stricken background in rural Wyoming. She and her husband deploy separately for Iraq, where she loses her right arm to an IED and her husband suffers catastrophic injuries, including a severe brain injury, which leave him unable to speak or care for himself. Despite her own losses, including the death of her child, Dakotah is expected to care for her husband, who was attempting to divorce her before his injury. That leaves them both, as she puts it, "tits up in a ditch," like a cow that has fallen on its back and is stuck dying in the mud. Dakotah is a complex character, like others "not represented or perceived within their narrative worlds as victims or heroes; rather, they invert old narratives in order to trouble a prosthetic illusion of military masculine wholeness" (239). And in *You Know When the Men Are Gone*, Siobhan Fallon includes not only characters like Kit Murphy, a soldier permanently disabled by an IED, and Ted Wolenski, a company commander who is arrested for public intoxication and fighting after returning home from Iraq, but also Helena, Kit's wife, who eventually leaves Kit, and Carla, Ted's wife, who picks him up from jail and tries desperately to understand what drives her husband to this kind of behavior. Helena and Carla have their own war stories as military spouses, and Fallon's collection "drives home the difficulties of post-traumatic stress, whether you are a returning soldier or the surviving spouse," writes Kathleen Harrigan (176). The war story, then, is a broader one than has often been considered, and the fact that Fallon, Benedict, and Williams are writing at the outset of this wave of representations makes their intervention in and redefinition of the genre all the more significant.

You Know When the Men Are Gone: Women in Wartime

Fallon's book is an interconnected collection of short stories featuring the families of soldiers who live at Fort Hood, Texas, the biggest military installation of its kind in the world. It is a very different portrait of the military-civilian divide than *Billy Lynn*, because here, military wives are intimately aware of the pressures and the risks of their husbands' service, though they also suffer their spouses' absence and the uncertainty of exactly where their partners are and what is happening to them. In the title story, Meg waits on infrequent calls or messages from her husband: "*I miss our life together*, her husband would write over and over again, and it made Meg think that there were three lives between them: the life he was living in Iraq, the life she was living alone without him, and the dim fantastical life of them together, a mythical past and future that suddenly had no present" (14). Meg spies on her neighbor Natalya, a mother of two who is also waiting for her husband to return, but who one day has apparently had enough. Natalya is Serbian, and Meg realizes that she may have married her husband to get out of Kosovo only to find herself caught up in a different war: "Natalya had escaped one war and found herself caught up in the wake of another; perhaps she realized she could survive without her children but she couldn't take the waiting anymore" (35). Natalya disappears, leaving her children behind—she flees the intense pressures of her profound dislocation and all the fears of living through yet another war. But when Meg's husband finally returns from a deployment, Meg's own feelings are confirmed rather than shattered. "She stood and took a step toward him, knowing suddenly and without a doubt that he was, and always would be, worth the wait" (35).

 You Know When the Men Are Gone tends to lean toward the positive—there are more couples who stay together here, finding some moment of peace and contentment within the maelstrom of their military lives—though that maelstrom is depicted as affecting and far-reaching, particularly when it concerns spouses' fears about the other's infidelity during deployments. In "Inside the Break," Kailani Rodriguez deeply misses her home island of Oahu and her family there. While living at Fort Hood, she discovers that her husband Manny was likely unfaithful while deployed—as a result, she feels doubly displaced, untethered in her spatial reality. Nonetheless, she makes the choice to stay with Manny rather than leaving him and going home. In "Leave," on the other hand, Nick Cash doesn't tell his wife that he is coming home, instead breaking into the basement of his own house and staying there for several days, waiting to see if another man has taken his place. When his suspicions are finally confirmed, he creeps upstairs as they sleep, holding his knife at the ready. He thinks about his daughter Ellie's obsession with fairy tales—not the sanitized Disney versions, but the rougher, darker Hans Christian Anderson versions. The Little Mermaid, in the Anderson story, loses the prince to another woman, and then "brokenhearted, she went to the prince's room on his wedding night and looked down on his sleeping face, his arm thrown possessively across his new bride. If she killed the prince and his wife, she would be set free, back to the sea and the waves that would crash over her until all of this human awfulness had faded away and she was a soulless water creature again" (185–86). The story ends as Nick replicates this moment, watching the sleeping couple, his knife "mov[ing] from hand to hand, the blade catching the moonlight, a pendulum swinging from one side to the next, a judge's gavel raised, and Nick waited to see where it would land" (187). Fallon doesn't tell us what happens, though in the original "Little Mermaid," she refuses to kill the prince and his bride, even though she knows it will cost her life, and then is surprised to be transformed into one of the daughters of the air, who can do good for three hundred years in hopes of finally receiving an immortal soul. One suspects that Nick also refrains from murder, since, in this collection of interconnected stories, a man's murder of his wife and her lover is never mentioned by another character.

And that restraint would be wanly positive at best, rather like the moment that ends the collection as a whole. In the final story, "Gold Star," Josie Schaeffer has lost her husband Eddie, who was killed by an IED while in Iraq. She is consumed by grief yet also suffocated by the base's gestures of support, like the Gold Star Family parking spots at the commissary. "Family members [of fallen soldiers] received a few special privileges like this lousy parking space, but that meant the pity rising from the asphalt singed hotter than any Texas sun" (210). Josie is more attuned to a visit by Kit Murphy, the man her husband had saved during the attack. She wants to know if Eddie deliberately sacrificed his life for Kit's, because if so, "then he had deliberately sacrificed his own; he had been conscious and in agony, and he had known he was leaving her behind" (218). Kit can't answer—all he knows is that Eddie's body protected him from the worst of the fire, and he's alive because of the "best noncommissioned office I ever met" (216). And Kit himself was badly injured, later suffering through multiple medical procedures, the loss of his career as he knows it, and the end of his marriage, as detailed in an earlier story, "The Last Stand." Josie and Kit both seem to understand that "pain was something you lived with as best you could" (219). At the end of Kit's visit, Josie stands in front of him, and suddenly sits in his lap. He's alarmed at first, and then loosely embraces her, "and Josie Schaeffer clung to him, knowing this man was not her husband, that her husband was never coming back, but for now she was as close to him as she could get and she would not let him go" (220). Her husband is gone, and Kit is not him, but at that moment, the blurring of categories is a comfort rather than a tempest.

Nick Cash's and Kit Murphy's experiences are important here, and Fallon gives them considerable attention in the collection. But the overall focus leans female, as the title of the book suggests. The drama of Nick's possible murder of his wife and her lover is matched, and I would say overtaken, by the pain and poignancy of "Remission," when Ellen Roddy is interrupted in her wait for cancer test results by news that her teenage daughter Delia and young son Landon are missing. Her husband John is a rear detachment commander, working at Fort Hood rather than deployed overseas because of Ellen's previous breast cancer diagnosis, and is busy dealing with news of an attack—likely the same one that killed Eddie Schaeffer and injured Kit Murphy. Ellen finally finds her children and is furious and despairing over Delia's disregard for the rules and rude behavior toward her mother. Finally, Ellen sobs in her daughter's room, overcome with her fear about her children's safety, and Delia asks her what the doctor said about her cancer. Ellen doesn't know—she had to leave before her appointment. "I'm so sorry," Delia says, and Ellen pulls her into a ferocious hug. "They stayed like that in the darkened, dismantled room, Delia's ear against her mother's heart, trapped and holding tight, both astounded by the pounding of the other's blood, the life in each of them as unknown, as magnificent and as frightening as the sea" (101).

Brian Williams makes a good point about the power of Fallon's collection. It is not that these stories have never been told—it is that they are so often told from the man's perspective. "Rather than recreating the unidirectionality of the traditional trauma narrative (men fight, women wait)," Williams argues, "Fallon imagines war-related trauma that flows in multiple directions, acknowledging the complex injuries that war creates across fronts and genders" ("War at the Home Front" 512). Soldiers aren't the only ones, for instance, wondering if their spouses are staying faithful, wondering what's happening where their loved ones are, and they aren't the only ones who fear another attack, another explosion, another rupture in the lives they had wanted for themselves. Soldiers aren't the only ones who would like everything to just stay in place for once, recognizable and predictable.

Fallon's recognition of trauma coupled with a generally positive tone echoes her own perspective, that of "a military insider full of knowing sympathy," as Molin puts it ("2011"). It is fitting, then, that the epigraph she chooses for *You Know When the Men Are Gone* is from the *Odyssey*, the moment when Penelope recognizes that her husband has returned after twenty years of war and travails:

> She turned to descend the stair, her heart
> in tumult. Had she better keep her distance
> and question him, her husband? Should she run
> up to him, take his hands, kiss him now?
>
> . . . And she, for a long time, sat deathly still
> in wonderment—for sometimes as she gazed
> she found him—yes, clearly—like her husband,
> but sometimes blood and rags were all she saw.

The moment aptly captures the military spouse's double consciousness, her fragmented vision of the man she knew before the war and the man she sees now, her simultaneous desire to embrace him and pull back, the indecision about what might be the right course of action. Fallon herself, it seems, has the answer—the book is dedicated to her "best friend, husband, father, soldier, you are always worth the wait."

Sand Queen: Women at War

Fallon's book strikes a much different tone from Benedict's *Sand Queen*, the epigraph of which is no less classical but much darker in affect: from Shakespeare's Sonnet 94, "For sweetest things turn sourest by their deeds; / Lilies that fester smell far worse than weeds." The stories that follow are indeed ones of disintegration and descent. The novel follows the interwoven narratives of three characters: Kate Brady, an American soldier in Iraq; Naema Jassim, an Iraqi woman and a former medical student whose father and brother are taken by the Americans in a raid; and a nameless soldier recovering from serious injury in a hospital. In the first of the soldier's cloudy, impressionistic vignettes, a nurse helps the soldier when she realizes the bed has been soiled. "Come on out now, or I'll pull you out myself, like I did yesterday," the nurse says. "Yesterday?" thinks the patient. "The soldier can't remember yesterday" (13). The soldier has, quite literally, been fragmented, broken apart both physically and mentally, and is living in a temporally undifferentiated state. The soldier is fairly quickly revealed to be Kate, after some future traumatic event has occurred. When in the next vignette a man visits and calls her Katie, she flinches, scooting to the far side of the bed in fear. "You do know who I am, don't you?" he asks, but clearly, she doesn't, nor does she know herself (28). When the man, Kate's former boyfriend Tyler, talks to her during another visit, he tries to delineate Kate's life for her: "You're home now, remember? The war's gone. You're not with those people anymore. It's over now, you're safe." But Kate, the soldier, thinks and feels no such thing. "He's lying," she insists (64).

As the novel continues, the three characters' stories all come together with tragic momentum. Kate joined the Army because she wanted to "do something impressive" and follow in her father's footsteps. She liked boot camp, liked "feeling strong and capable. I liked proving myself" (40, 43). But once in Iraq, in 2003, she misses home, hates the work, hates sharing a tent with thirty-three men and only two other women, hates that two of those men in particular call her "Tits" despite her lean frame. When Naema visits the prison camp where Kate is stationed, she observes the same disjunct that Kate often feels:

> We stand, my sad companions and I, until the sun has crept from the horizon almost to the top of the sky, and finally I see a tiny soldier plod up to the fence where we are waiting. He looks as though he can hardly walk under all he carries, with his helmet large on his little face. He looks like a child in his father's clothes. But of course he is no child. He is a killer and an occupier.
>
> I watch him approach, shouting and waving his silly little arms, and I feel such hatred bloom in my heart I do not know myself. Then I notice there is something odd about him, something wrong. I look again.
>
> It is a girl.
>
> I would laugh out loud if there were any laughter left in me. How desperate the Americans must be to send their girls to war. (19)

Naema manages to show Kate a photo of her brother and father and offers to help translate for Kate if she will help Naema locate them. For a moment, it seems as if this could become a story about two women from very different backgrounds helping each other in the chaos and destruction of war. But as it turns out, that chaos and destruction is too great. Naema describes the sadness of her family fleeing Baghdad, destroyed both by the

American military and by the thieves and looters who swarm the city after the initial bombing. She had to leave behind her home and possessions, her fiancé, her studies, and her familiar life, only to see her father and brother Zaki be taken in a brutal raid. She can't understand why the soldiers are so rough with her father, who's clearly physically frail, the result of repeated torture under Saddam Hussein's regime. Naema appeals to the soldiers in English, but one of them shoves her away, "his face . . . a twisted grimace of hatred and fear" (16). When she and her mother attempt to take her grandmother to the hospital after she's had a stroke, the place is pandemonium. "All about me are the wounded and dying, the victims of cluster bombs and machine guns, of mines and explosives, of poisoned air and filthy water" (219). Naema volunteers to help, using the medical training that she had before the war, but the hospital has no water, no electricity, and no resources or equipment. She works and works, becoming drenched in blood, "until I lose all awareness of my body, and all sense of time" (252). Her grandmother dies, and Naema wonders at the incomprehensible losses: "Why must we go through these things? Why can't we and all those other suffering people in the hospital be left alone to lead peaceful, ordinary lives?" (280).

The experiences begin to erode Naema's fervent hope that her former life will be restored, even as she retains her empathy for those around her. Kate, on the other hand, loses both hope and empathy as well as her physical and mental health. She is sexually assaulted by a sergeant and another soldier, and when she reports the assault to a female superior officer, that officer seems sympathetic but later denies the validity of her claims. Someone writes slurs about her on a Porta-John, saying that "TITS BRADY" is a "SAND QUEEN," and others sign underneath if they've "FUCKED HER" (104). Sand Queen is "one of the worst things a female can get called in the Army," Kate reflects. "It means an ugly-ass chick who's being treated like a queen by the hundreds of horny guys around her because there's such a shortage of females. But she grows so swellheaded over their attention that she lets herself be passed around like a whore at a frat party, never realizing that back home those same guys wouldn't look at her twice. In other words, she's a pathetic slut too desperate and dumb to know she's nothing but a mattress" (105). Kate is trying to be tough, to bear up under everything as her father told her to, but she's starting to crack under the impossible, absurd pressures of being a female soldier. Too sexual, not sexual enough—she has no place to occupy, no defined identity that she can comfortably inhabit.

When Kate confronts a detainee whom she thinks is the man who has repeatedly masturbated in front of her, she relishes the opportunity to make someone else feel as bad as she's felt. She shoves his face in the sand—"I want him to know that a girl is doing this to him, one of those females he thinks is no better than the shit he's been throwing at me. I want him to know how it feels to be treated like you're not even human" (190). It feels great, until she pulls back his head to see his face and has the horrible realization that the man is instead Naema's father. Everything falls apart. Kate is consumed by rage and guilt, which is then amplified by her discovery that Naema's brother Zaki has also died. She has nothing but negative emotions left: "I know who I hate and I know who I want to kill. All the rest is bullshit" (283). She shoots a donkey just to kill something, and when the man she calls "the jerk-off" returns to masturbate at the base of her guard tower, Kate aims her gun and shoots him in the groin. Then she passes out and falls, sustaining the injuries that result in "the soldier's" stays in hospitals and psychiatric wards. Physically, she's broken: "After that, it's a blur of hospitals and drugs and doctors. Kuwait for a few days, X-rays and needles. Interviews with doctors, interviews with shrinks. Diagnosis: Two cracked vertebrae and a bunch of wrenched muscles from the fall. Spine compressed from the weight I had to carry day and night. Neck fucked from jolting around in the Humvee, banging my head on its goddamn roof. Brain injury from the mortars. Dehydration, malnourishment, hearing loss, depression" (298). But she's broken mentally and emotionally as well: "Blood is in my eyes and in my soul. . . . I look in the mirror. Pale skin, empty eyes. Half robot, half fucked-up human being, the two sides fighting to the death. I have no idea which one will win" (299).

Even Naema, whose hope and ability to dream about a better life seem unshakeable, has been reduced by the seemingly unending tragedies of the war. The novel ends with her grandmother's funeral, and though Naema vows to press on—"Granny's death makes me all the more determined to find my brother and father, to bring our family back to what it once was" (309)—the reader knows that such resolve will be forever unrewarded. The words of mourning that her mother speaks over Granny's body "seem determined to extinguish, one by one, each tender flame of my hope":

> *I am the house of remoteness.*
> *I am the house of loneliness.*
> *I am the house of soil.*
> *I am the house of worms* [italics in the original]. (310)

As different as they are, Kate and Naema's identities can be understood as fragments of the same person. As Jennifer Haytock has argued, they are both women traumatized by war: "While Kate's story is the imagining of a woman undergoing a soldier's transformation, Naema's story parallels Kate's as that of the civilian who must accommodate the violence of war"

("Women's/War Stories" 2). Haytock calls *Sand Queen* a version of the female Gothic, in which "women's lives are rendered as horror tales," noting that the novel "insists on the similarities between Kate's and Naema's experiences as women in cultures that practice compulsory heterosexuality, insist on distinct gendered identities and roles, and rely on violence to enforce those roles" (3). Despite those attempts at gendered delineation, Benedict shows how it fails. For both women, there's just no way to make their lives work in the environment of violence and war—the novel is a broad and visceral condemnation of what war does, particularly to women. As Peter Molin puts it, "[Benedict is] not thanking anyone for their service; for her the Iraq war and military service in general corrupts at every level—badly conceived and planned on high, Operation Iraqi Freedom in *Sand Queen*'s view unleashed slaughter upon people who didn't deserve it and caused nominally good Americans in the ranks to treat each other like animals" ("No Thank You").

Plenty of Time When We Get Home: The War at Home

Although Benedict is a civilian rather than a veteran writer, several of her previous nonfiction books have clearly given her material she used to tell Kate's story in *Sand Queen*, including *The Lonely Soldier: The Private War of Women Serving in Iraq* (2009), *Recovery: How to Survive Sexual Assault* (1994), and *Virgin or Vamp: How the Press Covers Sex Crimes* (1992). Benedict has a reporter's background, and Siobhan Fallon draws on her own experiences in her fiction, but of the three, Kayla Williams is the most direct. Williams is likely the most prominent contemporary female war memoirist, having followed her first book, *Love My Rifle More Than You: Young and Female in the U.S. Army* (2005) with a second, *Plenty of Time When We Get Home: Love and Recovery in the Aftermath of War*. The first is, as I have argued in *Welcome to the Suck*, ultimately an ambivalent portrait of her service in the Army as an Arabic linguist, a story that "reveals Williams' experience of war to be less a hybrid space than a site of vacillation. . . . She praises her brothers in arms, and serves for them, but never gets to feel quite like a brother" (96). The second memoir chronicles her relationship with husband Brian McGough, who suffers a traumatic brain injury, or TBI, during his own service. They meet in Iraq, and she's impressed with him immediately. "He was tough, strong, and a good soldier," and he neither hits on her nor is put off by her own talent and toughness (15). She recognizes that her inability to be "soft and girly" as well as the "independence and ambition [that] were core components of my personality" can sometimes intimidate men—but not Brian (10). She's eager to start a relationship, though he suggests waiting until after their deployments is a better idea. "Don't worry," he assures her.

"There's plenty of time when we get home" (15). War first, then romance—war, and then life. But that's not how it happens.

Williams finds Brian's statement sufficiently ironic to use it for the title of her book. A few months later, Brian's convoy is attacked and shrapnel rips through his skull, injuring his cortico-temporal lobe and tearing the middle meningeal artery, which further causes blood to build up and put pressure on the brain. Brian is medevacked and receives excellent, timely care that almost certainly saves his life, though the doctor is not optimistic about his long-term prospects for both cognitive and physical functioning. After he is transported back to the United States and released from the hospital, they begin a relationship, delighting in each other's company. Problems soon become apparent, however. Brian suffers from insomnia and nightmares, struggles with his short-term memory, and has difficulty keeping up with his bills. He can suddenly erupt in rage, moments that Williams calls "Code Black." "Get the fuck out," he orders her, and she goes, blaming herself for pushing him (49). "He would be oblivious to my pain, indifferent to my tears, lost in his own rage and suffering, headed for a Code Black meltdown followed by days of isolation," she writes, but adds that "I had my own Code Black moments" (50).

Brian's condition makes the relationship increasingly difficult. "He wasn't always an asshole," she tells herself, especially when Brian's public behavior is rude or even cruel. The Army offers no rehabilitation or treatment, and trying to care for him herself leaves her "overwhelmed. Angry. Scared. Exhausted" (63). The result is a crisis of identity on several levels: "I was trying so hard to cling to my memory of the man Brian had been, the one I'd met all that time ago in the mountains of Iraq and had gotten to know in that idyllic first month home. I was trying equally hard to get away from the desperate, lonely, overwhelmed Kayla I had become. What it required was an active state of denial" (65). Denial seems the only way that Williams can delineate her life and keep the Code-Black Brian and the posttraumatic Kayla separate from where she wants to be.

Despite their difficulties, the two decide to get married and commit to a future together, an act of definitive identification and a break with their past, though precisely why they make that decision "wasn't clear, even to me," she notes (77). She reveals a similar ambivalence about the Army when she writes her first memoir (a story she tells here, in her second) and the Army reviews it before publication, to ensure that Williams didn't violate OPSEC (Operations Security) or reveal anything that might affect troops still stationed in Iraq. The reviewer flags a chapter in which Williams describes her sickened reaction to the sight of detainees being mistreated, and suddenly she is threatened with jail time for dereliction of duty. With a lawyer's help, she gives a sworn statement about the event and escapes punishment but is embittered by the experience: "The heavy-handed measures and the threats had left a bitter taste in my mouth. Sure, the Army had sometimes pissed me off—but ultimately I loved the Army—and here, on my way out, it was trying to fuck me. I was angry" (92). The emotions of love, betrayal, and anger are all blending together in her most important relationships—with the Army, and with Brian.

Williams's book comes out, she and Brian get married, and then Williams leaves on a book tour. During her absence, Brian "completely fell apart," which makes Williams feel as if her life is "splitting" (113). Not long after that, on their "worst night," he puts a gun to her head, and she asks him to pull the trigger (123). "Let his rage take him, wash over him and drown us both" (125). He pulls the trigger, but there's no bullet in the chamber, and Williams calls 911 and leaves the house. This is, I think, the most profound blurring of war and home possible—a weapon, the threat of violence between loved ones, the wish for it all to be over.

It's a nadir that is eventually ameliorated by marriage counseling, which feels like "crawling out of a pit towing a weight" (182). Brian finally gets access to better care, and they adopt one child and then Williams gives birth to a second. Williams adds "mother" to the list of identities with which she has both owned and struggled: wife, veteran, *female* veteran, caregiver. In her epilogue, Williams notes that she and Brian "still wonder what we want to be when we grow up," but that they are "living proof that for many struggling with physical and psychological wounds of war, there is a path back from the brink of despair to a meaningful new existence" (239–40). She ends her book on that note of strength and determination. Brian's war experience quite literally affects every aspect of his life, and Williams's—he carries the war with him and then fights it at home as well. The book is a testament to how dramatically war can shape your life, even if, like Williams, you have the strength to resist allowing that shape to be your ultimate definition as a person.

Fallon, Benedict, and Williams present a multiplicity of vantages on and definitions of the war story, often from viewpoints that, as Sanfilippo argues, have often been considered prosthetic at best or simply not been considered at all. These women's responses to their war experiences are as varied as the experiences themselves: the quiet, grasping grief of a war widow in "Gold Star," the unintentionally devastating rebellion of a teenager growing up on an army base in "Remission," the utter disintegration of a disabled female soldier and the hopeless tenacity of an Iraqi civilian in *Sand Queen*, and the steely determination of a female veteran and wife of an injured soldier in *Plenty of Time When We Get Home*. Although in the next chapter I will follow the practice of renunciation as a particular response to the blurred boundaries and fragmentation evident in these contemporary war narratives, it is precisely the diversity of experiences and responses in these female-centering and female-authored works that makes them invaluable to consider as a whole. The image of military masculine wholeness was always an illusion, as Sanfilippo writes, one that is dismantled consciously by the fragmented narratives of Ben Fountain and Phil Klay and unintentionally by the intertwined stories of Taya and Chris Kyle. That image is more profoundly challenged, however, by Fallon, Benedict, and Williams, who show that the male soldier was never the only one being made by war—or being taken apart by it.

CHAPTER 3

No More Borders

Giving In and Giving Over

As I noted in the last chapter, Kayla Williams ends her second memoir with a sense of resolve, even defiance: "The wars we fought, both overseas and at home, may have shaped us, but they will not define us" (240). Although the experiences that precede and motivate this statement are vastly different from Chris Kyle's, Kyle demonstrates a similar resolve at the end of *American Sniper*, insisting that he has a "clear conscience" about his work in the war, and that the biggest change that war has made in him is his sense of perspective, that he no longer cares about "all the everyday things that stress you here" (429, 430). Although Williams is refusing to allow her marriage to be haunted by the trauma of war, and Kyle is refusing to acknowledge that that haunting can happen—killing someone is "no big deal," as he says—they both display a desire to push forward, to keep going, and to close the door on negative thinking and move ahead (429). (Although the resolve is there, achieving that kind of definitive closure can be difficult or impossible, as tragically demonstrated by Kyle's death at the hands of a troubled veteran.)

Siobhan Fallon's works display a similar kind of determination. Although they aren't memoirs like Williams's and Kyle's, her two books are based on her own life as a military spouse living in Fort Hood and then overseas. Appearing after *You Know When the Men Are Gone* in 2011, her 2017 novel *The Confusion of Languages* follows two expat couples living in Jordan. The husbands are stationed at the US embassy there—a setting that, like Fallon's stories about life on a military base, echoes her own life, as she moved to Jordan in 2011 and has been part of the expat community there since then. The wives struggle with cultural differences and a sense of isolation, and both marriages are under a great deal of strain: Crick and Margaret have a young child while Cassie and Dan suffer the challenges of infertility; the men are away for long stretches as part of assignments they can't always talk about; both women consider, though do not actually pursue, the idea of having an affair. The novel takes place in 2011, during the Arab Spring, when protesters swarm in the streets and men set themselves on fire in Tunisia, Algeria, Egypt, Saudia Arabia, Mauritania, and Syria. They do so to draw attention to the resistance, to spur people to overthrow oppressive regimes. Margaret is moved by the collective expression of hope and identifies with the desire to break out of old restrictions, as frightening as that may be: "So many attempts to change your life," she thinks, "every desperate action worth it in order to find the smallest bit of freedom, of meaning" (250).

But by January 2012, Cassie thinks it was all for naught. "So much hope, and so much failure. A year that seemed on the verge of freedom and greatness, devolving into so much crisis, displacement, blood. So much meddling that led to more death" (315). She is speaking about the Arab Spring, but like Margaret, also about her own life. Cassie, frustrated by Margaret's flouting of societal customs and attempts to exert some independence, voices her suspicion that Margaret is having an affair with Hassan, a Jordanian who works as a guard at the embassy. Her suspicion is misguided, but it results in a devastating series of events. The rumor spreads, and Hassan is fired. When she finds out, Margaret drives alone to his house to try and make things right. The conversation doesn't go well, and Margaret is distraught. As she is returning to her home, she gets into a serious car accident, which kills her.

All four of the major characters are complicated and flawed, but in the end, Cassie and Dan's marriage is reaffirmed. When Margaret dies, Cassie begs Dan to return to her in Jordan, and he finally shows up for Cassie in the way she has been hoping for:

Dan was waiting for me the same day Crick returned home from Italy. I walked into our apartment, smelling the hospital in my clothes, smelling death and every fetid thing I should have done differently, and saw him. He had come when I asked. He was there. "Of course," he whispered, catching me in his arms. "I couldn't let you deal with this alone." I told him everything: he listened, he believed. I told him about Margaret. And I told him I felt like he was blaming me for not having a baby, that I was afraid he had stopped loving me a long time ago. Perhaps I was wrong about Dan too. He accepted everything, he accepted me, the way he always has, though somehow I didn't see it. (322)

Cassie is undone by Margaret's death, but at novel's end, she is on her way to making new decisions and new plans. She and Dan stay together, with plans to move back to the States and to start fertility treatments. "We do not know what the future will bring," Cassie says, "but we are willing to keep trying, together" (322).

Despite the shattering events that each experiences and the confusion that follows—the devolution into crisis, displacement, bloodshed—Williams, Kyle, and Fallon all end their stories by emphasizing this personal resolve to move forward, refusing to allow war and conflict to be the dominant element of their life story. Helen Benedict and Phil Klay, on the other hand, strike different notes. In *Sand Queen*, both Kate and Naema are consumed by war. Naema watches her grandmother's funeral and experiences the death of the hope she had so ardently felt, a flame slowly extinguished into darkness. Kate suffers the breaking of her body and her mind, and in the last few pages, discovers that the second of only two other women in her platoon has committed suicide—the first, Yvette, was killed by a bomb—and Kate collapses under the weight of the war that will never leave her: "I didn't protect her, Jimmy," she tells her unrequited love. "I didn't protect Yvette either, or Naema's dad or her little brother. I've killed so many of them. Oh God, when will it stop?" (305). Kate is safe—she is back in the States and receiving care—and yet her own war seems endless. She is in pieces, overtaken by her experiences and emotions, and the book ends on a note of overriding despair.

While Benedict's novel reaches a kind of crescendo of pain at its end, Klay's *Redeployment* ends in silence—an absence of emotion rather than a tidal wave. The final story, "Ten Kliks South," focuses on a soldier in an artillery unit that has just fired a presumably lethal barrage on a smuggler's checkpoint ten kliks (kilometers) south of their base. "We took out a group of insurgents and then we went to the Fallujah chow hall for lunch," the story opens. "I got fish and lima beans. I try to eat healthy" (271). The speaker is perhaps unintentionally flippant—mainly, he and the others are excited that they finally got to execute a mission rather than just shooting illumination rounds. "It's about time we killed someone," a soldier named Sanchez says, and they laugh (271). They are frustrated, however, that they don't *know* if they killed anyone, given the distance, and they debate about whether this is good or bad. The speaker becomes a bit obsessed—he hopes to have killed someone, "a man who lived and breathed and maybe murdered and maybe tortured, the kind of man I'd always wanted to kill. Whatever the case, a man definitely dead" (280). But without evidence, who knows? He asks around, wondering if a patrol might have found the bodies, and then goes to find an old gunnery sergeant working in Mortuary Affairs. He doesn't realize that Mortuary Affairs only deals with US casualties, not Iraqis, and so there is no information to be had there either.

In an interview, Klay describes this reaction as "a failed search for the dead, which is also a search for the sight of something which the narrator hopes will reveal to him the authentic emotional and moral response he should be having to his participation in a collective act of killing, but which he is unable to feel at a visceral level" (Jammes 6). In the end, the soldier is unable to find the information, and thus the closure or satisfaction, that he wants. He doesn't even feel a confused reckoning. Overall, he is mostly blank, numb. Finally, as the story and the collection come to a close, he latches on to the memory of seeing a fallen American soldier being transported on a stretcher from the surgical area to Mortuary Affairs. He imagines the old gunny working the wedding ring off of the corpse and visualizes the corpse's progress from there: "a C-130 to Kuwait. And they would have stood silent and still in Kuwait. And they would have stood silent and still in Germany, and silent and still at Dover Air Force Base. Everywhere it went, Marines and sailors and soldiers and airmen would have stood at attention as it traveled to the family of the fallen, where the silence, the stillness, would end" (287–88). The imagined scene might seem like an expression of reverence, but it is hollow—the speaker doesn't know who that fallen soldier is. He was trying to find a way to think about the bodies that he may have had a closer connection with, the people he might have killed. Instead of being overwhelmed, here he has hardly any emotions at all—he doesn't know what war and killing are supposed to mean to him. He feels that the silence will end when the body reaches home, but he doesn't imagine that outpouring of emotion. For him, it is still just silence.

These works by Williams, Kyle, Benedict, and Klay portray a spectrum of reactions to the all-consuming devastation of war. We see resolve in *Plenty of Time When We Get Home*, *American Sniper*, and *The Confusion of Languages*, despair in *Sand Queen*, and emotional blankness in the final story of *Redeployment*. In this chapter, however, I focus on a different kind of response evident in some of these post-2011 works. Kevin Powers, Brian Castner, and Brian Turner work in different literary forms—novel, memoir, and poetry—and to differing emotional effects, but these writers all describe a way of accepting the temporal and spatial disorientation and the sense of personal fragmentation that war can engender, of living with the ambiguity of boundaries that can't be delineated. That acceptance is a kind of failure, but a comfort as well, a mode of understanding that I refer to as renunciation.

The Yellow Birds: Things Fall Apart

Kevin Powers joined the Army at age seventeen and served in Iraq in 2004 and 2005. After his service, he went to college and then graduate school, receiving one of the coveted spots at the Michener Center for Writers at the University of Texas at Austin, and graduated with an MFA in poetry. His first novel, *The Yellow Birds*, was one of the crop of 2012 publications that got everyone talking, and of those it is probably the most searing, the work that highlights the devastation of war to the most extreme degree. One of the book's epigraphs, from which the title is taken, suggests that emphasis, quoting from a marching cadence, or Jody. (Cadences are often called Jodies, after one that includes the lines "Ain't no use in going back / Jody's got your Cadillac / Ain't no use in calling home / Jody's got your girl and gone / Ain't no use in feeling blue / Jody's got your sister too." Jody, a civilian, moves in on the soldier's property and loved ones while he is away at war—but there is nothing the soldier can do about it, so he may as well fully commit to the military and his new identity.) The Jody quoted in *The Yellow Birds* similarly depicts the abandonment of old ideals:

> A yellow bird
> With a yellow bill
> Was perched upon
> My windowsill
>
> I lured him in
> With a piece of bread
> And then I smashed
> His fucking head . . .

There is no place for beauty or delicacy in war, according to this Jody—though by titling the book after that bird, Powers suggests a grief for the beauty that the soldier eliminates. That is a fitting characterization of the book's protagonist, John Bartle. The novel's nonlinear story follows Bartle and his friendship with fellow soldier Daniel Murphy, or Murph. It begins in Iraq in 2004 and alternates between other places and times: Fort Dix in 2003 as the soldiers prepare to be deployed; Germany in 2005, when Bartle is on his way home after his service; Virginia in 2005, where Bartle lives after his service; and finally, Fort Knox in 2009, where Bartle serves a three-year term in prison.

The reader learns early in the book that Murph dies in the war, but how and why his death happens remains a mystery for the reader until the end of the novel. Similar to *The Hurt Locker*, the novel moves through a series of episodic vignettes that gradually accrue more force. Reviewers noted how the fragmented structure makes sense for a portrait of fragmenting people. In the *New York Times*, Benjamin Percy praised the book, saying that the "fractured structure replicates the book's themes. Like a chase scene made up of sentences that run on and on and ultimately leave readers breathless . . . the nonlinear design of Powers's novel is a beautifully brutal example of style matching content. War destroys. It doesn't just rip through bone and muscle, stone and steel; it fragments the mind as a fist to a mirror might create thousands of bloodied, glittering shards."

Percy characterizes the novel's fragmentation as a corollary for physical or mental trauma, and indeed both Murph and Bartle experience eventual breakdowns. That fragmentation becomes evident, however, because of the lack of delineation that the war causes in their lives, an amorphousness that Bartle eventually gives in to. In the novel's opening passage, Powers personifies the war's destructive force in a way that is deliberately unfamiliar and similarly amorphous:

> The war tried to kill us in the spring. As grass greened the plains of Nineveh and the weather warmed, we patrolled the low-slung hills beyond the cities and towns. We moved over them and through the tall grass on faith, kneading paths into the windswept growth like pioneers. While we slept, the war rubbed its thousand ribs against the ground in prayer. When we pressed onward through exhaustion, its eyes were white and open in the dark. While we ate, the war fasted, fed by its own deprivation. It made love and gave birth and spread through fire. (3)

It is a poet's paragraph, featuring that rough, slouching beast of war as well as "greening grass" and "the plains of Nineveh," a name with both ancient and modern connotations. In the Hebrew Bible, Ninevah was an ancient Assyrian city considered to be a place of ungodliness, though contemporarily the name can also refer to the eastern part of Mosul. The soldiers are exhausted, but the war flourishes. Nothing can stop it, as Bartle reiterates on the following page: "While I slept that summer, the war came to me in my dreams and showed me its sole purpose: to go on, only to go on. And I knew the war would have its way" (4).

Murph's death, though neither its cause nor circumstances, is revealed bluntly in the first section: "I didn't die. Murph did" (14). But it quickly becomes clear that of all the deaths Bartle has seen, this is the one that he can't shake. They were together for ten months, in Fort Dix and then Iraq: "Ten months, give or take, from that day to the day he died. It might seem like a short time, but my whole life since has merely been a digression from those days, which now hang over me like a quarrel that will never be resolved" (30). Murph haunts him, in part because of something he says to Murph's mother before their deployment, something he thinks is casual but turns out to be anything but that. "John, promise me you'll take care of him," she says. "Promise that you'll bring him home to me." "Of course," he responds. "Sure, sure, I thought. Now you reassure me and I'll go back and go to bed" (47). He promises to bring Murph back. What else, he thinks, would he say? When Sergeant Sterling calls him on it later and says he shouldn't have made that statement, Bartle doesn't understand. "I was just trying to make her feel better," he says. "It's not a big deal." For that, Sterling knocks him down and punches him twice in the face.

It turns out to be a very big deal, a "war promise," as David Buchanan calls it, of the kind that features in *Saving Private Ryan* (1998) and Leslie Marmon Silko's *Ceremony* (1977)—a soldier promises to bring another soldier back from war, and then his life is ever after defined by that eventual success or failure (63–64). In *Private Ryan*, as the title suggests, Captain John Miller (Tom Hanks) is tasked with finding Private First Class James Ryan (Matt Damon), whose three brothers have all been killed in World War II, and sending him home so that his family won't lose all their sons. Although Miller initially seeks to fulfill those orders against his own wishes, he comes to admire Ryan's commitment to his job as a soldier. Before Miller loses his life as a result of that mission, he urges Ryan to "earn this," and Ryan spends the rest of his life wondering, hoping, that he does, as the opening and closing scenes of an aged Ryan visiting Miller's grave make clear. *Ceremony* is tragic in the opposite respect, as Tayo promises his family that he will make sure his cousin Rocky—who is everyone's favorite—comes home from World War II. When Rocky dies during the Bataan Death March, Tayo is undone and suffers a breakdown that leads to institutionalization and further alienation from his family. "I'll bring him back safe," he tells his aunt before they deploy. "You don't have to worry." But deep down, "He knew that she always hoped, that she always expected it to happen to him, not to Rocky" (67). After he returns from war, he sees "the accident of time and space: Rocky was the one who was alive, buying Grandma her heater with the round dial on the front; Rocky was there in the college game scores on the sports page of the *Albuquerque Journal*. It was him, Tayo, who had died, but somehow there had been a mistake with the corpses, and somehow his was still unburied. He started to cry" (25).

Although Bartle and Murph aren't related the way that Tayo and Rocky are, Bartle is similarly haunted by his promise and what he sees as his failure. For Bartle, "Murph's always going to be eighteen, and he's always going to be dead. And I'll be living with a promise that I couldn't keep" (32). Particularly after his service is over and he travels through Germany and then back to Virginia, everything about the war is still with him. It starts immediately: "Though I was only a week removed from [the war], and unbeknownst to me at the time, my memories would seem closer the farther I got from the circumstances that gave birth to them" (51). His fingers grasp again and again for his absent rifle, he sees "the ghosts of the dead" at every airport gate, and looking out a car window, he "watched myself patrol through the fields along the river in the yellow light" (104, 110). The war is like a movie that he watches and lives in at the same time. And as a result, he doesn't feel like a real person anymore: "I was disappearing," he says. Later, "I was disintegrating." "I was becoming spectral" (111, 120, 156). The war takes over everything, and Bartle dissolves into pieces.

So what, then, happened to Murph? When, in Iraq, Murph begins acting more distant, talking less to Bartle and wandering off by himself, Sterling says he knows what's happening. He also knows what will happen as a result: "If you get back to the States in your head before your ass is there too," he tells Bartle, "then you are a fucking dead man. I'm telling you. You don't know where Murph keeps going, but I do. . . . Murph is home, Bartle. And he's gonna be there with a flag shoved up his ass before you know it" (156). Just as the war later follows Bartle home, Murph is going home while he's still at war—and that, Sterling says, is a fatal conflation. Bartle is worried and tracks down Murph, finding him watching from afar as a pretty female medic works on incoming patients, some of whom are grievously wounded. Murph seems moved by her beauty and by her compassion, her sense of care for others. When that medic is killed in a mortar attack, it seems to be the last straw for Murph. After the blast, Bartle finds her body next to the chapel, "her hair blowing in small wisps behind her, in and out out of the dust in a manner both fantastic and actual. Her eyes were half-lidded." As two young soldiers go to move her, Murph is silent, agape. "The new private grabbed the back end near her feet while Murph curled up helplessly in the still-smoldering ruins of the chapel, muttering to himself, over and over again, 'What just happened.' As we walked her up the hill, his litany faded from our ears" (171–72).

Then Murph disappears. He's gone, but Bartle and Sterling don't realize what happened until after the fact. Murph left the base, naked and dazed, moving "as a ghost, his feet and legs bleeding from his walk through the wire and detritus" (195). A beggar led Murph into an alley, where he was apparently abducted and the beggar was killed. Bartle and Sterling finally find his severely mutilated body at the base of a minaret, where he was thrown from a window, likely already dead. "He was broken and bruised and cut and still pale except for his face and hands, and now his eyes had been gouged out, the two hollow sockets looking like red angry passages to his mind. His throat had been cut nearly through, his lead hung limply and lolled from side to side. . . . His ears were cut off. His nose cut off, too. He had been imprecisely castrated" (205–6). Bartle and Sterling both fear that if the body is sent back to the States in its grisly, woeful condition, his mother could see it—a possibility that they refuse to allow. And so, with the help of a hermit and his cart, they take the body to the river and release it into the current. "Like it never happened, Bartle. That's the only way," Sterling tells him (211). And then, without warning, Sterling kills the hermit.

Like it never happened—and Bartle even writes a letter to Murph's mother pretending to be her son, to keep her believing that he's okay. (Daniel O'Gorman notes that Bartle's name is a possible reference to the title character in Melville's "Bartleby, the Scrivener," a depressed, unreactive man employed at the Washington Dead Letter Office, drifting among thousands of undeliverable letters. Bartle's letter to Murph's mother is, then, "a grimly literal take on the notion of the 'dead letter'" [550].) But the illusion that everything is fine can't last, of course, and after Murph was undone in Iraq, Bartle comes fully undone back in the States. He loses control of Murph's narrative as well as his own: "Everything I could recall about the war flashed kaleidoscopically, and I closed my eyes and I felt the weight of time wash over my body. I could not pattern it. None of it made sense. Nothing followed from anything else and I was required to answer for a story that did not exist" (182). Eventually a Criminal Investigation Division (CID) officer finds Bartle and shows him the letter. Bartle admits to writing it, but that is not what gets him arrested. Instead, he is arrested because of stories from other soldiers, none of whom really knew what had happened to Murph. "So it was a rumor that had brought the captain to see me," Bartle realizes, "the underlying truth of the story long since skewed by the variety of a few boys' memories, perhaps one or two of them answering with what they wanted the truth to be, others likely looking to satisfy the imagined needs of a mother, abused and pitied as a result of that day in Al Tafar, which sometimes seems so long ago" (186–87). And Sterling—the one person who could have corroborated Bartle's story about the circumstances of Murph's death—commits suicide, so he is no longer alive to either give an account or be held accountable.

Bartle doesn't fight it—he doesn't respond with the resolve apparent in Kayla Williams, Chris Kyle, or Siobhan Fallon's narratives. Bartle goes to prison, and while there, he gives in, and gives up on trying to make sense of it all:

> My first few months inside, I spent a lot of time trying to piece the war into a pattern. I developed a habit of making a mark on my cell wall when I remembered a particular event. . . . Eventually, I realized that the marks could not be assembled into any kind of pattern. They were fixed in place. Connecting them would be wrong. They fell where they had fallen. Marks representing the randomness of the war were made at whatever moment I remembered them: disorder predominated. Entropy increased in the six-by-eight-foot universe of my single cell. I eventually accepted the fact that the only equality that lasts is the fact that everything falls away from everything else. (216–17)

Bartle finally accepts the nondelineation of his own life. After he has completed his prison sentence, he settles into a cabin and unpacks his belongings, including a map of Iraq that Murph's mother gave him when she visited him in prison, seeking answers about her son that no one had been able to give her. He thinks about how the map would be soon out of date, "only an idea of a place, an abstraction formed from memories too brief and passing to account for the small effects of time," similar to the way that language never exactly expresses the intended meaning. "It wasn't much in the way of comfort," he admits, but it does comfort him a bit: "Everything has a little failure in it, and we still make do somehow" (225). The novel ends with Bartle's vision of Murph, as present as he ever was, floating by on the current of the Tigris, to the meeting of the Tigris and the Euphrates, and finally to the Persian Gulf, where his bones are swept out to sea, "toward a line of waves that break forever as he enters them" (226). The body passes a pair of soldiers, who don't know its identity, but one calls out to it, a kind of farewell. Joelle Mann writes that here, Bartle is envisioning the "reactions of estranged soldiers who mirror the trauma of both Murph and Bartle's experience," a "literal and figurative separation" of those characters, echoed by the breaking apart of Murph's body as it passes (348). Everything is in pieces, but Bartle finally seems to achieve a kind of peace with that, an acceptance of failures small and large: of intention, of promises, of coherence, of delineation. He renounces it all and finds that he may still be able to "make do." Geoffrey Wright contrasts that acceptance of ambiguity with the modernist writers of World War I as discussed by Paul Fussell in *The Great War and Modern Memory* (1975), who "used irony as a means of casting the experience of war in a fresh light and, by doing so, of comprehending it" (108). Although *The Yellow Birds* has elements of irony in it, Bartle's vision of Murph is something different: "Whereas modernist writers seek to explain the past by detaching themselves from it, postmodern writers [like, in Wright's argument, Powers] admit the inscrutability of the past and reconstruct it in a way that bears meaning for them" (111).

The Yellow Birds is an ambitious novel, consciously poetic in its use of language, although Patrick Deer has praised it for "its willingness to disfigure its own aestheticizing tendencies by showing Bartle's disillusionment and disintegration," a "pursuit and subsequent failure of recovery" (322–23) that he also sees in *The Hurt Locker* and *In the Valley of Elah* (2007). A film adaptation directed by Alexandre Moors and released in 2017 takes something of the same approach, with a plot that flashes back and forth between Iraq and the United States. Beautiful mise-en-scene portrays the characters' unraveling—in fact, the film won a Special Jury Award at Sundance for its cinematography. The film features a number of high-profile actors: Alden

Enrehreich as Bartle, Tye Sheridan as Murph, Jack Huston as Sterling, Jennifer Aniston and Toni Collette as Murph's and Bartle's mothers, respectively, and Jason Patric as the CID investigator. Despite that impressive pedigree, *The Yellow Birds* received mixed reviews and grossed only $57,946—a miniscule amount in box office terms ("The Yellow Birds (2017)"). In these ways, Powers's novel is another excellent example of these second-wave Iraq War stories—it features blurred temporal and spatial boundaries that lead to dramatic structural and thematic fragmentation, it portrays a kind of renunciation as a response to that confusion, and it is adapted into a film that is high quality and almost no one sees.

The Long Walk: IEDs and TBI

Murph's torture and death is the grisly secret at the heart of Powers's novel, but in Brian Castner's memoir *The Long Walk*, he writes about more subtle damage, particularly the changing understanding of how physical trauma can overlap with emotional trauma. In World War I, soldiers with no visible injuries who were nonetheless suffering in the aftermath of war were said to have "shell shock," a term that implied a physical cause for emotional distress; later, particularly in the Vietnam War years, that reaction was labeled post-traumatic stress disorder, a condition that could indeed be purely psychological. But now, with new research on concussions, it turns out that shell shock can, in some cases, be an appropriate diagnosis. Like James in *The Hurt Locker*, Castner led Explosive Ordnance Disposal units during his service in Iraq in 2005 and 2006, disarming IEDs or other bombs that often detonated in the process, effectively exposing him to dozens, maybe hundreds, of explosive impacts of the kind that can cause concussion-induced TBI. Soldiers experienced blasts, but body armor, helmets, and armored vehicles kept their bodies protected and they walked away seemingly unhurt, only to later experience problems with memory, headaches, sleep disruption, and impaired functionality, among other symptoms. His job, Castner notes, consisted of incremental and cumulative damage, which he describes as a kind of disassembling of himself. "Every day, something is blowing up," he says. "Every day, your brain rips just a little bit more. Blast waves tear up memories and functions. They leave holes where your identity used to be. You lose parts of your past and have trouble retaining the present or remaking a future. The strong, capable soldier now can't sleep, can't discern or differentiate among voices and noises, becomes easily distracted, gets tired, cries randomly in public, and doesn't know what to order for dinner. Where does Crazy stop and TBI begin? Who knows?" (154).

Castner begins his memoir with an open statement of identity dysphoria that characterizes his life after war: "The first thing you should know about me is that I'm Crazy. . . . The second thing you should know about me is that I don't know how to fix it. Or control it. Or endure from one moment to the next. The Crazy is winning" (1). The Crazy is a lack of delineation, what he literally describes as failing to behave correctly in the correct context or understand the differences between voices and noises, but which is clearly descriptive of other aspects of his life and mental state as well. So, Castner says, he runs—a daily, intense exercise regimen he undertakes in hopes of tamping down the Crazy. But other things intrude—thoughts of the friends he has lost and an oblique, unexplained image: "The foot sits in the box. Because why not? Where else would you put it? The foot sat in the box" (2). Castner's memoir is divided into short sections separated by line breaks, and this opening one—titled "Whirl Is King"—is a portrait of temporal confusion: "I run, and run, and run, and in the Is try to pound out of my head what once Was" (3). The Was, to use Castner's terms, threatens to take over the Is, to counter all his efforts at psychological or narrative delineation.

As we have seen with others of these second-wave works, Castner structures his narrative in a nonlinear series of vignettes that alternate between his time in Iraq, where he served three tours, two of them as the head of an Explosive Ordnance Disposal (EOD) unit, and his time at home, struggling with the Crazy. But even within these individual vignettes, his chronology is blurred. In the second section, he arrives in Kirkuk, which reminds him of his previous service in Balad. "I'm back," he writes. "I'm still here. I never left. It was less than a year and I was back in Iraq. It was less than a minute and I was back in Iraq" (4). Just two lines later, in the third section, Castner lies in bed, the Crazy "fill[ing] me to the brim in the darkness of my bedroom, alone next to my sleeping wife. . . . High, full, boiling sea" (4).

Like Powers, Castner alludes to traumatic events that he will only describe in detail later in the memoir—names of dead friends, for instance, and the phrase he keeps repeating, "the foot in the box." These function as touchstones that he returns to often, as does the line, "Don't be scared of the soft sand." That's a friendly command from Boatswain Mate First Class Jeff Chaney, who was "my number two, my partner, my problem solver and my confidant" in EOD school (23). Jeff leads the students' physical training sessions, urging them to run up a punishing hill of sand. Castner finds a strip of grass to stabilize his stride, but Jeff sends him back: "Don't be scared of the soft sand," he chides (32). Initially it serves as a mantra for the toughness he needs to develop in order to succeed, but it eventually becomes a metaphor for the engulfing, quicksand Crazy that he longs to escape.

Castner uses this structure of alternation throughout the book, which has the effect of contrasting the deep appeal of military service with its devastating consequences. Castner writes about "the Brotherhood" that he found in EOD school, "a new family . . . [who] are all that will sustain you," and then, after a section break, describes Jeff's death in Tikrit from an IED (33). Later, he lists the members of his family who had served—an uncle, two grandfathers, a great-great-grandfather—and describes that legacy in mythic terms: "What blood runs in my veins? Am I from a Line of Old? What may rise in me, unbidden and unknown, to meet this oldest of challenges? How many battlefields has my blood made wet, in empires made and gone, on bare green islands and cold forested mountains of myth, in lands whose names have changed countless times? . . . How many helmets have I worn? In the line of my people, all the way back to the beginning" (64). But then, two lines later: "In the darkness of my bedroom, at night, when I try to fall asleep, the top of my head comes off." A spider crawls out of his head and over the foot in a box. He laments the effect on his marriage, now that they sleep "in a bed full of rifles and helicopters and twitching eyes and Kermit's blue skin and the foot in the box" (91). He is without boundaries. "I came home, but what follows?" he asks. "I never considered. But I chose it all the same" (200). When his struggles with the Crazy are at their most acute, he says that he died in Iraq—the war self is all that's left. As Castner commented in an interview, "I was really writing a ghost story, but I thought I was crazy" (Goolsby 3). He misses the war, which in its own way is easier than life at home: "I think about going back every day. Back to the job. Back to the clarity of thought, the singleness of purpose, the mundane details of the world falling away and only the essential remaining. No bills. No to-do lists. No children asking for attention. No tear-filled marital counseling with my wife. . . . No clutter" (189–90).

So what can help? He is not implicated in criminal matters the way that Bartle is, so he doesn't end up in a cell, an isolated spot where he can try to work it all out. Instead, he goes running, often with someone named Ricky, a talented runner who offers him companionship and conversation. He tries counseling, both individually and with his wife. When everything fails to offer relief, however, he finds a surprising outlet. His new counselor suggests a yoga class, and he goes. It works, or at least starts to: "The muscle strain boils off the Crazy. The repetition dulls, then frees, the mind. . . . On a good day, the flow reverses the Crazy for a moment and my healing mind is present beneath and apart from the movement" (158–59). The yogini, his young, female yoga teacher, instructs him in the poses and in chanting Om.

Finally, this is what works: yoga and Om, particularly the release these practices offer from the constraints of traditional notions of identity and time (and, I would add, masculinity). "My mind follows my Om, of breath and flecked with spit, released into the universe, back through time, no time, the continuum of the river flowing, no start or end" (164). The spider, he says, crawls out of his forehead. Late in his memoir, Castner finally tells the story of the foot in the box, of investigating the site of a bomb set off in a crowded market. Debris and body parts are everywhere, and Castner discovers a cardboard box into which someone had placed a torn-off foot. First he laughs at the absurdity of it, and then the image settles in. He can't separate himself from the devastation of war—the foot is in the wrong place, and everything indeed is in the wrong place. "The foot sat in the box. My foot sat in the box" (181).

Castner also reveals that Ricky has been long dead—he died of a brain aneurism on an airplane, and now exists only in Castner's mind as his nearly constant companion on runs. He is angry about Ricky's death, even though it seems like it was just the result of "random bad luck" (206). He wonders, though, if the aneurism was really "a remnant of his own traumatic brain injury, a time bomb left dangling on a thread waiting for the right moment to let go." He finally decides, "They killed him. He made it back from the mission . . . and was finally safe. But he wasn't. None of us are. They can still kill us anytime" (207). That threat of death, the danger of whoever Castner means by "they," is ever-present, and won't go away. But in some sense, neither does Ricky, as much as Castner misses him. He is still around, even though sometimes he runs so fast that Castner can't keep up with him. By the end of the memoir, Castner comes to a kind of peace with those blurred categories, the confusion that has dogged him throughout the book. At last, it seems acceptable. Like Bartle, Castner has found a way to renounce his attempts to bring everything about his life into order, and that renunciation finally seems to free him. "The Om Is and the Om Was," he writes in the book's closing passage. "It returns from the universe, with the universe, with the pain and hope and the blood and the helicopters and the artillery rounds falling on Habbaniyah. . . . It brings the mountain to my feet. Ricky sits to my right. The line of my grandfathers sits to my left. The Om is my Is and my Was. I am my Om. The next day, I put on my shoes and go for a run" (220). He finally understands running as a way not to escape the Crazy or get away from the memories and emotions that are crushing him, but as a way of existing—if not comfortably, then at least more calmly—with both Was and Is.

Castner's might be the first war story to use yoga, and the chanting of Om, as a way to reconcile the fragmenting forces of war. But it does work, and seems a happier kind of acceptance than Bartle's, which doesn't alleviate his profound alienation. Castner goes on to publish a number of other works—the nonfiction books *All the Ways We Kill and Die* (2016), *Disappointment River* (2018), and *Stampede* (2021). He coedited a collection of short fiction about contemporary war with Adrian Bonenberger, *The Road*

Ahead (2017), and somewhat improbably, *The Long Walk* was commissioned as an opera by the American Lyric Theater. It premiered at Opera Saratoga in 2015 and has also been performed in 2017 and 2018. C. J. Chivers reviewed the opera positively in the *New York Times Magazine*, comparing the story to Greek tragedy, or to the story of Odysseus' fraught homecoming. Chivers quotes an exchange in the opera between Castner's wife and her grandmother that delineates the narrative tension in a different way than Castner does in his book, but with the same central motif, that war follows you everywhere:

> "How do I help him
>
> When he comes home?" [Castner's wife asks]
>
> "He won't come home," my grandmother said.
>
> "The war will kill him either way.
>
> He's as good as dead.
>
> I hope for your sake he dies over there.
>
> Because if the war doesn't kill him,
>
> It'll take him here.
>
> The war will kill him at home. With you."

It's a threat and a danger, one of the central motifs of Castner's memoir, and one that he finds an unlikely way to accept.

My Life as a Foreign Country: Living with Ghosts

I have argued that Brian Turner's first book of poetry *Here, Bullet* reveals a soldier fascinated with Iraqi culture and history, and a "desire—thwarted as it may be—to reach across the cultural and political divide" (*Welcome to the Suck* 102). In the imagery and narrative arc of that collection, Turner explores "the possibilities for transcendence, or ultimate and total illumination, but finds that they are coupled, seemingly irrevocably, with moments of destruction." The book ends with "the failure of that possibility, and figures that failure as a kind of afterimage, the blinding absence of a mode of communication that might salve the ruptures that war brings" (120). Turner's poetry, especially in that first collection, is the most striking example of the phenomenon I trace in the first wave of Iraq War literature: this desire, on the part of soldiers in the stories, to transcend traditional notions of categorization, and the subsequent thwarting of that desire by the experience of war.

Ironically, the boundary crossing that Turner desires, but fails to achieve, in *Here, Bullet* is discovered in a different way in his memoir, *My Life as a Foreign Country*—the very title of which can be taken not as an assertion of multicultural hybridity but rather of alienation, of an experience of oneself as foreign. While Castner's narrative blurs time periods and experiences—the Was and the Is—Turner's goes further and presents his postwar identity as an assemblage of his own experiences as well as other people's. "I am a drone aircraft plying the darkness above my body," the book begins, "flying over my wife as she sleeps beside me, over the curvature of the earth, over the glens of Antrim and the Dalmatian coastline, the shells of Dubrovnik and Brčko and Mosul arcing in the air beside me, projectiles filled with poems and death and love" (ix). Turner is his own body as well as a drone above it—an unmanned aircraft by definition, its operator unknown. (The drone has become a potent symbol of the reimagined spaces and dislocation of contemporary warfare, which I will discuss further in the Conclusion.) Turner's drone traces the sites of battles ancient and modern, the clashes of other weapons and other peoples: the Delmatae's resistance of the Roman empire, the Battle of Antrim in 1798, artillery from the siege of Dubrovnik in 1991, the site of war crimes in Bosnia, and the Iraq War filling the air with both destruction and creation.

While Powers and Castner make use of nonlinear narrative to create interest and suspense, and to reflect the damaging effects of war on one's identity, Turner pushes that device to an even greater extreme. His memoir is divided into short, numbered sections, and Turner alternates between descriptions of his service—living through mortar attacks on a firebase in Iraq and the devastation of house-to-house searches—with other vignettes, some of which are events from his life, and many which are not. In one, he remembers an oil painting in a museum in Kyoto, Japan, of an archer preparing to shoot: "The point is to become one with the moment," he writes of the image. "To meld with the motion of the instrument. To become the archer and the bow combined" (11). In another, two Iraqi boys, Zaid and Malik, accompany their father as he transports an improvised mortar, which they will fire near the American base. Malik thinks that the cannon means that "nobody, but nobody, is allowed to fuck with him"; his father "wonders if another man's son will have just woken from a dream as the round pitches over and begins its descent, spinning" (35). Turner imagines inhabiting other existences: feeling the tension of the bow both as the archer and as the bow itself; feeling the tension of violent strategy and execution as an American soldier and also as an Iraqi father and son, each with their own motivations for and understandings of that violence. Turner even builds that same "other-imagination" into his vignette about the father, who himself wonders about the consequences for "another man's son"—which, perhaps, would be Turner himself. His identity here is framed far differently than in the home/war/home narrative so common in the classic war memoirs that Alex Vernon describes, as I discuss in the Introduction. Instead, it is hardly framed at all, just a collection of diffuse pieces.

Even when Turner addresses one of the standard questions inherent to the genre—why he joined the military—his answer is both direct and refracted. He did it, he says, "for reasons I won't tell you, and for reasons I will" (39). Because of heroic expectations, he says. And because he hadn't fought in the First Gulf War, and because he'd lived in South Korea. He describes his father, a tough-as-nails man's man, scarred by a serious car accident, who converted their garage into a dojo, a space to pursue martial arts. He joined the infantry, he says, to prove himself, because "I was from Fresno and people from Fresno can take it, can take it in spades and shovelfuls" (44). He joined because one great-grandfather was gassed in the Battle of Meuse-Argonne in 1918 and another served in the Union army (55). Finally, though, he says that "I signed the paper because I knew that on some deep and immutable level, I would leave and I would never come back" (57).

And indeed he doesn't, at least not in his telling. The "landscape of ghosts," as he describes his imagining of places in Iraq, eventually includes him as well. A rocket-propelled grenade hits his Stryker, "a great shot. A direct hit. Right in line with me" (146). The next section begins, "Sgt. Turner is dead" (149). As the driver speeds away, Turner describes "the dead Sgt. Turner" left behind, in shock and wandering the streets, making his way to the Tigris with the other dead. What does a near-death experience do, after all, but create the ghost of a deceased self? And those ghosts can be hard to shake. "How does anyone leave a war behind them," Turner writes, "no matter what war it is, and somehow walk into the rest of his life?" (154). Because indeed the dead will follow you home, the "ruined world will call its home inside of me" (156), old shrapnel will "weep" from the body (159), and old bombs will resurface and detonate decades after the conflicts they were manufactured for. "Maybe it isn't that it's so difficult coming home," he muses, "but that home isn't a big enough space for all that I must bring to it" (173).

In response to war's eternal presence, to his inability to leave the war behind or eject it from his bedroom and his marriage, Turner undergoes a sweat lodge ceremony—the heat, ritual, and repetition similar in many ways to Castner's description of his yoga practice. In sections titled with the four cardinal directions—important elements of the ceremony—Turner summons memories and engages with them, imagining a series of events: that he is being asked to take a man he killed into the next world; that he visits a hospital with a collection of living and dead family members; that he digs graves in his backyard for Iraqi dead; that his wife Ilyse walks into the war to retrieve him as he points "off into the distance, to the past, or to the future, or to a dream, perhaps, there's no way of telling, but I point to where the first raid of the night in already in progress" (192).

"Sgt. Turner is dead," the book's final section begins, and that dead iteration of himself visits both other dead and the living. The dead Turner observes as the drone circles a sleeping couple—the living Turner and his wife Ilyse—and watches. "He will monitor the heat signatures of the living. And, because Sgt. Turner is dead, he will remain at his post. There is nothing strange in this at all" (201). It might seem as if the author of this memoir has left his war self behind—Sgt. Turner is dead, after all—but in a book in which the dead populate the landscape as vividly as the living, he suggests instead that war has indeed created a new self, and that self now exists alongside and inside of the self that would simply like to sleep peacefully with his wife. Ultimately, however, acceptance of the ghosts—of yourself and of others, and the way that time slips perhaps all too easily between past, future, and dreams—seems the only possible response. "At first I can think of nothing other than the heat," he says of the sweat lodge. "I remember how we'd been instructed not to worry and panic, that we'd by okay, that the heat would seem too much, too crushing, and more" (187). Initially, the oppressiveness is unendurable, and the only real solution is to let go—to renounce an identity bound to temporal linearity and the idea that a "real man" (or, for that matter, a tough woman) should be able to leave it all behind and drive on. This may be the best way, Powers, Castner, and Turner suggest, to live with the wars you fought: let go, and let them come with you.

Imagining Others

Turner followed his memoir with three collections of poetry that were, remarkably, all published in fall 2023: *The Wild Delight of Wild Things*, *The Goodbye World Poem*, and *The Dead Peasant's Handbook*. In the third of those, *The Dead Peasant's Handbook*, Turner offers a glimpse of a different kind of response to the loss of coherence and sense of fragmentation engendered by war. This isn't renunciation, but rather a response that is similar to the collective imagining that I trace in literature by Iraqi authors, which is the subject of the following chapter. Turner's collection is divided into four sections, the titles of which give a sense of the collection's subject matter and progression: "On War & Conflict," "On Dream," "On Love & Loss," and "On Survival." As in his memoir, there are ghosts, and there is war that isn't neatly confined to a historical time and place. The poem "Historians" in the first section makes this clear:

> What they don't tell you about war
> is how it outlives us. Or, how they get it wrong,
>
> framing each war in parenthesis, like stonecutters
> in the graveyards of memory, as if war isn't inscribed
>
> into our DNA, then handed down, one generation
> to another.
> [. . .]
> And what happens to the ghosts?
> [. . .]
> That's what they don't tell you about war.
> And I'm thinking about how it all comes home.
>
> The way it sleeps. The way it dresses up the police
> in its hand-me-downs, its assault rifles, ghillie suits,
> armored personnel carriers.
> [. . .]
> The silence after.
> The years and decades of that silence. The way
>
> it lingers in the body. Lingers on the tongue. (10–11)

War is more fluid, and more present, than the history books suggest. The silence after destruction is long-standing and stays with you. Ghosts linger. The war comes home with you both psychologically and socially, in dreams and the patterns of one's life as well as in the militarized armament of police. And all of this is what experts don't tell you. The opening poem of the collection, "Sunflowers," emphasizes this as well—it also begins with "What they don't tell you about war." That includes details like how budgets can impact military strategy, how bullets can skip across stone, that war "is born of the obscene." Then Turner puts it succinctly: "These things we do. These ghosts / we live with" (3–4).

War, and war's ghosts, are not the only presence in Turner's collection, however. In *My Life as a Foreign Country*, Turner writes about his wife Ilyse—in the sweat lodge ceremony, she walks into the landscape of war that he envisions and leads him out of it, and in the book's closing, she is curled next to Turner as his soldier-self, the dead Sgt. Turner, observes a drone's overhead footage. If the war stays with him, Ilyse is in that room too, and that matters deeply. (In the ceremony, Ilyse leads Turner home, out of his war gear, and into a shower, echoing repeated imagery of water as a cleansing or purification.) Ilyse is Ilyse Kusnetz, a poet whose collection *Small Hours* (2014) won the T. S. Eliot Prize for Poetry. Ilyse died of cancer in 2016, at age 50. In some poems in *The Dead Peasant's Handbook*, Ilyse is a dreamlike presence, still appearing alongside ghostly soldiers and weapons, as in the end of *My Life as a Foreign Country*. In "Metal Fume Fever," Turner again joins with her in a mind's-eye landscape:

> You are trying to wake me,
> but I don't want to leave this, even
> if it never happened this way, the details
> of past and present blended
> one into another, as small combat teams
> crouch in the dunes beyond, launching
> shoulder-fired missiles into the sky,
> each round bursting into a tree
> of lightning, your body
> silvered with it as you draw near,
> saying, Sleepwalking, you're sleepwalking,
> and that's when I promise to always find you,
> I promise to wade into the curling waves,
> I promise to submerge into the night-blue waters,
> I promise to hold my breath
> so that we might share it
> at the bottom of the ocean,
> and I'll ignore the journalist's voice
> describing the war, the simmering
> misanthropy of strangers passing . . . (28–29)

As in his memoir, Ilyse approaches him in an envisioned landscape of war and draws him out of a benumbed existence, but here, he promises to find her as well, in whatever different landscape she occupies. "Metal Fume Fever" is a long poem with ten numbered sections, and it is the sole poem in the "On Dreams" segment of the collection. Dreaming here is a submerging, the "work we do / in sleep, searching under an acetylene sky / for all that has begun to slide under: / lovers, friends, strangers . . . / We must do what we can to keep them / before the breakers, close to shore" (23).

The war is still with him, but so is Ilyse, and for Turner her presence connotes grief as well as possibility. In the "Love & Loss" section, the poem "On This Harvest Moon" includes the lines, "What they don't tell you about love / is how our bodies house the dead / until we breathe the last words /

we carry within, a poem" (35). It's a different configuration of the ghosts that populate *My Life as a Foreign Country*—these aren't ghosts of war, but of love. In another poem in this section, "The Weight," Turner writes about men's tendency to hold emotions inside themselves, unexpressed, but existing here within the weight of their bodies. That "grief and anger and regret" is stored "within the rounded half globe of the belly," even if they don't fully realize it. Turner takes that image and then makes it multivalent, describing the odd, alchemic potential of grief, loss, and living with ghosts:

> Still, they fail to connect how loss is tethered
> to love, how they carry the weight
> until it transforms into something startling,
> if we're lucky, and goddamn if it isn't
> one of the most beautiful things we might ever do. (47)

More people should try to reach that understanding, he suggests, and reiterates that message in the final section, "On Survival." In "Central Park in the Spring," Turner recasts the voices of the dead as birdsong, echoing the book's epigraph from Jolie Holland, "The littlest birds sing the prettiest songs." Here again, if people paid attention, they could hear it:

> I'm listening to the dead
> and how they sing within the throats
> of finches and sparrows too numerous
> to count, their bright embellishments
> pleasing to the ear, though tourists wander on
> as if the dead they love, too, aren't filling the air
> with song (71)

The final poem in the collection, which is placed after the end of the last section, is titled "All Our Lazy Sundays." Both war and Ilyse are here, destruction and love:

> the journalist saying   *The front line has collapsed   Civilians*
> *trapped in the fighting now flee for their* lives   and as we rest here
>   in these cloud-like sheets   the long travail of the dispossessed walks
>   a hard road newly drafted through our bodies   and we offer
>   no aid or comfort   we do not ease their burdens or call out
>   their names   we only kiss and hold each other   as the world moves
>   through us [. . .]

[. . .]
    and though you are surely only a vision   I see you   here
right here   alive and human   the universe singing through you
     the closest I've ever come to what others might call   a god. (73–74)

The world that moves through the two of them here, the universe singing through that love, is divine, "a god," which is the final word in the collection. Although Turner is an individual poet, these final images are more communal, an imagined space that includes the voices of the living and the dead. The collection as a whole is suffused with loss, but that loss results in an imaginative expansion rather than a contraction. This somewhat paradoxical maneuver echoes what many Iraqi writers emphasize, a kind of collective imagination in response to the devastation of war.

The Trauma Hero

Regardless of the variety of responses that different representations emphasize, all these American second-wave authors are offering portraits of trauma, the personal sense of fragmentation that results from war—although as I have argued, the fragmentation is multivalent, evident in a number of representational characteristics, and can be understood as a symptom of a larger failure of delineation. In a 2015 essay for the *Los Angeles Review of Books*, Roy Scranton takes issue with the emphasis on psychological damage to American soldiers and critiques the representation of what he calls the "trauma hero." In this all-too-common myth, he explains, a boy goes to war, "sees, suffers, and causes brutal and brutalizing violence," only to return home to a world that doesn't understand, wracked by "the struggle between the need to bear witness to his shattering encounter with violence, and the compulsion to repress it." The soldier's story becomes a kind of "mystic truth," elevated beyond the banal or ordinary and almost incommunicable; Scranton finds this narrative pattern in canonical war writers like Wilfred Owen, Ernest Hemingway, and Tim O'Brien.

Scranton doesn't deny the power of their writing, but that is, in some sense, the problem. Owen, for example, in his poem "Dulce Et Decorum Est," "means to malign war, but according to his logic, it is his very experience of war that gives him privileged access to moral truth beyond anything civilians . . . can ever hope to achieve." Owen is at least drawing on real experience, Scranton writes, noting that Hemingway "lasted only a few weeks as a noncombatant before being wounded and returning to the US" and yet "stands in American letters as the high priest of combat Gnosticism." Scranton is dismissive of Hemingway here, not considering Hemingway's experience in the aftermath of an explosion of a Milan munitions factory in

1918. Hemingway was just nineteen, and on the scene as a Red Cross ambulance driver. About sixty were killed, many of whom were young women, and Hemingway helped locate and move mutilated corpses and body fragments, which he later wrote about in his short story "A Natural History of the Dead." Although his style is ironic, his point is not: "The first thing that you found about the dead was that, hit badly enough, they died like animals."

It is hard to fault the famed writers of earlier conflicts because of how well they conveyed their experiences or how those representations have been understood in later years. Scranton's critique is sharper regarding more recent war writers, however, and that deserves further consideration. Another reason to call out the trauma hero myth, he writes, is because it serves "a scapegoat function, discharging national bloodguilt by substituting the victim of trauma, the soldier, for the victim of violence, the enemy." Privileging one's own perspective is arguably more problematic now than it was in, say, the early twentieth century. Scranton focuses on this tendency in Klay's *Redeployment*, Powers's *The Yellow Birds*, and the film adaptation of *American Sniper*. The last is the most egregious, as I discussed in chapter 1, since both memoir and film offer one-dimensional portrayals of Iraqis as bad guys and evildoers, and Kyle as a white-hat hero who only regrets the Americans he couldn't save. But Scranton points out these emphases in Powers and Klay as well. Bartle's entire consciousness is focused on Murph and Murph's death and barely registers the death of an Iraqi translator, Malik, in the opening pages—"I didn't think about Malik much after that," he comments (12). Nor does he give much thought to the hermit that Sterling kills in the wake of Murph's death, a cold-blooded murder of an Iraqi civilian. Bartle's trauma is Murph's trauma and no one else's. Although I identify renunciation as a notable and, in its way, admirable response to the sense of confusion and personal fragmentation that war can engender in Powers, Castner, and Turner, it is worth noting that renunciation of this sort is a privilege, and only an option for those who aren't still quite literally living in a war zone.

Scranton spends more time talking about the title story of *Redeployment* and the striking opening sentence, "We shot dogs." This, Scranton argues, "allows American readers to ignore the unpleasant fact that we shot people." When Sergeant Price confronts his own dead dog, Vicar, at the end of the story, Scranton points out that if a vicar is a representative or substitute, then the dog could be standing in for the narrator's trauma, but also for all the Iraqis killed in the war. "The sad fact Klay plays on," he writes,

> is that most American readers will care more about a dead dog than they will about a dead Iraqi, and in this way "Redeployment" opens up an emotional conduit for those readers to feel the pang of grief that

can come with killing, but without having to connect that feeling to the political reality of the war in Iraq. Whereas an Iraqi victim would have to be reckoned with as a fellow human being, with all the complexity that entails, a dog can simply be pitied and his killer simply empathized with. This moral simplification comes at a cost.

While Scranton concedes that the title story of Klay's collection constitutes just one perspective among many in *Redeployment*, he notes that neither Powers nor Klay portrays Iraqis with any depth or detail. That is an important consideration, though I would argue that Powers and Klay are after a different kind of portrait than *American Sniper*—not of a hero literally eliminating Iraqi "savages," but soldiers becoming savages themselves and unsure how to deal with the fact that they can no longer feel emotions like compassion or empathy. When reflecting later on his absence of feeling about the death of Malik the translator, Bartle says, "I was not surprised by the cruelty of my ambivalence then" (11); compare that to the narrator's utter blankness about his successful artillery mission in Klay's "Ten Kliks South." Focusing on a different story, "Psychological Operations," Paul Petrovic argues that Klay as well as Brian Turner and Eliot Ackerman have "deepened their engagement with the colonized subject, utilizing transgressive narrative strategies by placing Arab, Copic American, and Persian narration at the forefront of their texts" (1). "Psychological Operations" centers on Waguih, an Egyptian American Copt and a veteran, enrolled at Amherst College, who is at odds and in conversation with Zara Davies, a Black student who has recently converted to Islam. Ackerman's 2015 novel *Green on Blue* tells the story of Aziz Iqtbal, an Afghan boy caught up in the violent and conflicting allegiances within Afghanistan as well as those that arise after the US invasion. Petrovic writes that as a result, these authors "refuse to make an exception out of American suffering; instead, their very narrative strategies suture together their combat trauma under a more constitutive lens of globalized suffering that takes into consideration Arab and Persian perspectives" (22). And as I will discuss in the Conclusion, Klay's next work, *Missionaries*, takes an even more broadly multivocal approach to violence and conflict.

Joseph Darda has extended Scranton's critique to focus on what he terms "military whiteness," an emphasis that he argues emerges in the wake of the Vietnam War. That emphasis has been attributed to "a conservative backlash to the racial reforms of the civil rights era that orchestrated a reinvestment in whiteness," as well as the "remasculinization of America" that Susan Jeffords has described ("Military Whiteness" 78). But Darda also identifies the "positive pluralism of multiculturalism" as an influence, as veteran status began to be considered a form of diversity—even though the effect was one of "maintaining white racial dominance" (78–79). Darda describes, for example, Larry Heinemann's surprise receipt of the National Book Award for his novel *Paco's Story* in 1987, the year that Toni Morrison's *Beloved* was expected to win. Darda argues that Heinemann's novel reflects the project of military whiteness, "in which writers, filmmakers, and artists render white enlisted men as, at once, deracinated universals and minoritized outsiders, or 'veteran Americans.' The American veteran is figured as the victim of his own acts of military violence, as both victimizer and victimized in a circular account of the war" ("Ethnicization" 413)

While, as I noted earlier, I think that more recent multivalent and multivocal literature serves to mute that emphasis on military whiteness to a degree, it is certainly the case that there are few mainstream works about contemporary war by non-white authors to consider. As Peter Molin has put it, "Given the scarcity of published writing by Black American vets in the post-9/11 era, Darda's critique merits consideration on quantitative grounds alone" ("Wayward Warfaring" 4), a problem that has also been noted by Matthew Komatsu. Molin does note two autobiographies cowritten with M. L. Doyle, herself a Black veteran—*I'm Still Standing* (2011), about Shoshana Johnson, a soldier who was wounded and captured alongside Jessica Lynch in 2003, and *A Promise Fulfilled* (2014), about Brigadier General Julia Jeter Cleckley, the first Black woman to attain the rank of general in the Army. Molin also draws attention to Nicole S. Goodwin's collection of poetry, *Warcries* (2016), which wrestles with issues of race and gender in the military. Johnson's book was published with a small imprint, Touchstone, that is no longer in operation, and Cleckley's and Goodwin's were independently published with CreateSpace. "The publishing industry record regarding African-American veteran-authors does not impress," Molin affirms, "but the vibrant vet-writing/spoken-word and performance/theatrical scenes in New York City and Philadelphia, in which Goodwin participates, offers access to many Black voices and perspectives" (6). Molin mentions authors like Johnson Wiley, Donna Zephrine, and Maurice Decaul, whose work he has sought permission to publish or link to on his website, *Time Now* ("Black Voices").

In his *Los Angeles Review of Books* piece, Scranton only mentions Brian Turner in passing—he doesn't include Turner in the list of authors that he critiques most strongly. For Scranton, Turner is an example of a writer who understands the war experience as revealing a deeper, profound truth, a potentially problematic position if it conveys singular authenticity on the white veteran-author and contributes to the trauma hero myth. For Turner, however, "poetry itself is already experience-as-revelation," Scranton writes.

The fact that he is a war poet, then, is "practically incidental." Turner has been notably intentional about taking up Iraqi perspectives and cultural context in his work, and critics have praised him for his consideration of subjectivities beyond that of the white American male soldier. His doing so, notes Petrovic, "allows him to undo a simplistic persona of the Other and enables him to create a more complex, and empathetic, worldview of the colonized subjects occupied by U.S. military forces" (4). And in an article published in the *Journal of Arabic Literature*, Mara Naaman reads Brian Turner's poetry alongside iconic poets of the Arab world, Badr Shair al-Sayyab, Mahmud Darwish, Sadi Yusuf, and Sinan Antoon. Naaman notes that much of this poetry maintains the lyric tradition of representing a "heroic, sensual Iraq of some epic past" rather than chronicling the decades of war and occupation, but that Antoon and Turner take a different approach, portraying Iraq as "ever-elusive" and ravaged by war (337, 338). Ultimately, Naaman argues, considering Iraqi and American works together is more productive, because "by reading these poems alongside American works responding to the Iraq war, it becomes evident that this sense of ambivalence over the issue of representation—the tension between humanizing and essentializing the other within the poem—is common across cultures and texts. . . . America and Iraq respectively are represented as contradictory spaces of humanity as well as barbarism, spaces of possibility and of deep despair" (342). This is an apt recommendation, and one that I take up in earnest in the following chapter, which focuses on Iraqi authors writing about contemporary war and many works that have only recently been available in translation.

CHAPTER 4

Imagining an Archive
Contemporary Iraqi War Fiction

In 2016, Sinan Antoon published his fourth novel, titled *Fihris*, which means index or catalog. The English translation appeared in 2019 with the title *The Book of Collateral Damage*. Antoon writes about a man not unlike himself, Nameer al-Baghdadi, who grew up in Iraq but now teaches Arabic at New York University (NYU). Nameer is fascinated to the point of preoccupation with a man named Wadood, who still lives in Baghdad. As he grapples with the alienation he feels in living so far away from his homeland, Nameer speaks to a therapist and ends up telling her about Wadood. Wadood is a secondhand book dealer who writes obsessively, collecting stories and news reports of the war's devastation, all for a project he calls *Fihris*. The therapist approves of that project and tells Nameer, "Writing can be therapy! This has been an important development in recent years—but supervised by a specialist, of course. Many of the soldiers coming back from Iraq write as part of their psychological therapy." All true. But Nameer laughs dismissively. "Why are you laughing?" the therapist asks him. "Because my friend is still in the throes of war. The troops come back here, while he can't 'come back.' And that's what he's actually writing." "Yes, but the soldiers are victims too at the end of the day," the therapist counters. "I don't want to get into an argument with you now," Nameer responds. "The troops here volunteer to join the army. Iraqi civilians don't volunteer. They don't have a choice" (267).

Although I have considered literature about American soldiers like Billy Lynn, whose military service is a choice only because, for him, it is the Army or jail, Nameer obviously makes a salient point, and undermines the therapist's apparent understanding of soldiers as what Roy Scranton would call "trauma heroes." In fact, most Iraqi-authored literature about contemporary war doesn't feature soldiers' perspectives but rather characters like Antoon's Wadood, a civilian living in the midst of war, and Nameer, an Iraqi living in exile from his home nation. And the throes of war, as Nameer puts it, are indeed different when they so completely encompass your home, your family, the entirety of your life. It makes sense, then, that the blurred boundaries and fragmentation I have been tracing throughout this book are all the more extreme in these contemporary Iraqi works, emphases that are taken further in terms of both subject matter and narrative style. The response to the devastation is also different and builds on the idea of Wadood's catalog—his archive, his ongoing history and story—to suggest a kind of collective imagination as both the substance of and counter to grievous loss.

All these writers are working within a very long tradition as well as reimagining it in dramatic ways. Since the seventh century, when the Arabic script used today first began to appear, it has been a language characterized by diglossia—speakers know both a vernacular language of everyday use and a "prestige language" used in literature or formal settings. The prestige language is Classical Arabic, which Robert Irwin describes as "*fasih* Arabic": "chaste, free from barbarisms; the usage among Arabs of pure speech of which the beauty is perceived by hearing; eloquent; following the rules of desinential syntax" (xii). Modern Standard Arabic is basically the same as Classical Arabic, though there are some altered grammatical constructions and vocabulary—the changes began in the nineteenth century largely as a consequence of developments in media, such as the printing press and mass marketing. But neither Classical nor Modern Standard Arabic is used in common speech. Rather, people use a variety of localized, vernacular dialects, some of which are unintelligible to each other.[1]

In the Arabic literary tradition, poetry is the earliest and highest literary form, a form that is not only considered prestigious but also revered within societies. The most famous poems in Arabic might be the *Muʿallāqāt*, a collection of pre-Islamic verse from the sixth century considered to be the most excellent. The poetry is written in the form of a *qaṣīda*, a long poem that adheres to strict rules about length, rhyme, and meter, and which dominates Arabic verse until the twentieth century (Irwin 6–7). In prose, one of the great influences on Arabic literary styles is a book of animal fables, *Kalīla wa-Dimna*, which Abdallah ibn al-Muqaffaʿa translated from Persian in the eighth century. Before that, it had been translated from Sanskrit to Persian (Irwin 75–76). This is the book that begins the tradition of nested and interwoven stories, a device that the contemporary authors Ahmed Saadawi, Hassan Blasim, and Sinan Antoon use in works I cover in this chapter. These three authors also use degrees of Iraqi vernacular, a deliberate choice based on what they want to convey in their narratives—a corollary effect of this choice is that, in the Arabic, aspects of the texts may not be intelligible to non-Iraqi readers, and that in translation, the text finds a wider, more global audience.

In Iraq, the novel as a literary form developed in the twentieth century, against the backdrop of decades of political instability and violence. In her 2015 study *War and Occupation in Iraqi Fiction*, Ikram Masmoudi traces the novel's establishment back to Sulaymān Fayḍī's 1919 *al-Riwāya al-īqāẓiyya* (*The Story of Awakening*) and Maḥmūd Aḥmad al-Sayyid's 1928 novella *Jalāl Khālid*, the latter of which depicts the Iraqi revolt against the occupying

British forces. (Under a League of Nations mandate, the British joined three provinces into a single client kingdom, the State of Iraq, in 1921, which attained independence in 1932.) Ghā'ib Tu'ma Farmān published *al-Nakhla wa al-jīrān* (*The Palm Tree and the Neighbors*) in 1966, a realist novel by an author who became central to the literary scene for some years to come, and firmly in the midst of several cycles of violent conflict: the monarchy was overthrown by a coup in 1958; that was followed by bloody disputes between the Communists and the Nationalists; and the Ba'ath party rose to power in 1968 (Masmoudi 8–9). Saddam Hussein became head of state in 1989, inaugurating a series of new wars: the Iran-Iraq War, the first Persian Gulf War, and the Iraq War. "One might advance the argument that the Iraqi novel has become a representation of the manifestation of sovereign power," Masmoudi writes, "examining how the individual Iraqi has coped with and withstood the subjugation of life to the power of death and killing during three decades of raw power, murderous wars and, more recently, a war of occupation within the context of the war on terror" (2).

While many writers were inspired by and depicted the violent struggles of the 1950s and 1960s, under Saddam Hussein, citizens were required to embrace the Ba'ath party, and thus artists were drastically restricted in what they could portray. As a result, many writers left the country, a wave of expatriation that was repeated during the wars. "The main characteristic of this literature of exile," writes Masmoudi, "is that it addresses clearly and unequivocally the trials, ordeals and suffering of the Iraqi people in the face of daily death during the years of the dictatorship and throughout the different wars that it had brought upon the people. It was impossible for these kinds of novels to be published inside Iraq" (14). All of this history demonstrates the need for studies like hers: "the world's relationship to Iraq has been dominated by the West's own military, political and academic discourses on Iraq; there remains a significant gap in this knowledge that can be filled by the testimony of Iraqi writers, told in their own voices, and, to date, *only in their own language*, offering their own perspectives on the events that have shaped their history and changed their lives" (1; emphasis added).

Since Masmoudi's writing, however, a number of those testimonies and perspectives have been published in translation—which means that the popular readership and critical conversation can now include non-Arabic speakers. Ahmed Saadawi's novel *Frankenstein in Baghdad* was first published in 2013 and then translated in 2018. Hassan Blasim's collection of short stories, *The Corpse Exhibition*, originally published in 2008 and including stories from his previous works *The Madman of Freedom Square* and *The Iraqi Christ*, appeared in translation in 2014, as did Sinan Antoon's novel *The Corpse Washer*, originally published in 2013. Antoon also published *The*

Baghdad Eucharist in 2013, translated in 2017, and most recently *The Book of Collateral Damage*. Blasim's novel *God 99* appeared in 2018 and was translated in 2020. Finally, Inaam Kachachi's 2008 novel, *The American Granddaughter*, was also translated in 2020. (Jonathan Wright, a British journalist and translator, was responsible for a number of these English versions and has won acclaim for some of them.)

As many of these titles suggest, Iraqi literature does not shy away from depicting the death and destruction caused by war. To put it bluntly, there are a lot more bodies in Iraqi war fiction, and not ones that are hidden as traumatic secrets to be eventually revealed or uncovered, as they are in so many American works. Near the end of Joseph Heller's *Catch-22*, Yossarian patches up Snowden's leg wound and assures him he'll be all right, only to realize, when he opens up Snowden's flak suit, that he has a hideous abdominal injury as well. Yossarian hears himself scream as "Snowden's insides slithered down to the floor in a soggy pile," and this horrific revelation is Snowden's "grim secret": "It was easy to read the message in his entrails. Man was matter, that was Snowden's secret" (449, 450). But Snowden's secret in *Catch-22* is not a secret in Iraq—everybody already knows that story and that reality. Roger Luckhurst has examined the absence of bodies, particularly of Iraqi civilians, in American reporting, photography, and fiction: "The American military and government steadfastly refused to issue even basic figures on the number of Iraqi civilians killed, perhaps learning from the disastrous effects of the so-called kill lists issued during the Vietnam War" (356). Luckhurst also notes the strict embed agreements that had to be signed by photographers working with the military in Iraq that controlled the kinds of images that could be captured and distributed, restrictions that applied to both Iraqi and American dead. American literature that seeks to represent the trauma of violent death often does so using "the horrific detail, the delayed traumatic kernel" that is revealed late in the plot, as in *The Yellow Birds* or the novels Luckhurst discusses, Pitre's *Fives and Twenty-Fives* and Atticus Lish's *Preparation for the Next Life*. Luckhurst admires these novels and adds that "Lish's interweaving of [a] veteran's life with that of an illegal Chinese immigrant in New York attempts to extend, complicate, and interleave global networks of displacement and trauma" (366–67). That exploration of trauma, however, is again usually focused on white American protagonists. Iraqi-authored fiction, on the other hand, "seems expressly designed to bring the absent bodies back into focus" (357), and Luckhurst uses Antoon's *The Corpse Washer* and Saadawi's *Frankenstein in Baghdad* as potent examples: "For all its abstraction and apparent vanishing in the scopic regime of the War on Terror, here the body returns finally, demanding to be counted, remembered, and honored" (370).

Frankenstein in Baghdad: A Horror Classic Reimagined

Those bodies return in a way that is uncannily horrific in one of the best-known and most acclaimed works about the Iraq War, Saadawi's *Franken-stein in Baghdad* (2013). Something of an exception to Masmoudi's rule about writers' ability to publish in their own country, Saadawi continues to live and work in Baghdad. He is the author of two other novels, *The Beautiful Country* (2000) and *Indeed He Dreams or Plays and Dies* (2008), and one poetry collection, *Anniversary of Bad Songs* (2000). In 2010, Saadawi was one of *Beirut 39*'s list of thirty-nine best Arab authors under forty years old. He remembers an idyllic childhood in Baghdad in the 1970s, the beautiful Zawra Gardens, and the cinemas on Saadoun Street. Then after Saddam Hussein took power, "my memories from the 1980s are of dead bodies and women screaming in my neighbourhood when a young man arrived in a coffin." When the war began in 2003, he had served in the Iraqi Army three times and considered emigrating with his family but thus far has chosen to remain in the country. "I am still anxious about ensuring my family's safety in the unstable conditions in the country," he said in 2018. "On the other hand, I benefit [creatively] from the advantages of being in the chaotic 'boiler room' of the real world of Iraq" (Devi).

Masmoudi writes that the "spiral of violence and revenge killings" during the Iraq War in the midst of the continually destabilized nation "is nowhere better described and dramatized" than in *Frankenstein in Baghdad* (16). The novel won the International Prize for Arabic Fiction, it was shortlisted for the international Man Booker prize, and its 2018 English translation was advertised as coinciding with the 200th anniversary of Mary Shelley's novel. As Tasnim Qutait notes, Saadawi achieves both regional and international fame, and his work can be understood as a "refracted national literature" as well as the more widely familiar monster story. As the title itself suggests, it is operating on both the local and the global stages.

The plot of *Frankenstein in Baghdad* begins with an explosion:

The explosion took place two minutes after Elishva, the old woman known as Umm Daniel, or Daniel's mother, boarded the bus. Everyone on the bus turned around to see what had happened. They watched in shock as a ball of smoke rose, dark and black, beyond the crowds, from the car park near Tayaran Square in the center of Baghdad. Young people raced to the scene of the explosion, and cars collided into each other or into the median. The drivers were frightened and confused: they were assaulted by the sound of car horns and of people screaming and shouting. (5)

Explosions, as we've seen, are common occurrences in American literature of the Iraq War, but here, of course, they happen amid the characters' daily lives. Elishva, however, doesn't even hear the blast—old and frail, she continues to stare out the bus window, lost in her gloom. She thinks about her son, Daniel, who fought in the Iran-Iraq War but never returned home. He's one of three beings she believes she lives with, "three ghosts, with so much power and presence that she didn't feel lonely" (15). The chapter about Elishva is called "The Madwoman." The next chapter is "The Liar," and it follows Hadi al-Attag, a junk dealer who is telling his story to a group of journalists. "That guy's recounting the plot of a movie," one journalist comments to another. "He's stolen his story from a Robert De Niro film" (19). Hadi is, in fact, telling his own story, including "all the details of the things that happened to him" but working to make it "more interesting," and he had gotten as far as "the first" explosion, which is the same one that detonates near Elishva (18, 20).

Hadi picks something up from that explosion site and puts it into a canvas bag. When he gets home, the description of what he does is unsparing, and indeed reminiscent of a particular De Niro film:

> He went to the shed, which he had assembled out of scraps of furniture, iron bars, and sections of kitchen units he had leaned up against the piece of wall that still remained, and squatted down at one end. The rest of the shed was dominated by a massive corpse—the body of a naked man, with viscous liquids, light in color, oozing from parts of it. There was only a little blood—some small dried patches on the arms and legs, and some grazes and bruises around the shoulders and neck. It was hard to say what color the skin was—it didn't have a uniform color. Hadi moved farther into the narrow space around the body and sat down close to the head. The area where the nose should have been was badly disfigured, as if a wild animal had bitten a chunk out of it. Hadi opened the canvas sack and took out the thing. In recent days he had spent hours looking for one like it, yet he was still uneasy handling it. It was a fresh nose, still coated in congealed, dark red blood. His hand trembling, he positioned it in the black hole in the corpse's face. It was a perfect fit, as if the corpse had his own nose back. (26)

Hadi has been collecting body parts from explosion sites and works to assemble them into a full corpse. "I wanted to hand him over to the forensics department," he explains to those listening to his story, "because it was a complete corpse that had been left in the streets like trash. It's a human being, guys, a person. . . . I made it complete so it wouldn't be treated as trash, so it would be respected like other dead people and given a proper burial" (27). Once the corpse is complete, however, Hadi realizes that he isn't sure what to do with it. After Hadi is himself blasted by another explosion that leaves him in shock, he goes home to sleep, and wakes to find that the corpse has disappeared. It's been animated by "A Lost Soul" (the title of the next chapter), a hotel guard named Hasib Mohamed Jaafar who was killed by a suicide bomber. Finding the body, Jaafar "lodged inside the corpse, filling it from head to toe, because probably, he realized then, it didn't have a soul, while he was a soul without a body" (40).

This, then, is the Frankenstein story set in Baghdad. The comment about "a Robert De Niro film" refers to Kenneth Branaugh's 1994 adaptation *Mary Shelley's Frankenstein*, starring De Niro as the creature. Saadawi's novel is not a retelling with the same level of fidelity to the original that the title of Branaugh's film suggests, however. Here, the creature—called, among other things, the "Whatsitsname"—is also summoned into being by Elivsha, who thinks the creature is her long-lost son Daniel, finally returned to her. As Sinéad Murphy notes, "This misrecognition connects the animated corpse formed in post-2003 conditions of war with the ten-year conflict between Iraq and Iran, gesturing to a longer history of sectarian violence in Iraq over the past several decades" (274). That longer history, and the Whatsitsname's multifaceted origins, suggest the complications to follow. Murders begin to occur in the area, and the Whatsitsname tells Hadi that "the soul of Hasib Mohamed Jaafar was demanding revenge, and he had to kill the person who had caused Hasib's death" (129). It seems, too, that it's not just Hasib who demands revenge: "The Whatsitsname was made up of the body parts of people who had been killed, plus the soul of another victim, and had been given the name of yet another victim. He was a composite of victims seeking to avenge their deaths so they could rest in peace. He was created to obtain revenge on their behalf" (130). But the creature soon realizes that his body is starting to decay, to fall apart, and he needs "new flesh from new victims" to replace it. Despite his claims that "I'm the only justice there is in this country," his killing becomes indiscriminate (135).

The Whatsitsname insists that no one need "take up arms with me" and asks only for support, as there is a "moral and humanitarian obligation to back me, to bring about justice in this world, which has been totally ravaged by greed, ambition, megalomania, and insatiable violence" (143). He accrues followers nonetheless: mysterious characters known only as the Sophist, the Magician, and the Enemy, and three madmen, young, old, and eldest. The creature is called other names: Criminal X, The One Who Has No Name. He is whispered about, and the fear grows. No one knows quite what or who is committing the murders, and a brigadier is stymied in his attempts to track down and arrest the perpetrator: "In Sadr City they spoke of him as a Wahhabi, in Adamiya as a Shiite extremist. The Iraqi government described him as an agent of foreign powers, while the spokesman for the U.S. State Department said he was an ingenious man whose aim was to undermine the American project in Iraq. But what project might that be? As far as Brigadier Majid was concerned, the monster itself was their project" (268).

In the end, Haji is disfigured in a fire, and after his bandages are removed, he looks in the mirror and sees "a horrible creature." He looks closer, and screams: "It was the face of someone he had convinced himself was merely a figment of his fertile imagination. It was the face of the Whatsitsname" (267). Is Haji crazy? Is he just "The Liar," as the previous chapter title denotes? Or is he actually the murderer? The community seems to think so. Haji is arrested for the killings, but his friend Mahmoud al-Sawadi doesn't believe he's guilty. "It was impossible that Haji was the Whatsitsname," he concludes (279). The novel ends in appropriate horror-movie fashion—the killer is (perhaps?) not in custody after all, but appears as "the specter of an unknown man" moving quietly around a room in an abandoned hotel, peering out the window at the crowds outside celebrating Haji's capture (280).

The lack of delineation and resulting fragmentation in *Frankenstein in Baghdad* operate at a number of levels. The novel features similar psychological struggles and narrative nonlinearity that we see in recent American texts, but Saadawi's use of Shelley's gothic horror story also invites considerations of political fragmentation and even the fragmentation of the origin story itself. Hadi quite literally works with bodily fragments, trying to create some sort of whole, and as Patrick Deer argues, trying to ensure that those many, many losses will be seen and acknowledged. The Whatsitsname, too, makes it his mission to force an accounting, and accountability, in the midst of senseless acts of violence. The creature's body is, Murphy writes, "a striking metaphor for the instrumentalization of human bodies in conditions of contemporary violent conflict" (278). The creature consists of people, and people's lives, torn apart by war. Rather than achieving a reconstitution or violent restitution, however, the creature continues to fall apart, and the violence spirals out of control. Similar to Murphy, Qutait argues that the creature is "an allegory for the fragmented national body," occupied by a foreign military, riven by factional violence, and stymied by broken bureaucracy (97). But even that allegory falls apart, as Saadawi strays further from Shelley's story and the retelling "disintegrates into an absurd, fragmentary tale, finally eroding the structural sympathy of allegory" (100).

Both Murphy and Qutait comment on Saadawi's engagement with the horror genre, an approach he shares with Hassan Blasim, whom I will discuss next. (Other critics have talked about *Frankenstein in Baghdad*'s use of magic realism and science fiction, depending on how they wish to classify Shelley's 1818 novel.) Horror, a genre focused intently on bodies, has long drawn narrative power from fragmentation and blurred boundaries, from the damage and uncanny transformations that bodies can undergo. Film scholar Barbara Creed uses Julia Kristeva's conception of the abject to explain what disturbs us about horror movies—in Kristeva's words, the abject is that which "disturbs identity, system, order. What does not respect borders, positions, rules. The in-between, the ambiguous, the composite" (4). Horror films, Creed explains, create monsters out of blurred boundaries: between human and animal (*The Wolfman* and *Dr. Jekyll and Mr. Hyde*); normal and supernatural (*The Haunting* and *Poltergeist*); good and evil (*Carrie* and *Rosemary's Baby*); life and death (*Dracula* and, of course, *Frankenstein*). That failure of delineation is what creates monsters, and so Saadawi's interweaving of contemporary war and classic horror makes sense.

Murphy and Qutait note that horror is an perfect genre for writers like Saadawi and Blasim not just because, as Qutait writes, its tropes can represent "the dislocating and disorienting force of violence," but also because it is a genre that is applicable to many different cultural contexts (89). That wide applicability further means that writers can veil or refract their political commentary, which can be crucial for an author like Saadawi, living in Iraq. Murphy argues that Frankenstein's creature, that much-adapted icon, works as a symbol of what Judith Butler calls precarious life—a life that, because of intersecting social and political conditions, becomes fragile or unsustainable, unvalued by the powers that organize populations. Precarious life "exists on a global scale," Murphy writes, but "is iterated differently in specific national and regional contexts" (284).

The Whatsitsname is precarious, abject life, the epitome of unreconstituted fragmentation, and *Frankenstein in Baghdad* is, as its title suggests, a story of and about horror. But it becomes a story about something else, too. We saw, in writers such as Phil Klay, Michael Pitre, and Brian Turner, a multivocal approach to contemporary war narratives in the various literary forms of short story collection, novel, and most unconventionally, memoir. That multivocality necessarily invites the reader to think about different perspectives on war and, particularly in Turner's case, to consider the reasons an author might decide to include voices other than their own. In that sense storytelling itself becomes part of the subject matter—though not nearly to the degree that it does in Iraqi-authored war literature. In Saadawi's case, his novel's title already suggests some level of self-awareness, as *Frankenstein* is one of the more frequently adapted of the classic horror stories and Frankenstein's creature one of the most iconic (and parodied) characters. (A journalist's mention of "a De Niro film" also gestures toward not just the original but

the subsequent flood of variations.) Saadawi takes the self-reflexive emphasis on narrative further right at the book's outset, in a section titled "Final
Report" that precedes chapter 1 and the bomb explosion that sets the plot's
events in motion. The report is a document from the "Tracking and Pursuit Department" concerning events in 2005, events that led the department
to "[operate] outside its area of expertise, which should have been limited
to such bureaucratic matters as archiving information and preserving files
and documents. Under the direct management of Brigadier Majid, it had
employed several astrologers and fortune-tellers, on high salaries financed
by the Iraqi treasury, not by the U.S. authorities" (2). Instead of just docu-
menting the past, the department was trying to predict the future. Worse,
documents in the department had been leaked to someone known only as
"the author." That person was identified and arrested and found to be "in
possession of the text of a story he had written drawing on material contained in documents belonging to the Tracking and Pursuit Department."
Experts read the text and concluded "that it does not violate any provisions of
the law, but for precautionary reasons they recommended that the information in it should not be published under any circumstances and that the story
should not be rewritten" (2).

This Final Report riffs on the classic horror frame story, presenting the
events of the narrative as something that has already occurred and that is
being recounted, the authenticity of those events confirmed by documents,
letters, or other records. Mary Shelley does this in *Frankenstein* by using
the epistolary format, telling Victor Frankenstein's and the creature's story
through the letters of Robert Walton; similarly, Bram Stoker narrates
Dracula through letters and journal entries of the main characters. This isn't
a device that is only seen in horror—the first Arab American novel, Ameen
Rihani's *The Book of Khalid* from 1911, purports to take its story from a
manuscript discovered in the Khedivial Library of Cairo. "Needless to say
we asked at once the Custodian of the Library to give us access to this Book
of Khalid, and after examining it, we hired an amanuensis to make a copy
for us. Which copy we subsequently used as the warp of our material; the
woof we shall speak of in the following chapter. No, there is nothing in this
Work which we can call ours, except it be the Loom." And the tradition of
Arabic literature generally frequently features nested stories and storytell-
ers.² Saadawi's use of the frame story, then, echoes both the Arabic literary
tradition and the global horror genre, but that is not the only way Saadawi
emphasizes the act of narration.

In *Frankenstein in Baghdad*, the frame story is already complicated by the
uncertainty about the author's identity noted in the Final Report, and questions about storytellers and authorship become more complex as the novel

goes on. The journalists in the novel both pursue and doubt the story of
the Whatsitsname. One of them, Mahmoud, records the story that Hadi
told, though in doing so he "is aware that he was paraphrasing the words
that Hadi had attributed to the Whatsitsname and that he was adding his
own personal gloss as well" (131). In chapter 10, the Whatsitsname speaks
directly into the recorder, amusingly ensuring before he begins that everything will be captured correctly:

> "Hello, hello, test, test, test."
> "I've started recording."
> "I know. Hello, hello, test, test."
> "Mind the battery."
> "Please be quiet. Hello, hello, yes." (142)

But the creature takes a bit too long, and the battery does indeed die.
"Yes, no problem," he says, and then commands: "Leave the building and
don't come back till you have a big bag full of batteries" (144). He talks
and talks, speaking about the many people he has killed. The chapter ends
somewhat ambiguously, implying that the Whatsitsname kills the person
doing the recording. Contradictory statements imply both that the story has
been completely told and also that it's not nearly over:

> "The battery's going to run out, sir."
> [. . .]
> "I know. I won't need any more batteries. I've finished recording."
> "The recording's finished? What will you do now?"
> "Only one thing—this."
> "No, sir. No, master. I'm your slave and your servant. Why are you
> doing this? No, sir. I'm your slave, your sla . . . ve."
> "Hello, hello, hello, yes."

"Jeez, I'm running out of time. You wasted so much time, damn it!"
(163–64)

Near the novel's end, "the writer" shows up—perhaps the one who will
master all these stories and wrestle them all into submission, who will create
a single, clear, marketable narrative, as we imagine writers do. He brandishes
his own recorder and starts asking questions, first to an old man who lived
near Hadi and Elivsha. At last, there is someone to listen—the old man had
been "like a broken record, going on and on about everything he had seen
from his balcony over the years." "What would you like me to tell you?" the

old man asks. "Tell me everything," the writer responds (248). The reader doesn't get to hear that story, but the writer does narrate the novel's penultimate chapter. Everyone's talking about the Whatsitsname, the murderer, and the stories are as powerful as they are variable: "No one knew who his next victim would be, and despite all the assurances from the government, people grew more convinced with every passing day that he would never die. . . . The definitive image of him was whatever lurked in people's heads, fed by fear and despair. It was an image that had as many forms as there were people to conjure it." The writer concludes, "Although I had been immersed in this story for a long time, even I started to feel afraid" (268). The writer mentions his arrest, related in that opening Final Report, and that he is being pursued for a second interrogation—and one reason why he knows about the pursuit is that someone sends him that same Final Report. And so he tosses his fake identity card and flees.

Everything here is stories—reports, the prophecies of fortunetellers, the bodies of the dead, the characters' understanding of themselves and others. There are so many overlapping narratives that they even get the best of the writer. All that collective imagining, however, has power. When Hadi is telling Mahmoud about the creature, and Mahmoud finally "surrendered himself to Hadi's crazy story," he realizes that Hadi is speaking as if he's telling secrets rather than "playing the role of the old storyteller" (118). Qutait observes that in the original Arabic, Saadawi uses a specifically Iraqi term here, *alqaṣkhūn*, "to refer to the dying profession of the storyteller (referred to elsewhere in the region as the *ḥakawātī*)" (98). Saadawi writes his novel using Modern Standard Arabic for descriptive passages and vernacular for dialogue, in addition to a number of words that are specifically Iraqi, thus fusing the classical Arabic tradition with this particular contemporary context. His choice of term for the creature is notable as well—in the Arabic, Hadi calls the creature "the *shesma*," which Qutait notes is "a contracted dialect word for an object whose proper name is forgotten (literally 'what-is-his-name')" (98). Qutait further argues that "According to Saadawi, this (un)naming signifies the monster as an amalgam or everyman representing national complicity in the post-invasion violence" (98). Ibrahim Al-Aboosi comments that this common Iraqi dialect word can refer to objects or people—something you would say if you had temporarily forgotten the word for something, for instance, but also someone whose name you don't know. Al-Aboosi is struck by Saadawi's choice to use a definite article with *shesma*, something you wouldn't normally do in casual speech, and finds that this choice "allows the definitiveness of the creature—its real existence, vengeance, and violence—to co-exist with the creature's indefiniteness, particularly the anonymity of its individual body parts" (Ibrahim Al-Aboosi, email message to author,

November 21, 2022). In that sense, the creature is itself like a story, both definite and indefinite, specific and universal, something that captures the imagination (for good or ill) and comes to life as a result. That is not an act of recovery or reconstitution—and indeed the Whatsitsname is neither of those things—but it does demand attention, and that the story continues to be told. That the novel ends by retelling the events noted in the opening Final Report emphasizes the endlessness of war—as we see in so many American works as well—but also the endlessness of the story, which circles back and begins again.

The Corpse Exhibition: Horror/Stories

Hassan Blasim's career has had a different and more unusual arc than Saadawi's. He grew up in Kirkuk and Baghdad, studying at Baghdad's Academy of Cinematic Arts and working in film production. Under Saddam Hussein's regime, however, this was a dangerous occupation. "Whenever we went out to film in the street," he says, "we would end up in the police station and in the offices of some other security agency. They deliberately intimidated us" (Holland). He fled first to Iraq's Kurdish territories in 1998 and out of Iraq entirely in 2000; in 2004, he settled in Finland. He first published stories in Arabic online but attracted little attention from publishers, an oversight perhaps attributable to both his subject matter and his literary style. Blasim avoids the extended use of Classical Arabic, which he considers "one of the prisons of the Arab world" (Holland), and like Saadawi instead uses a combination of Modern Standard Arabic with elements of the vernacular. Qutait writes that "Perhaps even more than the vernacular language, however, Blasim's use of unconventional structure and imagery deemed incoherent or vulgar proved an obstacle for Arabic publishing houses" (91–92). But Blasim was adamant:

> You learn something from the classics but your feelings and your imagination operate in the domain of the colloquial. We need to think seriously about reforming the Arabic that we use today. It's ridiculous and painful to use the Arabic of an Iraqi poet who lived centuries ago to describe what we in Iraq are suffering today, for example. How can one talk in a classical language about a child who's torn apart in an explosion in the market near his school? People in Iraq don't talk about their joys, their problems, and the destruction of the country in literary diction. (Holland)

Blasim became widely known as a writer only after his works appeared in translation. *The Madman of Freedom Square* made the long list for Britain's

Independent Foreign Fiction Prize in 2010, and in 2014 *The Iraqi Christ* won that award. *The Corpse Exhibition* received several accolades, including the English PEN's Writers in Translation Programme Award, also in 2014. Since those successes, his work has been published in Arabic, but he remains a writer known more globally than in Iraq.

In Blasim's most celebrated collection, *The Corpse Exhibition*, we see many of the same emphases as in Saadawi's novel. Although the central premise isn't the reimagining of a classic horror monster, the stories feature violence that is often extreme, an unsettling affect, and magical realist elements. The title story consists almost entirely of instructions given by an unnamed, unknown person in an organization whose members commit murders and then display the corpses in creative ways. When that person begins speaking, he sounds rather like a lethal bureaucrat: "Before taking out his knife he said, 'After studying the client's file you must submit a brief note on how you propose to kill your first client and how you will display his body in the city'" (3). But he makes clear that these killings are not politically or financially motivated: "Always remember, dear friend, that we are not terrorists whose aim is to bring down as many victims as possible in order to intimidate others, nor even crazy killers working for the sake of money. We have nothing to do with the fanatical Islamist groups or the intelligence agency of some nefarious government or any of that kind of nonsense" (4). The goal, at least in the man's explanation, is art—a kind of art achievable in Iraq because there are so many violent factions and so much instability. "Every body that you finish off is a work of art waiting for you to add the final touch, so that you can shine like a precious jewel amid the wreckage of this country. To display a corpse for others to see is the ultimate in the creativity we are seeking and that we are trying to study and benefit from" (5). As the story ends, the speaker describes an absurdly horrific display achieved by an admired colleague—a platform made of pulped bones and flesh, a man's skin entirely removed from his body, and an eye set into the fleshy pulp. A triumph, the speaker asserts. And then the story ends with an unaccountable conclusion: "Then he thrust the knife into my stomach and said, 'You're shaking'" (10). Many of the stories are like this—they take a sudden turn, they defy the interpretive hypotheses that the reader might have been mulling. For Blasim, this is completely apt. "In Baghdad," he says, "it can happen that someone goes shopping—food, apples—and suddenly a car bomb explodes. Life is like that sometimes: you pass a car, and the direction of your life changes completely. . . . You think life is simple, but it gives you big surprises, lots of changes" (Heath).

Subsequent stories contain striking, sudden changes of plot and of narrators—it can be hard, at times, to tell who is speaking, especially since both living and dead, realistic and fantastic characters are given a voice. The story "Crosswords" is narrated by a longtime friend of Marwan, a crossword writer who is hit by the blasts of a double explosion that kills at least two dozen people, as well as three policemen who arrive to render aid. Marwan is wounded, though not seriously. But after being treated at the hospital, he hears the voice of one of the policemen, possessing him. "I saw you under the rubble," the voice tells him, "so I went inside you and I felt warm again. And here I am, smelling what you can smell and tasting what you taste, hearing what you hear, and aware of you as a living being, but I can't see anything. I'm in total darkness. Can you hear me?" (60). Marwan does. It unhinges him, after a while. Those who know him begin taking his odd behavior as a matter of course. "They treated him as a victim of the explosion. Just another madman" (61). Eventually he dies, vomiting blood after swallowing a razor blade. An italicized sentence earlier in the story asks, *Why couldn't it have been the policeman who incited Marwan to swallow the razor blade?* (61). Italicized sentences like this one seem to be coming from the perspective of a third, unknown friend of Marwan and the speaker, and the query suggests two different meanings: that perhaps the policeman was *not* the motivation for Marwan to commit suicide in such a way; or it could be someone asking, well, why *couldn't* this have been the case? Which is the story that you hear in your head?

Iraq is full of victims, people made mad by the constant violence and suffering. Khaled Al-Masri traces Blasim's representation of madness in the collection, noting that the term and idea are sometimes used to signify mental illness but also as a way to interrogate received notions about war and narratives that elide or negate the experiences of those who are most affected by it. Al-Masri situates this in the broader history of Arabic literature, in which characters who violate social norms are often called mad, as far back as the story of *Majnūn wa Laylā* from the seventh century. A young man falls in love with Layla and writes poetry about her—he is so taken with her, so obsessed, that others begin to call him *majnūn*, which can mean crazy as well as "possessed by a jinn," or genie. Tarek El-Ariss argues that the madman figure is often "the rebel, the entertainer, and the prophetic figure" (299). And so by including madmen frequently and prominently in his stories, Blasim "critiques the 'sane' discourse of cultural and political authority, and the social institutions and structures that seek to enforce social stability by 'muffling' and marginalizing madness" (Al-Masri 275).

"The Madman of Freedom Square" makes use of this trope most prominently. "In those unforgettable days before the miracle happened and I discovered the truth that everyone now denies or ignores," the story begins, "we used to guard the platform where the two statues stood" (81). That statement prepares the reader for a good story—the speaker knows, and will presumably tell, the real truth, even though others can't see it. He is guarding statues, which are disallowed and targeted by multiple factions. The "fanatical Islamists" want the statues removed because they consider them idols; the government wants the statues removed because they symbolize the period of dictatorship. But, the speaker says, his neighborhood loved the statues for other reasons. "Of course, there are dozens of versions of the statues story," he admits, "but perhaps the version that my grandfather told was the one closest to the truth" (82). This, then, the speaker relates. The statues are of two young blond men who appeared in the neighborhood mysteriously, passing through it daily in a beneficent silence. (In Arabic culture, having blond hair is sometimes said to be lucky.) Over time, the people in the neighborhood began to attribute the good things that happened to them to the two blond men, including, at last, the overthrow of the monarchy. But after a military coup, the blond men stopped appearing, and the statues were erected in their memory and the memory of this "golden age." That's the grandfather's story—but the speaker goes on. The new government's forces arrive to take down the statues, and violence breaks out as the neighborhood tries to protect them. The blond men themselves are said to have appeared again, fighting in the melee, and when the speaker is blasted by a missile explosion, it is the two blond men who pull him from the wreckage.

If the story ended there, then the speaker could be said to be undermining the various official understandings of the meaning of the statues, to be telling the real story, perhaps the people's story. But that, again, isn't all. "Some of the young men from the new generation in the neighborhood now call me the madman of Freedom Square," he reveals, because they say the violence in Freedom Square (what the new government has renamed the neighborhood) resulted in a blast that planted shrapnel in the speaker's brain (89). And then the story twists yet again—the speaker meets a stranger who listens to him tell about all this with a sympathetic ear. "But what I don't fully understand is the wide belt the man wrapped around my waist in his house this morning. I feel very hot because the belt is so heavy. I'll sit down in the shade of the tree. . . . Damn, the women and children have taken all the benches" (90). The speaker, the madman, has been tricked into donning a suicide bomber's belt and will unknowingly kill both himself and innocent civilians. This tricks the reader as well, who assumes they have been reading a considered, thoughtful recounting of the facts, but realizes in the end that the narrator suffers from a brain injury and has been ruthlessly manipulated. According to Al-Masri, this has the effect of destabilizing both the story and the collection as a whole:

At the start of "The Madman of Freedom Square," it appears that the "madness" of the story of the blonds is contained by the "rationality" of the disbelieving external narrator. When it is later revealed that the frame narrator has a piece of shrapnel lodged in his brain, has come to embrace the story of the two blonds, and is in fact "the Madman of Freedom Square," these borderlines are called into question. This reversal legitimates the truths of the "mad" narrators of the other stories in the collection at the same time that it questions the rationality of its "sane" narrators. The role of the latter as reliable witnesses is challenged, just as the ability of the former to bear witness is validated. (295)

The borderlines between sane and mad become blurred—this is another common characteristic of the horror genre, a loss of distinction driven by constant violence. In "The Hole," a man fleeing three gunman falls into a deep, dark hole, and away from the chaos at the surface—protests, looting, killing, gangs, extremists, the army, and armed civilians all fighting each other. In the hole, the speaker finds an old man who says he lives there, occasionally eating the flesh of a dead Russian soldier who lies nearby. The speaker calls him disgusting and punches him, but the old man is unmoved—"he said there was no need for me to be upset, because he would leave the hole soon and I would fall into another hole from another time" (75). The old man does die, and now the speaker confronts a young girl who falls in. "I'm a jinni," he tells her (77). The boundaries continue to blur, and the stories proliferate and become byzantine. In "An Army Newspaper," the speaker talks about supervising the cultural page of an army newspaper and publishing war stories and poems. A soldier sends in some stories, and the speaker decides to publish one under his own name after discovering that the soldier had been killed in an attack. The stories, he says, are of the highest literary quality: "a transparent and cruel exploration of sexual beings from a point of view that was childlike and satanic at the same time" (41–42). The published piece rockets him to fame and wide acclaim, and he relishes the thought of publishing the others and eventually receiving the Nobel Prize in Literature. But the speaker receives a package with twenty more stories—and then more, and then more. They pour in by the hundreds, even though the soldier is confirmed to be dead, and the speaker resorts to hiding them in a vast warehouse. Finally, the speaker finds and burns the soldier's body, and then burns the stories in an incinerator. But all of this is, in fact, a story told by a dead man. He ended his life some time before and relates all these events to someone he refers to both as "Your Honor" and "dear writer." "So now," the story concludes, "before I'm put back in the mortuary, I know you are the Omnipotent, the Wise, the Omniscient, and the Imperious, but did you also once work for an army newspaper? And why do you need an incinerator for your characters?" (47). A writer can be a judge, a god, a creator, and a destroyer all at the same time.

"An Army Newspaper" has an unmistakably fantastical bent. But Blasim communicates too that stories have real-world, life-or-death consequences. In "The Reality and the Record," refugees vie for asylum, and the way they do that is by telling their stories—and so the stories need to be the right kind, the kind that will convince a listener that they are deserving of a new life. *"Everyone staying at the refugee reception center has two stories,"* "The Reality and the Record" begins, *"the real one and the one for the record. The stories for the record are the ones the new refugees tell to obtain the right to humanitarian asylum, written down in the immigration department and preserved in their private files. The real stories remain locked in the hearts of the refugees, for them to mull over in complete secrecy"* [italics in the original] (157). After this initial framing, a new Iraqi refugee arrives in Sweden, and tells his story—he has been a victim of kidnapping in which he was forced to be videotaped claiming to be an Iraqi army officer who killed, raped, and tortured people. Then he was traded to another group and told to say he was a soldier in the Medhi Army who killed many people with support from Iran. Over the course of a year and a half, "I was moved from one hiding place to another. They shot video of me talking about how I was a treacherous Kurd, an infidel Christian, a Saudi terrorist, a Syrian Ba'athist intelligence agent, or a Revolutionary Guard from Zoroastrian Iran. On these videotapes I murdered, raped, started fires, planted bombs, and carried out crimes that no sane person would even imagine" (168). The story ends by returning to the frame narrator, who notes that three days after the man told his story, he was committed to a psychiatric hospital. *"The ambulance driver summed up his real story in four words: I want to sleep"* (170). As Nadia Atia notes, Blasim's story here is deeply ambiguous: "framed by an anonymous narrator, told by a nameless and endlessly reinvented man, to an anonymous (presumably Swedish) worker whom we assume is interviewing the asylum seeker and assessing his claim" (323). In the story's opening, the narrator says that when thinking about the reality and the record, *"[it's not] easy to tell the two stories apart"* (157). In the original Arabic, Atia writes, the meaning is a bit different: "that it is not necessarily possible to distinguish *al-hudood* (الحدود), the boundaries, or borders, of each tale; الحدود seems particularly apt for a story about what it takes to successfully cross borders to safety, but it also further complicates the distinction between 'the reality and the record.' Instead of one false and one true, the stories blur ever more complicatedly into one another" (329).

Despite all that ambiguity, Blasim's story still emphasizes how important narrative can be for those affected by war, and particularly for refugees. Atia notes that the word *"Ersheef* in 'الإرشيف و الواقع,' the Arabic title of Blasim's story, translates as record, but also simply 'archive.'" Archive can refer to bureaucratic records and files, but also to repositories, places where scholars go to try and reconstruct the past, to investigate old stories. That Jonathan Wright translates *ersheef* as "record" also connotes the idea of legitimacy, of a story told "for the record," and the high stakes of telling the right story at the right time—a reminder that "the stories told in these liminal spaces have the power to transform the lives of displaced people" (323).

A displaced person, one who goes to impossible lengths to change his own story, is the subject of the final story in *The Corpse Exhibition*. "The Nightmares of Carlos Fuentes" is about a man named Salim Abdul Husain who works in Iraq cleaning up in the aftermath of explosions. He works hard in the hope that he will earn enough money to buy a visa to go to Holland and "escape this hell of fire and death" (187). One day he finds a man's finger with a silver ring, which he wears and likes so much that he keeps it rather than selling it. When he finally makes it to Holland, he changes his name to Carlos Fuentes—following the advice of his cousin, who said to avoid having an Arab name in Europe, and to choose something that would still "suit your complexion, which is the color of burnt barley bread" (188). Salim sees the name Carlos Fuentes in the newspaper and so adopts it as his own, with no awareness that he then shares a name with the famous Mexican author. He also adopts an entirely new identity—he learns Dutch, pays his taxes, works hard, marries a Dutch woman, gains Dutch citizenship. He scoffs at those immigrants who don't work as hard as he does: "He felt he was the only one who deserved to be adopted by this compassionate and tolerant country, and that the Dutch government should expel all those who did not learn the language properly and anyone who committed the slightest misdemeanor" (190). But "the wind did not blow fair for Fuentes," despite everything (191). He begins to dream of Iraq—of people speaking to him in an Iraqi dialect, of children making fun of his new name, of being accused of planting bombs. He tries everything to dispel the dreams, resorting to ever more absurd techniques including eating more chicken, wearing an overcoat to bed, dying his hair and toenails green. But it is all to no avail. In the end, he dreams of coming "face-to-face with Salim Abdul Husain!" (195). Fuentes screams and aims a rifle at Husain, but Husain just smiles, and says derisively, "Salim the Dutchman, Salim the Mexican, Salim the Iraqi, Salim the Frenchman, Salim the Indian, Salim the Pakistani, Salim the Nigerian" (195). Fuentes shoots, but Salim jumps out an open window and escapes. But when Fuentes's wife wakes up and investigates, she finds that "Carlos Fuentes was dead on the pavement, and a pool of blood was spreading slowly under his head" (195). He might have forgiven the newspapers, Blasim writes, which wrote that an Iraqi man committed suicide, not a Dutch national. He would have never forgiven his brothers, however, who had his body taken back to Iraq and buried in Najaf. A photographer captures a picture of Fuentes's outstretched hand on the pavement, wearing the silver ring, the stone "glowing red in the foreground, like a sun in hell" (196).

Brian Turner's memoir also ends with an image of the doubled self, the Sgt. Turner who is always present and watching, surveilling his bedroom landscape. And Turner frames himself as something of an exile, having the sense of one's life as a foreign country. But the final image of Blasim's collection intensifies those associations and is more colored by irony and despair. Husain is the exile whose new self kills the old one, or maybe vice versa. That ending also echoes the story's beginning—a dead man's finger wearing a ring lit up by fire and death.

The story of Husain and Fuentes is both sad and satiric, a kind of absurd tragedy that is nonetheless affecting. But although it ends with the same violence and death that pervades the collection—the horror of a dream life and a waking life blurred lethally together—scholars have noted that, taken as a whole, Blasim's writing affirms the power of all these storytelling voices even as it portrays the violence in a way that is both dark and unflinching. The madness of many of these characters, Al-Masri writes, is not a mere failing or sad end, but is also "used as a trope to question interior and external perspectives of war and exile, represent complex realities, and complicate linear narratives that fail to adequately portray the experiences and consequences of war and its refugees." In that sense, "Madness can have the effect of expanding reality, rather than distorting it" (273). Similarly, Qutait writes that in the world of Blasim's stories, "The narrators think constantly about representation as a form of fabulation, producing rather than reflecting the world" (104). Salim Abdul Husain does, after all, create his identity as Carlos Fuentes, the Dutchman, even if he is ultimately unable to completely erase his past.

The Book of Collateral Damage: Archiving War

Some of these more recent Iraqi works, then, acknowledge loss as loss, but include the imaginative act of narration as a potent element of their own chronicling, their own storytelling—whether it is the story of the story of Frankenstein in Baghdad or the aptly named Carlos Fuentes dreaming a story about who he was and is. The novel that does the most with this idea is Sinan Antoon's *The Book of Collateral Damage*, originally published as *Fihris*, meaning index or catalog. Antoon was born in Iraq and lived in Baghdad, earning a BA in English from the University of Baghdad. He left Iraq for the United States after the first Gulf War began in 1991 and completed an MA at Georgetown University in 1995 and a PhD in Arabic and Islamic Studies at Harvard in 2006. Antoon is known for both his poetry and his novels—his poetry collections include three in Arabic, *Mūshūr Muballa bi al-Ḥurūb* (*A Prism: Wet with Wars*, 2003), *Layl wāḥid fī kul mudun* (*One Night in All Cities*, 2010), and *Kamā fī al-simā'* (*As in Heaven*, 2019), and one in English, *The Baghdad Blues* (2006). His novels are *I'jaam* (2002), *Waḥidha Shajara al-rumān* (*The Pomegranate Alone*, 2010), which was translated by the author and published as *The Corpse Washer* in 2013; *Yā marīm* (*Ave Maria*, 2012), which was published in English as *The Baghdad Eucharist* in 2013; and *Fihris*. He has also published a scholarly study, *The Poetics of the Obscene in Pre-modern Arabic Poetry* (2014). Antoon is an associate professor at New York University, where he teaches Arabic literature.

Antoon is well known both as a poet and a novelist and has written about the dramatic changes in the Arabic literary tradition that happened in the twentieth century, particularly in Iraq. Writing about the Arabic prose poem, he says that its emergence constituted "the most radical break with an established poetic tradition going back to the sixth century CE," and notes that new forms of poetry in Iraq were developed "against the backdrop of decolonization and a growing desire for political and cultural independence"—the struggle against British occupation ("Arabic Prose Poem" 281). Increased contact with other parts of the world and access to translation, in addition to that destabilized political context, were enough to inspire change even to a long storied and celebrated tradition:

> Poetry had long been the most potent and privileged space in which to construct new individual and collective selves and to deconstruct old ones. The *qaṣīda*, the Arabic ode, was the iconic and classical form par excellence. Its symbolic capital as an aesthetic reservoir of a glorious history was unparalleled and undisputed. It represented a long and deeply-rooted tradition dating back to pre-Islamic times. While neoclassical poets had injected it with new themes and concerns in the early twentieth century, its form had remained the same, dictating adherence to meter and symmetrical hemistitches and monorhyme. (282)

Antoon discusses poets such as Jamīl Ṣidqī al-Zahāwī (1863–1936), who experimented with poetry that retained meter but not rhyme; Rūfā'īl Buṭṭī (1901–1956), who encouraged al-Zahāwī to go further and eliminate meter as well; and Ḥusayn Mardān (1927–1972), who not only experimented with form but with subject matter as well, leading to a trial for obscenity in 1950

(283). Antoon's own work is indebted both to the classical tradition and to the modernists. As he put it in an interview,

> I write prose poetry, but my poetic genealogy is diverse. One root is pre-Islamic and classical Arabic poetry which I have read a great deal of and still do and which I studied as a graduate student. It has an ocean of imagery and metaphors. The other root is world and modern poetry which any contemporary and young poet has to read and be aware of. So Neruda, Lorca, Cavafy, Hikmet, Whitman, Auden, William Carlos Williams, Rimbaud, Eluard and so on, are all ancestors. So my poetry is fed by various traditions and I translate a lot of American poetry to Arabic. (Iğsiz)

In his description, his poetry brings together these various traditions, a diverse genealogy. His most famous novel, *The Corpse Washer*, depicts a character, Jawad, who is similarly educated in ancient and modern traditions, though he experiences that as more of a clash than a productive mix. Jawad is from a family of corpse washers, who ritualistically bathe the dead to purify them before burial. His father and his brother Ammoury work together in that practice until Ammoury is killed fighting in the Iran-Iraq War. His father then begins to teach Jawad when Jawad is a teenager, and gradually he learns the honorable profession. But he feels a "slight boredom" with it all, a boredom that is in contrast with the thrill he experiences in art classes (27). The teacher at his local school tells the class that art is "intimately linked with immortality: a challenge to death and time, a celebration of life," very different from what he sees of his family's business. And not only that, "Iraq was the first and biggest art workshop in the world . . . the first works of art and statues had appeared in ancient Iraq during the Sumerian era and now fill museums all over the world" (31). Five years later, Jawad enters the Academy of Fine Arts, a decision that disappoints his father. "He never forgave me for straying from the path and favoring art over the useful profession he had inherited from his ancestors" (39).

After the beginning of the Iraq War in 2003, Jawad's father has a heart attack and dies. Shortly thereafter, Jawad learns that in addition to lootings at the national library and the national museum, the United States has bombed the Academy of Fine Arts, and its library has burned. Jawad goes there and is overcome by the loss: "I remembered the hours I had spent reading and leafing through glossy art books there," he thinks. "This is where I had been captured by the works of Degas, Renoir, Rembrandt, Kandinsky, Miró, Modigliani, and Chagall, de Kooning, Bacon, Monet, and Picasso. This is where I spent hours poring over images of statues by Rodin and

Giacometti, my beloved Giacometti" (73). His father's assistant, Hammoudy, who continued the corpse washing after Jawad's father's death, suddenly disappears, and his mother becomes ill and needs expensive medical care. Jawad can't find a job to pay the debts and agrees to take up the business just for a while, not realizing that he will end up doing it for years amid the increasing tide of bodies that war brings. He suffers from nightmares, always about bodies and the dead, and attempts to flee to Jordan. But he is turned away at the border because, as a single man, he arouses suspicion that he might be a member of a militia. Jawad goes back to Baghdad, back to the bodies and the nightmares. In the final chapter, he washes the body of a nine-year-old child killed in an explosion and feels the weight of all that immense loss: "The living die or depart, and the dead always come. I had thought that life and death were two separate worlds with clearly marked boundaries. But now I know that they are conjoined, sculpting each other. My father knew that" (184).

Jawad at last understands that these are false boundaries. For him this is a tragic knowledge, since he feels like a dead man himself, and his nightmares are not so different from his waking life. This takes the story back to where it began in the first chapter, when Jawad dreams of washing the body of the woman he loved and lost. He wakes trembling and sweating: "Death is not content with what it takes from me in my waking hours, it insists on haunting me even in my sleep. Isn't it enough that I toil all day tending to its eternal guests, preparing them to sleep in its lap?" (3). Jawad further uses the image of the archive for death: "If death is a postman, then I receive his letters every day. I am the one who opens carefully the bloodied and torn envelopes. I am the one who washes them, who removes the stamps of death and dies and perfumes them, mumbling what I don't entirely believe in. Then I wrap them carefully in white so they may reach their final reader—the grave" (3). It is an image that Antoon will expand on in more elaborate detail in the final work I will focus on in this chapter.

When Hārūn al-Rashīd was caliph of the Abbasid Caliphate, the capital of which was Baghdad, he adopted the use of paper for state business—it was a sign of expanding literacy in the middle of the eighth century. He is said to have founded the legendary library Bayt al-Ḥikma, or House of Wisdom, perhaps the most impressive of numerous libraries of the period. As Robert Irwin puts it, "Besides the large public libraries founded under the patronage of caliphs and viziers, and those attached to the great mosques, there were smaller circulating libraries run by scribes, from which books—often of a popular and entertaining nature—could be rented out. . . . During the Abbasid period a reading public came into being" (69). The Abbasid period centered in Baghdad lasted from 750 CE until 1258, when the city was sacked by the Mongols. At that period's height, in 987, a Baghdadi scribe and bookseller decided to bring together all of the great learning and knowledge. Ibn al-Nadīm's goal was to include a list and summary of "the books of all peoples, Arab and foreign, existing in the language of the Arabs, as well as of their scripts, dealing with various sciences, with accounts of those who composed them and records of their times of birth, length of life, and times of death, and also of the localities of their cities, their virtues and faults, from the beginning of the formation of each science to this our own time" (qtd. in Irwin 68). He called this compendium of knowledge his *Fihrist*—his index.

It was, as Irwin says, "a map of the literary world." Ibn Al-Nadīm divided his book into nine chapters, "and it is evident from the way the chapters were divided that Ibn al-Nadīm's categories are not ours":

> The first chapter dealt with language, calligraphy and scripture; chapter two dealt with grammar; chapter three encompassed historians, genealogists, government officials who wrote books, cup companions, jesters and singers; chapter four was consecrated to poetry; chapter five was on the literature of Muslim sects; chapter six, on the writings of jurisconsultants and experts on religious law; chapter seven dealt with philosophy and the sciences; chapter eight was a sort of ghetto reserved for "story-tellers and stories, exorcists, jugglers, magicians, miscellaneous subjects and fables"; in the last chapter, Ibn al-Nadim discussed non-Islamic sects as well as literature on Asia. (69–70)

Sinan Antoon pays homage to this work and its unusual categories in his fourth novel, which was published in English as *The Book of Collateral Damage*. Its original Arabic title, however, is *Fihris*. (The connection is made explicit in the book's first epigraph, which notes of Ibn al-Nadīm's book, "He left many blank pages in it"—a hint, perhaps, that others might come along to pick up the project.) In the world of the novel, the title refers to the project of Wadood Abdulkarim, whom the protagonist Nameer al-Baghdadi discovers overseeing a collection of rare books and other artifacts when he makes a visit to Baghdad in 2003. Nameer is from Iraq but emigrated to the United States in 1993 and now teaches at NYU (much like Antoon himself). He is also a writer, though he is stuck: "I can't even begin," he says. "And all this concern, or rather obsession, with writing rituals and instruments only ends in blank pages and silence" (6). He hopes that he'll be inspired by the trip to Iraq, where he is helping translate for a team of documentary filmmakers, but all his memories coupled with the devastation of war are too much to process. He visits an aunt and other family members and is struck by the way that "time seemed to have crushed them like a steamroller, as if they had had to live through the last ten years several times over, back and forth, and had endured massive doses of pain" (16).

Instead, what gets him thinking about writing is Wadood. Nameer is fascinated by Wadood's collection of books: *The Collected Works of al-Rusafi*, *Hamlet* translated by Jabra Ibrahim Jabra, and especially a 1953 edition of the third volume of *The Collected Works of al-Jawahiri*. Among the old and first editions is a shelf full of notebooks and clippings. Nameer asks about them, and Wadood responds that he is writing a "circular history," "the project of a lifetime, an archive of the losses from war and destruction. But not soldiers or equipment. The losses that are never mentioned or seen. Not just people. Animals and plants and inanimate things and anything that can be destroyed" (46). Nameer thinks Wadood says that title of the project is *Fihrist*, like Ibn al-Nadīm's, but Wadood clarifies: *Fihris*, he says (47).³ Wadood's approach is unconventional both in subject matter and in scope. When Nameer sits down to read the first chapter, Wadood explains: "I'll write down the history of the first minute of the war, which wasn't the first war I've seen. Most of the people who tackle history record centuries, decades, and years. I'm interested in minutes, especially the first minute. . . . There are people who write in order to change the present or the future, whereas I dream of changing the past. This is my rationale and the rationale of my catalog" (22–23).

In addition to Ibn al-Nadīm, Wadood's character alludes to the author behind Antoon's second epigraph, Abū 'Uthman 'Amr Baḥr al-Jāḥiz (c. 776–868/9), who said of books that "They speak for the dead and translate the speech of the living." According to Robert Irwin, al-Jāḥiz was "the leading literary and intellectual figure of his age, who in the course of his long life covered most of contemporary human knowledge in his writings" (84). He was also a bibliomaniac who paid to be locked in bookstores at night so that he could read to his heart's content. "It is reported," writes Irwin, "that he was killed when an avalanche of books collapsed on top of him" (86). Wadood, the book lover, archivist, and chronicler, has a touch of this madness and dark fate about him.

Nameer reads Wadood's writing with interest and hopes to help Wadood publish the project. Antoon's novel is interspersed with some of its parts, called colloquies. The colloquy of a tree in a house's courtyard whose long life is finally ended by a bomb. The colloquy of a Kashan carpet woven with great artistry that is buried under a house's rubble. The colloquy of a stamp album given from one friend to another that is destroyed in a fire after a missile strike. There are many—of a beloved clay oven, a recording of a father and son speaking to each other, a series of photographs of two lovers. They are written in the first person, as in "The Colloquy of the al-Zawraa." In that one, a manuscript is inscribed with great care by a creator, who says, "You are going to preserve the most beautiful poetry that has ever been written about this city, and you will live long after me and after what comes after me" (34–35). The manuscript is given to a wealthy person, whose "descendants passed me on and then the descendants of those who killed them" (36). It is hidden in dark vaults, occasionally read, though it misses the eyes and hands of its creator. "When someone's eyes fall on my body or their lips move as they read me, I remember only his eyes and I long for him" (36). Then one day, the earth trembles and the manuscript feels heat, even though it is winter. Fire laps at its edges. "Before shedding a tear I gasped a one thousand-year gasp and saw myself rising up as a cloud of smoke in the sky over Baghdad" (37).

As Ghyath Manhel has said of Antoon's novel, "Against statistical rendering of victims into numbers in news coverage, the novel revives the losses by imagining their accounts of the war, by retrieving their histories that collectively make for the lost memory of a destroyed country." In this sense, the novel is certainly about loss, but rather than a kind of renunciation of that loss, it responds with a reimagining. Where things can't be literally recovered, Antoon reimagines them back into history, into existence. Nameer notes at one point that "in Arabic the words for hope and pain were almost the same, with just the two consonants transposed—*amal* and *alam*" (188). And Wadood, chronicling that first minute of the war, uses a metaphor that captures the twin forces of destruction and creation. In "The Colloquy of the Catalog," he writes:

> In the beginning was the explosion.
>
> Isn't that what the prevalent, accepted theory says? But maybe that massive explosion was the universe screaming and weeping as it emerged from the womb of nothingness into the pain of existence. This universe that expanded at the speed of light. Instead of crawling, it began to fly in every direction with a million wings and stars.
>
> In the beginning was the explosion. (263)

In the colloquies, the explosions are annihilation, the darkness of disappearance, but Wadood's colloquies bring back those stories, and Wadood explains writing not as an individually therapeutic exercise but as collective, collaborative, and ongoing: "All I did then was read and sell books," he says. "I hid in a dark tunnel and came out only when I grasped a simple truth: there are no real endings, just as there are no real beginnings. There are just imaginary borders, signs, and marks that we put in place in order to structure our irrational existence in this random universe. . . . And I am writing this book, which may never end, as all books (don't) end. It won't end even with the death of the author. Other writers can go on writing its other parts after me" (282–83).

And indeed that happens. The novel's three final sections are titled "An Ending," "Another Ending," and "The End of the Novel . . . and Its Beginning." In the first, Nameer describes applying for and receiving a grant to bring Wadood to NYU, to be part of a workshop on restoring old manuscripts. Wadood arrives, and Nameer is delighted. But the narrative trails off:

> I should describe his meeting Mariah [Nameer's girlfriend] and his impressions of New York . . .
> but I'm not satisfied with this ending and I don't think it works.
>
> I have to write another ending. (290)

In the second ending, Nameer receives a letter from Wadood in which he says that he will burn his catalog, that he wishes to "be the master of my ending" (290); he encloses pages torn from a book that concern a character who seeks to burn his own books rather than "leave my books to people who have been my neighbors for twenty years, when none of them has shown me true affection or been protective" (294). But neither is this ending satisfactory: "I think this ending is slightly better than the first, but it isn't the end. . . . We have to admit that the endings we imagine and hope for are only suggestions. Sometimes, when it is kind to us, which is rare, life adopts them. Or life's own endings resemble or are identical to the ones we imagine, and then we are overjoyed. But our endings do not belong to us" (297). In the final ending, Nameer hears about a bomb that went off in Baghdad near where Wadood lived. Nameer is frantic for news, but devastated when he gets it: Wadood died in the explosion. He finds an article online that an old friend of Wadood's writes about him, which laments his death and honors Wadood, who "chose to live and die with books"—another nod to al-Jāḥiẓ (302). Antoon's book concludes with Nameer's final actions: "I wiped my tears away and printed out the article. I wrote 'Wadood's Colloquy' on it by hand, added it to the catalog, and decided to write this novel" (302). This is another story, then, in which the end returns to the beginning.

In writing about themes of loss and recovery in contemporary war literature, Patrick Deer argues that the obsession with recovery in US culture "has as much to do with confronting official failures to represent and document the ongoing material losses involved in the wars in Iraq and Afghanistan as it does with a profound loss of historical certainty about the conflicts" (312). He notes the uncertainty about the wars in Iraq and Afghanistan—their timelines, costs, meaning, and consequences—uncertainties that has been "heightened by a combination of official negligence, secrecy, and disregard for civilian involvement" (314). Deer cites investigations, most notably one by *ProPublica* and the *Seattle Times* in 2012, revealing that many US military units did not keep operational records of their Iraq deployments. "It was commonplace, journalists discovered, for units in the field to erase hard drives, fail to preserve documentation, or only keep the last 60 days of their field records to hand over to the incoming units replacing them" (317). The record of the war, its archive, is woefully incomplete, a loss compounded on the Iraqi side by the destruction of facilities and the undoing of the bureaucratic state.

Deer reads works by Kevin Powers, Brian Turner, the Iraqi blogger Riverbend, and Sinan Antoon and argues that although their narratives chronicle profound losses, they actually speak "against recovery in striking ways, whether in terms of recovering bodies, archives, or nationalist (or imperialist) narratives" (312–13). Particularly in Antoon and Riverbend, these stories don't patch over those losses with a notion of premature recovery, but rather engage in "projects of fierce, melancholy, and ongoing reflection about the wars' vast costs to American and Iraqi society" (331). Writing about Antoon's *The Book of Collateral Damage*, Sami Alkyam makes a similar point, understanding the novel as "[bearing] witness to the trauma of writing and narrating this history, suggesting the impossibility of its healing. The excavation of the archive—whose past is no longer traceable—is an act of interpretation of an effaced past and erased history" (54).

The final epigraph to *The Book of Collateral Damage* is from a Jorge Luis Borges poem, "Cambridge":

> We are our memory,
> We are that chimerical museum of shifting shapes,
> That pile of broken mirrors.

This hints at Antoon's approach, one that I think is shared by many of these recent Iraqi works and is a characteristic distinct to them—this emphasis on acknowledgment of loss and devastation coupled with collective imagination—not literal recovery, and certainly not a re-covering, and neither a renunciation nor a giving over. Those blank pages Ibn al-Nadīm left in his *Fihrist* are waiting for others to fill them, just as Nadeem finds a way to fill his own blank pages by writing Wadood's colloquy. Memory is a pile of broken mirrors, but the shapes are shifting, and the inquiry of Wadood's project is an apt one: How did the universe fly in every direction with a million wings and stars?

CHAPTER 5

The Fantasy of Endless War

The Marvel Cinematic Universe and Star Wars

In 2016, Walt Disney Studios released *Rogue One: A Star Wars Story*, produced by Lucasfilm and the first stand-alone Star Wars anthology film. The narrative follows Jyn Erso (Felicity Jones), who lost her family to the Empire at a young age and trained as a rebel soldier under the extremist Saw Gerrera (Forest Whitaker). As the Rebel Alliance learns of the Empire's development of the Death Star, Jyn urges them to steal the massive weapon's plans and exploit a vulnerability that her father surreptitiously built into it—which are precisely the events that kicked off the first Star Wars movie, *A New Hope*, in 1977. But in *Rogue One*, the Alliance is reluctant to take such a risk, and so Jyn leads a ragtag team of volunteers to do just that.

As their ship approaches its landing site, Jyn looks around at the men waiting to undertake the assault and registers their drawn, downcast faces. She then delivers a rousing speech that solidifies their resolve and thus their bravery, a speech of a military commander inspiring the troops. "Saw Gerrera used to say one fighter with a sharp stick and nothing left to lose can take the day," she begins, invoking the wisdom of her mentor. "They've no idea we're coming. They've no reason to expect us," she continues, as the camera cuts to their rapt faces. "If we can make it to the ground, we'll take the next chance, and the next. On and on until we win, or the chances are spent. The Death Star plans are down there. Cassian, K2 and I will find them. We'll find a way to find them." Cassian Andor (Diego Luna) follows up with specific instructions for different groups of soldiers, and then they're off, to execute their plan that will ultimately be successful, but at great cost.

It is a speech that wouldn't be out of place in a classic war film, delivered by Robert Mitchum or Lee Marvin. It is inspirational, tough, determined, and a touch fatalistic. It demonstrates the depth of Jyn's commitment to the mission and the cause, which she's had to develop over the course of the film. And she rallies her troops, a diverse group of soldiers who must acknowledge their differences in order to come together and fight. In interviews, Kathleen Kennedy, the president of Lucasfilm, compared the movie to a World War II film, and given all these elements, the comparison works ("Bonus Features"). But the film's implications can be tied to the contemporary moment as well. Fielding Montgomery has argued that just as George Lucas's first Star Wars trilogy can be read as "an implicit criticism of U.S. imperialism in the context of the Vietnam War" (as I mentioned in the Introduction), *Rogue One* provides "unique insight on today's political struggles and events in the waning stages of the almost two-decade long War on Terror" (29, 31). Part of what makes this possible, Montgomery argues, is the context of the film's 2016 release coupled with its chronological place in the Star Wars storyworld. Its events take place after Lucas's prequel trilogy—*The Phantom Menace* (1999), *Attack of the Clones* (2002), and *Revenge of the Sith* (2005)—and immediately before the original Star Wars, *A New Hope* (1977). Thus, "*Rogue One* positions Star Wars as more than just a historical criticism of the Vietnam War by bringing the story to bear on the present, critiquing U.S. hegemonic structures and warning of the potential consequences." Montgomery further notes that "*Rogue One* also cements its place in the saga as a whole by making the transition from overt political messages in the prequel trilogy to covert political messages in the original trilogy less jarring. This challenging task is accomplished by problematizing some of the most basic elements of the original Star Wars" (37).

Montgomery points to obvious political parallels in the prequel trilogy, such as Anakin telling Obi Wan Kenobi in *Revenge of the Sith* (2005) that "If you're not with me . . . then you're my enemy," an echo of George W. Bush's statement in 2001 that "Either you are with us, or you are with the terrorists." The prequel trilogy is staunchly anti-imperialist, and though in Montgomery's view, the Empire in *Rogue One* clearly represents "the military hegemony of the United States," it is not all black and white (31). Characters such as Saw Gerrera, Cassian Andor, Jyn, and her father Galen all demonstrate that the Rebellion is not unified on how best to fight the Empire or under what circumstances the ends justify the means—see, for example, Gerrera's use of torture, which in *Rogue One* he employs on an Imperial pilot who defects to the Rebellion. In this way, *Rogue One* capitalizes on its chronological and historical context to expand the Star Wars universe and tell a war story that is appropriately nuanced and engaging for those complications.

Rogue One, then, is an interesting example of the fantasy war stories that have captivated audiences (and made astonishing profits) during this second wave of literature about contemporary war. It is very much a Star Wars film—there are spaceships and droids, blasters and Storm Troopers, and the iconic Darth Vader. *Rogue One* is incontrovertibly fantasy, and fantasy, as Owen Gilman has argued, is not known for trafficking in the difficult realities of war and contemporary society. Rather, it is known for escapist simplicity, "distractions that serve to dull anxiety" (8). And yet *Rogue One* is not quite that easy or as familiar, for several reasons. The protagonist and skilled military leader is a woman. None of the men with whom she fights most closely—characters played by Diego Luna, Donnie Yen, Riz Ahmed, Jiang Wen, and Forest Whitaker—are white, and none of them question the ability of a woman to lead. The story is undeniably tragic—a narrative arc that Americans have never had much of a stomach for—as all of Jyn's force dies in their attempt to steal the Death Star plans, including Cassian and Jyn themselves, whom we last see embracing as a massive explosion spreads toward them. The embrace, it should be noted, is not a romantic one. Among a strong cast, Luna is particularly compelling as the Rebellion fighter with a dark past, and that past is later explored in the series *Andor* (2022–2024). *Andor* has won accolades for its "complex, mature story," following the lives of characters under an oppressive regime, most of whom "have never seen a lightsaber," as showrunner Tony Gilroy put it (del Barco).

Although we associate the worlds of fantasy films with satisfying good-versus-evil narratives that come to a conclusive, triumphant end—and those associations are not wrong, as a film like *Avatar* proves—it is also true that many of the newer iterations of these genres are more complicated, revealing some of the same narrative and thematic features as the literature I have been addressing in this study. Gilman laments Americans' tendency to "venture off to fantasyland, through whatever means it may be realized," a tendency he associates with Star Wars and superhero franchises as well as the short attention spans cultivated by Twitter, the accessibility of online pornography, and the frantic competition of modern sports (5). And while I don't disagree with the broader argument Gilman makes here, I do think it is worth considering what lessons these fantasy war stories are teaching about who fights, why, and to what effect, and also important to realize that not all those lessons are as simplistic as they might seem. In this chapter I explore how the Marvel Cinematic Universe (MCU) presents ongoing warfare with nuanced political context and implications, depicts the physical and emotional trauma caused by battle with what is at times surprising depth, and, particularly in its more recent introduction of the multiverse, reflects the blurred boundaries and fragmentation that I have identified in other contemporary war stories. And while it has taken the MCU a long time to catch up in terms of gender representation—Black Widow's origin-story film didn't appear until 2021, after her character's death in *Avengers: Endgame* (2019), and Captain Marvel didn't show up onscreen until her solo film in 2019—Star Wars has not only focused four of its five most recent films on female protagonists but also made female military leadership a significant part of the plot. *Rogue One* aside, the films often do revert to satisfying closure in the end and evince much less of an emphasis on fragmentation. That closure, however, happens against a backdrop of not just globalized but galactic warfare that is as endless as it is ubiquitous.

The popularity of superhero films in particular has been so immense that criticism of the genre is perhaps natural, though like the Western in the 1950s and 1960s—another genre that was essentially unavoidable in film and television during those years—not everything is as one-dimensional as a basic white hat/black hat template would suggest. Superman movies of the late 1970s and '80s, Batman movies of the late 1980s and '90s, and then Spider-Man movies of the early 2000s were all big money-makers and mostly well-received, but the superhero scene truly took off in the second two decades of the twenty-first century. Christopher Nolan's *Dark Knight* trilogy (2005, 2008, 2012) proved that superhero films could be auteur showcases, *Iron Man* initiated the MCU in 2008, the *X-Men* and *Spider-Man* films forged ahead with new actors and storylines, and oddball entries like *Deadpool* and *Suicide Squad*, both in 2016, also found wide audiences.

But not everyone is a fan. In 2019, Martin Scorsese gave an interview to *Empire* magazine and then followed it with an op-ed in the *New York Times* in which he said that Marvel movies aren't to his taste because they aren't cinema. Cinema is what he grew up with, he says, films that were "about revelation—aesthetic, emotional and spiritual revelation. Cinema is about characters—the complexity of people and their contradictory and sometimes paradoxical natures, the way they can hurt one another and love one another and suddenly come face to face with themselves." Cinema leads you to "[confront] the unexpected," and he mentions films like Sam Fuller's *The Steel Helmet* (1951), Ingmar Bergman's *Persona* (1966), Gene Kelly and Stanley Donen's *It's Always Fair Weather* (1955), Kenneth Anger's *Scorpio Rising* (1963), Jean-Luc Godard's *Vivre Sa Vie* (1962), and Don Siegel's *The Killers* (1964). It is not necessarily mainstream popularity that makes films less interesting, he says, and talks about his deep appreciation for Hitchcock—"*our* franchise," Scorsese calls him. But because today's superhero films are so market-driven, so beholden to the larger Marvel behemoth, they are inherently risk-averse, lacking "revelation, mystery or genuine emotional danger." While everyone's free to like the kind of movies that they want to, Scorsese worries that the superhero glut will crowd out smaller, more independent-minded cinema from theaters, from funding, and ultimately from audiences.

Given the effects of the COVID-19 pandemic on movie theaters and the rise of streaming services, Scorsese's concerns about which films and filmmakers receive access to resources and different modes of distribution are apt. He dismisses Marvel movies, however, more on the basis of their content, their lack of complication and emotional depth. Scorsese says that Marvel movies don't take risks, but I think they do, especially if you are seeing them as the war stories that they are. Scorsese misses the levels of complexity that these films are able to achieve in the era of the expanded cinematic universe, a storytelling format that goes beyond the linear narrative progression of the film franchise to allow not only contributions from multiple writers and creators but also extended character development, explorations of different perspectives on events, stories that take place in different places in the overall chronology (as with *Rogue One*), and even stories that take chronology itself, our perception of time, as part of the subject matter. This is a new development for cinema, though not for storytelling. Think about the way that Greek mythology is variously taken up and reimagined by Homer, Euripides, Sophocles, Aeschylus, and Virgil, and much later by writers as different as James Joyce and Rick Riordan. And, of course, Marvel and DC Comics constitute a labyrinthian, extensive, and multilayered body of narrative, which Nick Lowe has called "the largest narrative constructions in human history," exceeding, in his view, even Greek and Roman story production and adaptation (qtd. In Kaveney 25). That narrative construction gets even more intricate when the idea of the multiverse appears in both the comics and the films, about which I discuss more below.

Fantasy War, Real-World Implications

A genre bubble as profligate as the superhero surge is catnip for scholars, and superhero films have led to no small amount of pondering about what might be behind all that popularity and box office profits. Are these films a masculinist fantasy of impenetrable male bodies, for instance? A reimagining of America as a powerhouse of traditional industry, as names such as Iron Man and the Man of Steel suggest? Are they technological fantasy more broadly, space to think about renewable energy, impossibly strong metal, sentient artificial intelligence? Several scholars have argued that recent superhero films are responding to and rewriting the September 11 World Trade Center attacks. These claims can take a broad political or cultural view, as Annika Hagley and Michael Harrison do: "The post-September 11 resurrection of the superhero genre, particularly in film, is a direct response to the feelings of helplessness and terror that Americans experienced in the days and years following the attack" (120). Jeffrey Brown writes that the nature of that response is a gendered one, and that the superhero film "counters fears of a nation that has grown soft, weak, and vulnerable, instead offering a narrative of toughening up, of remasculinizing America" (*Modern Superhero*, 64). In addition to that, however, Brown notes that the narrative possibilities of the expanded cinematic universe have allowed films to "explore the lingering implications of post-9/11 anxieties from a range of perspectives beyond simple violent retribution" (64). And he points to the ways that the devastating alien attack on New York and the big superhero battle that follows in *The Avengers* (2012) get referenced and argued over, its aftermath

Figure 4. Steve Lombard (Michael Kelly) and Perry White (Lawrence Fishburne) are covered in ash and surrounded by the ruins of tall buildings in *Man of Steel*, clearly evoking 9/11. (Warner Bros., 2013)

discussed in social and political terms as well as in subsequent films and television series: *Iron Man 3* (2013), *Captain America: Civil War* (2016), *Spider-Man: Homecoming* (2017), *Daredevil* (2015–2018), and *Jessica Jones* (2015–2019). (Something similar happens in the DC Universe, with *Batman v. Superman* [2016] providing literally a new perspective on the battle that happens in *Man of Steel* [2013].)[1] Karen Randell notes not only the narrative and thematic implications of these 9/11-like elements but also the aesthetic: "There is now a generation that did not see the events of 9/11 play out in live action but that, I would argue, has been imprinted with the *effect* of 9/11, an aesthetic effect, through the repeated imagery of the destroyed city, in particular the vertically falling building, enveloping ash clouds, people running toward news cameras, paper raining, and the mangled metal wreckage, which in neurotic repetition within these fantasy movies refuses the notion of catharsis." Randell concludes that these "imprinted images of the events of 9/11 now really *are* a movie" (141).

Beyond the implications and aesthetic of 9/11, Marvel films in particular are entrenched in the context of the wars that follow. *Iron Man*, released in 2008, is the inaugural film of the MCU, and it begins with combat in Afghanistan. Tony Stark's (Robert Downey Jr.) larkish jaunt to Kunar Province to demonstrate his weapons company's new missile quickly goes awry when the convoy transporting him is ambushed. Before that moment, Stark isn't terribly interested, much less concerned, about what's actually going on with the war or even the military, expressing surprise that his driver is a female soldier. He tosses back drinks; he gossips with the soldiers about bedding models. But after the bomb goes off, the film suddenly changes tone, with quick, confusing cuts, a barrage of noise and the sound of bullets hitting the Humvees, and shots of Stark fleeing the firefight in a panic. He is injured by the explosion of one of his own weapons, taken prisoner, and recorded on video as a hostage. *Iron Man* then flashes back to the thirty-six hours leading up to the attack, after which we see the blast again, and Stark's total disorientation when he wakes after having been cared for by Ho Yinsen (Shaun Toub), a fellow captive.

Although Stark eventually escapes, it is this experience in Afghanistan that completely upends his life. Not only does he undergo torture when he initially refuses to accede to the captors' demands, he is now disabled, the shrapnel in his chest prevented from piercing his heart by an electromagnet devised by Yinsen. (Later, Stark replaces this with an arc reactor, a device his father created as an alternative energy source.) Previously, Stark wore the mantle of the wealthy genius because of his company's success, but in captivity, it makes him "the most famous mass murderer in the history of America," as one of the leaders of the terrorist organization puts it, and they are his "loyal customers." Stark's sense of his own identity has been summarily deconstructed. Stark and Yinsen build what will be the first of many Iron Man suits as a way of overcoming their captors and getting out. But Yinsen doesn't make it—he's fatally injured, and Stark watches his comrade die after finding out that Yinsen's family has already been killed in the war. "Don't waste your life," Yinsen tells him, an echo of Captain Miller's urging Private First Class Ryan to "earn this" at the end of *Saving Private Ryan* (1998). When he returns home, Stark shocks everyone by shutting down the weapons manufacturing division of his company, saying at a press conference that he's had his eyes opened: "I saw young Americans killed by the very weapons I created to protect them and defend them, and I saw that I had become part of a system that is comfortable with zero accountability." Stark wants to do something different, something worthwhile—and he begins by calling out the military-industrial complex that his family built its name on. Thus the MCU is on its way, with war as the context and the catalyst.

Despite Stark's criticism of the money and the systems that make waging contemporary war possible, the Department of Defense supported the film and its sequel, *Iron Man 2* (2010), and offered production assistance, including filming at Edwards Air Force Base. Such agreements are common in Hollywood history, going all the way back to the first Best Picture winner, *Wings*, in 1927, as well as other films like *Top Gun* (1986), *Black Hawk Down* (2001), and the *Transformers* series (2007–2023). Reuben Baron writes that "The Department of Defense has long had an arrangement that, if a producer wants to feature actual U.S. military equipment in their film, the department will provide them funding and resources in exchange for following strict regulations on how the military is portrayed. This is often connected to some sort of recruitment campaign." That was precisely the case when *Captain Marvel* was released. Before her transformation into a superhero, Carol Danvers (Brie Larson) is an Air Force pilot who can't fly combat missions in 1989 because she's a woman—that role in the military isn't open to women until 1993. Despite the film's critique of that policy and its suggestion of the military's history of sexism—at one point in her training, a fellow cadet sneers at her, "You do know why they call it a *cock*pit, don't you?"—the military was enough of a fan of Danvers's brash heroics that they arranged a flyover of Air Force Thunderbirds at the Hollywood premiere and included an Air Force recruitment ad titled "Origin Story" to run before the movie in cinemas (Baron). (However, the Department of Defense support did falter with *The Avengers*, reportedly because the Pentagon couldn't work out how the military related to S.H.I.E.L.D., the acronym for the Strategic Homeland Intervention, Enforcement, and Logistics Division, a counterterrorism and intelligence agency founded after World War II to maintain national and global security. In *Iron Man*, Phil Coulson [Clark Gregg] describes S.H.I.E.L.D. as a "separate division" from the Department of Defense, the FBI, and the CIA, one that has a "more specific focus." That definition and mission weren't clear enough for the Pentagon.)

In the case of *Captain Marvel*, the military was happy to be associated with the MCU's positive portrayal of a female soldier, especially if it helped recruitment. Carol Danvers and Natasha Romanoff/Black Widow (Scarlett Johansson), who was trained by the KGB, are the most prominent female characters in the MCU with a military background, but the MCU strove for racial diversity earlier and more broadly. Gerry Canavan has noted that both prior to and after the introduction of *Black Panther*'s African cast, "Every African-American featured prominently in the MCU has been an elite soldier or intelligence agent working for the U.S. government: Nick Fury (Samuel L. Jackson); Col. James "Rhodey" Rhodes (Terence Howard/Don Cheadle); the Falcon, Sam Wilson (Anthony Mackie); Maria Rambeau (Lashana Lynch); her daughter, Monica Rambeau (Teyonah Parris)" (215–16). Eric "Killmonger" Stevens (Michael B. Jordan), one of the villains of *Black Panther* who nonetheless has a moving backstory and an interventionist worldview that T'Challa (Chadwick Boseman) eventually adopts in a nonviolent fashion, was previously an elite super soldier, with dozens, perhaps hundreds, of confirmed kills in Afghanistan and Iraq denoted visibly on his body by raised scars. Although Steve Rogers/Captain America (Chris Evans) is the quintessential World War II soldier who must later reckon with the changing practices of war and politics, at the end of *Endgame*, an aged Rogers hands over the shield to Sam Wilson. At that moment, and in the later television series *The Falcon and the Winter Soldier* (2021), Wilson is reluctant to

Figure 5. Brie Larson as Carol Danvers, or Captain Marvel, as she strikes a confident pose in the cockpit in *Captain Marvel*. (Walt Disney Studios, 2019)

take on the moniker and the identity—as he says at one point, "Every time I pick this [shield] up, I know there are millions of people out there who are going to hate me for it. . . . No blond hair or blue eyes" ("One World"). Eventually, however, he does.

Of the original Avengers—Captain America, Iron Man, Thor, the Hulk, Black Widow, and Hawkeye—who are the most famous superheroes of this era, the only one trained as a solider in the US military is Steve Rogers. But the Avengers initiative as a whole is framed as a military endeavor. As Nick Fury famously puts it, "The idea was to bring together a group of remarkable people, see if they could become something more. See if they could work together when we needed them to, to fight the battles we never could." These are combatants, representatives, who fight for "us"—an "us" that is nebulously defined but most often means humanity, Earth, against hordes of invading aliens or threats from within. The foundation of the superhero film, especially the origin story, has a great deal in common with the soldier's memoir: Why do you fight? How do you develop your skills? What are your weapons of choice, and how do you train? How do you experience battle, and with whom? And finally, what are the effects of this war experience on your identity and your life?

That all makes it sound as if these superheroes' relationship to the military and the United States is straightforward, but again, the extended narratives of the MCU complicate that relationship repeatedly, as well as the political implications and context of the superheroes' actions, much as Alex Tankard argues about Star Wars and *Rogue One*. This goes all the way back to *Iron Man*—James C. Taylor observes that the Iron Man films "explore the obfuscating entanglement of military and commercial interests in the twenty-first century" in part because "Tony's relation to the military-industrial complex, the nature of his capitalist enterprise, and the ways in which nationality factors into these issues shift across the series" (140). Taylor notes that the real bad guys in these films are villainous businessmen, like Obadiah Stane (Jeff Bridges), Justin Hammer (Sam Rockwell), and Aldrich Killian (Guy Pearce), and how Stark's own capitalist enterprises are both compared to and differentiated from them. In the end, the films "[tread] a precarious path between critiquing and championing US power structures" (141).

Steve Rogers is Stark's foil, the sincere, righteous-minded war hero to Stark's "genius, billionaire, playboy, philanthropist," as Stark puts it in *The Avengers*. But just as Stark is forced to confront the dangers of capitalism—the damage his Stark Enterprises weapons are capable of, the corruption within his own company, and the ways that a combination of wealth, technology, and ambition can just as easily make a villain or a hero—Rogers has to confront the corruption of the military, the institution that made him Captain America and for which he seemingly sacrifices his life during World War II. In *Captain America: The Winter Soldier* (2014), he and Black Widow discover that S.H.I.E.L.D. has been infiltrated by Hydra, a Nazi-founded organization that Rogers fought against, presumably to its defeat, during World War II. As the consciousness of Hydra scientist Arnim Zola (Toby Jones) explains to them,

> Hydra was founded on the belief that humanity could not be trusted with its own freedom. What we did not realize was that if you try to take that freedom, they resist. The war taught us much. Humanity needed to surrender its freedom willingly. After the war, S.H.I.E.L.D. was founded, and I was recruited. The new Hydra grew, a beautiful parasite inside S.H.I.E.L.D. For seventy years Hydra has been secretly feeding crisis, reaping war, and when history did not cooperate, history was changed. . . . Hydra created a world so chaotic that humanity is finally ready to sacrifice its freedom to gain its security.

A villain's proclamation that freedom is a burden he will happily take from humanity is classic bad-guy behavior. The context and the implications here, however, are more nuanced. When Zola speaks about the extreme chaos of the modern world, images of conflict in the Middle East and surveillance technology flash on screen. The scene suggests that the War on Terror is a manipulation, violence manufactured for the purpose of better controlling the citizenry, creating fear in order to consolidate both information and power. This fantasy film about good battling evil nonetheless tells the viewer not to trust narratives that rely on easy categorization—that the truth is often more ambiguous and more difficult to discern. It is a stance that critics of the 2001 Patriot Act and the justification for America's 2003 invasion of Iraq would find familiar.

Winter Soldier goes further, however—it is not just an evil Nazi scientist espousing this scheme. Nick Fury shows Steve Rogers something called "Project Insight"—three next-generation helicarriers synced to a network of targeting satellites. The helicarriers are armed with long-range guns, and the satellites can "read a terrorist's DNA before he steps outside his spider hole," Fury explains. "We're going to neutralize a lot of threats before they happen." Rogers doesn't like it. "I thought the punishment usually came after the crime," he says, and characterizes this approach as "holding a gun to the head of everyone on earth and calling it protection." When Rogers says that this is not freedom, but rather fear, Fury parries: "S.H.I.E.L.D. takes the world as it is, not as we'd like it to be." Though in a subsequent scene we see Fury more in doubt about the project, his full-throated defense of it with Rogers brings the critique of America's international policy closer to home.

Rogers's suspicion of even his own military hierarchy turns out to be justified, and that leads to the position he takes in *Civil War*, when the Avengers are at odds with one another about legislation known as the Sokovia Accords, proposing United Nations' oversight of the Avengers. Ironically, Tony Stark, usually the iconoclastic rebel, is in favor of the Accords: "We need to be put in check," he tells the other Avengers. "If we can't accept limitations, if we are boundary-less, we're no better than the bad guys." But Rogers disagrees: the UN "is run by people with agendas, and agendas change," he says. "If we sign this, we surrender our right to choose. . . . We may not be perfect, but the safest hands are still our own." Stark's individualism has been challenged by his understanding of the collateral damage the Avengers' actions have caused, and Rogers's institutional loyalty has been challenged by his discoveries of corruption and infiltration. This film, as well as this argument, "initiates a discourse on America's role in international conflict," writes Taylor, and "contributes to an increasing engagement with issues of globalization in the MCU" (153). Who should make decisions about the use of violent force? A trusted leader, like Captain America (or America), or a group of global representatives (the UN)? The question has political implications, especially in the wake of the United States' invasion of Iraq without the support of the United Nations and ongoing conversations about freedom and security.

The original *Civil War* series in the comics has drawn no small amount of commentary for this debate, which sprawls beyond these two central characters and clearly engages the political context of the early years of the wars in Iraq and Afghanistan. In the collection *Marvel Comics' Civil War and the Age of Terror*, Travis Langley notes that while the comics' author Mark Millar was clearly writing a superhero story, he was also "[adding] depth and resonance along with some degree of political commentary regarding political and social realities of the post-9/11 world such as privacy issues, controversial wiretapping, and the wide variety of compromised civil liberties rising out of the Patriot Act." That depth and resonance gets complicated as boundaries are set and then defied—over the seven-issue series and in other series set in this world, "Heroes die, villains die, civilians die, government agents die, authorities release unrehabilitated criminals in order to sic them on rebel superheroes, the government funds construction of a massive extradimensional prison to hold the rebels even though they had never built such a structure to contain super-villains, anti-registration heroes defy laws the public expects them to uphold, and leading pro-registration heroes amass wealth from associated government contracts" (69–70). Even more than the films, comics' long runs, frequent publication schedule, and need for storylines make it all but inevitable that writers will mine political and historical contexts and play with any number of plot twists and character development.

Identities, affiliations, and relationships are always changing, even—or especially—among the most iconic characters. Joanna Nowotny and Bettina Jossen note that the conflict between Rogers and Stark is also a philosophical one, as "Captain America's deontology insists on the intrinsic moral value of certain acts, while Iron Man's utilitarianism holds that, in a climate of fear and distrust of superheroes, the people have a right to expect accountability" (180). Nowotny and Jessen write that, in the original comics series, the philosophical angle "somewhat dilutes the political virulence of the series, as it masks a concrete political issue in general terms where no right or wrong can be determined," though it's also true that "there is no simple evil to identify and fight against" (180). Nowotny and Jessen argue that in the broad scope of Marvel comics, whether Rogers or Stark is eventually proven correct is hotly debated—it depends, in one sense, on which comics you consider. The film, however, leans subtly, then more obviously, toward Captain America. As a character, he is usually portrayed as having an innate sense of morality, and psychological studies have shown that people making deontological judgments are preferred as social partners and leaders (Everett, Pizarro, and Crockett). That is, we tend to gravitate toward leaders whom we believe have a strong moral compass and trust their judgment. But it is also the case that the politician pushing the Avengers to sign the Accords is Thaddeus "Thunderbolt" Ross (William Hurt), a former Army general and now the Secretary of State, who has demonstrated pretty poor judgment himself in the past, as in *The Incredible Hulk* (2008). Thus this isn't a debate about how to defeat pure evil, but rather an acknowledgment about complicated questions regarding the use of force, collateral damage, oversight, and leadership, as well as how an individual's own background and experience can affect how they understand all of those things.

The identity of the enemy gets complicated, too, though that might not be one's initial impression. In many big set pieces of superhero films, they are hordes of invading aliens, insect-like and largely indistinguishable, commanded by some grand poohbah with a vision for mass destruction. Kristen Whissel has written about what she calls the "digital multitude," combat sequences with massive numbers of the enemy, made possible with CGI starting in the early 2000s. She covers films like *Starship Troopers* (1997), *300* (2006), and the *Lord of the Rings* trilogy (2001, 2002, 2003), but her comments seem made to order for *The Avengers*: "If the digital multitude foregrounds the dark side of collectivity (ie, extreme uniformity and submission to a single, authoritarian power), then the protagonists' temporary alliances bring into relief their own dark counterpart: the extreme differentiation, isolation, and self-interest that make civilization more rather than less vulnerable to annihilation by a homogenous, radically uniform mass.... To become the agents of a new history, the protagonists must temporarily prioritize the collective over the individual and trade self-interest for united, self-sacrificing, bloody engagement with the enemy" (774).

Of course, it is easy to mow down invading insect-like aliens with righteous impunity, but the Earth-based enemies are more interesting. *Iron Man* 3 features the intriguing villain known as the Mandarin, a bomber whose appearance is very much like Osama bin Laden's and who releases self-aggrandizing videos accusing America of atrocities and using imagery heavily coded as Middle Eastern. "Some people call me a terrorist," he intones in a video. "I consider myself a teacher." Eventually the Mandarin is revealed to be quite literally a racist caricature—he is actually Trevor Slattery (Ben Kingsley), an actor who has been "cast" by Aldrich Killian for the purpose of "manipulating Western iconography." "The second you give evil a face—a bin Laden, a Quaddafi, a Mandarin—you hand the people a target," Killian explains. And if he plays both sides, he will effectively "own the War on Terror," as he puts it, and profit accordingly. Here, Americans' media-stoked fears of a racialized Other are used against them to indefinitely extend a war because it is lucrative for those holding the reins. The Other is, as it has always been, an illusion, and the true villain is someone rather like the entrepreneurial rebel Tony Stark—only a bit more so. The story is fueled by the complication of categories.

And particularly with Marvel, the idea of simplistic good guy/bad guy dichotomies has already been complicated by the nature and history of the superheroes themselves. As Christopher McGunnigle has noted, many of Marvel's most famous superheroes were created after the end of the Golden

Age, roughly the late 1930s until the mid-1950s, when many comic book companies began publishing more horror, westerns, and crime comics. Atlas Comics, a division of Timely Comics (which is now Marvel), had titles like *Journey into Mystery*, *Strange Tales*, *Tales to Astonish*, and *Tales of Suspense*, which "repeatedly depicted humans encountering extraterrestrial, subterranean, and aquatic creatures that would later be called 'Marvel monsters'" (110–11). This was an important transition from the Golden Age to what is known as the Silver Age of the 1960s, which featured superheroes with monstrous epithets—Mr. Fantastic, the Invisible Girl, the Human Torch, the Thing. Now-iconic superheroes like the Incredible Hulk and Spider-Man are very much a product of this heritage. Not only did these monstrous superheroes give Marvel more marketable content, McGunnigle argues, but they made for complicated characters with rich storytelling possibilities, with "a tendency toward amorphism and category crisis" (111). Even Captain America, dosed with super serum and later pulled from the ice and reanimated, has elements of the monstrous about him. If the superheroes often challenge notions of category and classification, it only makes sense that the villains would as well. Furthermore, while these films don't delve into aspects of the horror genre to the same degree or in the same way as much Iraqi-authored war fiction, they are nonetheless similar in their use of echoes of the horror genre to tell stories about shifting categories, mutating identities, and violence and its multifaceted, fragmenting effects.

Fantasy War, Real-World Consequences

In a cinematic universe, stories aren't over-and-done by the end credits—and Marvel, more than any other studio, popularized the insertion of "credit cookies," or midcredit and postcredit scenes, typically used to indicate that the story, and the conflict in question, isn't yet over. That means that conflicts continue, but also that the consequences of all this turmoil and violence can be explored more fully. Sometimes those consequences include physical disabilities—Bucky Barnes loses an arm in *Captain America: The First Avenger* (2011), Thor loses an eye in *Thor: Ragnarok*, and James Rhodes's legs are paralyzed in a fall when Stark can't catch him in time in *Civil War*. In one sense, disability is fairly easily ameliorated in these films—lose an arm, an eye, or the use of your legs, and you'll quickly receive a perfectly functioning prosthetic that not only restores your physical abilities, but more often than not, enhances them. Alex Tankard has written that Marvel movies "celebrate transforming disabled people into living weapons," noting in particular how Tony Stark develops the arc reactor that powers his Iron Man suit in order to prevent shrapnel from penetrating his heart, Steve Rogers takes the super-soldier serum in part because he was initially rejected from serving in the military due to his general weakness and possible heart trouble, and Bucky Barnes is rebuilt into the Winter Soldier after he falls into a ravine and loses an arm (41).

In that sense, Tankard writes, these films are ableist. That's generally true, although they also contain elements of antiableist critique. Analyzing *Captain America* and *The Winter Soldier*, Tankard notes that the former "foregrounds ableist social pressures coercing Steve's 'choice' to eliminate his disability" and that in the latter, "using the Winter Soldier to reinforce disability hierarchy [backfires] because, once inserted into the story, the irreparably traumatized, mutilated veteran remains a disruptive presence—even hinting at an alternative disability future based not on technological transformation but on interdependence" (42–43). Tankard points to moments later in the MCU that suggest this critique as well, such as the postcredit scene in *Black Panther* that shows Bucky living peacefully in Wakanda without a prosthetic, and a scene in *Avengers: Infinity War* (2018) when he is presented with a new prosthesis. "In what should be a triumphant moment of rehabilitation," Tankard writes, "Bucky looks devastated; rather than thanking his benefactor, he just asks, softly, 'Where's the fight?' . . . The words in the script may celebrate weaponization, but Sebastian Stan's performance exudes resignation and despair" (53–54). What initially look like easy ways to "fix" physical disability and enhance the body are, upon further examination, more indicative of disability as a relative and social category.

Emotional trauma is treated in a more overt and sustained way. Christine Muller has written about how nearly all the superheroes in the MCU are defined by some kind of traumatic experience—Bruce Banner's struggles with the raging Hulk, for instance, or the Maximoff twins' loss of their parents. But some are specifically the result of war experience. In *Winter Soldier*, Rogers visits a veterans' support group run by Sam Wilson. A female veteran is talking about coming home but remaining on alert—she swerved to avoid a plastic bag on the road while driving because she thought it was an IED. Wilson describes her experience, and all their experiences, in terms echoing all the works in this study: "Some stuff you leave there. Other stuff you bring back. It's our job to figure out how to carry it." Talking with Rogers afterward, he comments, "We all got the same problems."

In *Iron Man 3*, much of the film's plot focuses on Tony Stark's PTSD after the Battle of New York in *The Avengers*. In that battle, after Rogers has repeatedly criticized Stark for never being the kind of guy to "lay down the sacrifice play," Stark redirects a nuclear missile fired by the World Security Council into a mass of attacking aliens positioned just through a wormhole. The missile detonates, and Stark falls back through the wormhole just as it closes, surviving by the slimmest of chances. In *Iron Man 3*, Stark experiences frequent anxiety attacks and insomnia—at one point, he stays up working obsessively for seventy-two hours. "I'm a piping hot mess," he tells his girlfriend Pepper Potts (Gwyneth Paltrow). "You experience things and then they're over and you still can't explain them"—a statement that could have been made by Billy Lynn, John Bartle, Kate Brady, or any number of other characters. At times, Stark's Iron Man suit becomes a cocoon he is afraid to leave. At others, he treats it like a beloved fellow soldier—when it is damaged and its AI system JARVIS can no longer communicate with him, Stark pleads, "Don't leave me, buddy," and drags the suit like a wounded comrade to safety.

By the film's end, Stark has destroyed all his Iron Man suits and undergone an operation to remove the shrapnel from his chest so that he no longer needs the arc reactor, all in an effort to address his trauma and move on with his life. He does assert, however, that even without all his accoutrements, he remains Iron Man. It is a triumphant ending, but Stark's problems aren't over. In *Civil War*, Stark once again takes up the suit and the public mantle of Iron Man, leading to a breakup with Pepper. He struggles with his emotions surrounding the collateral damage caused by the Avengers' actions in Sokovia—when they were fighting an AI that Stark himself created—and in Lagos, where an explosion kills a number of humanitarian workers from Wakanda. All of this is what leads him to argue with Rogers about oversight of the Avengers. It might appear that he is breaking character, as Stark has hardly been known for his prudence or submission to authority. But here, his decision-making is directly influenced by the emotional trauma of his experiences. In that sense, when he says of being Iron Man that "I can't stop, because the truth is, I don't want to stop," he is conveying damage as much as he is heroism. As Alysa Auriemma sees it, "This inability to get rid of his patterned response to trauma is not only seen in the *Avengers* films, but becomes a major plot point in *Civil War*. Tony signs the Sokovia Accords in order to assuage his survivor's guilt, which has grown ever larger with each adventure. He is completely incapable of seeing anyone else's side in this matter because he is incapable of viewing himself through the lens of his own trauma, and as a result, his single-mindedness splinters the team." Stark is stymied, and that emotional impasse isn't resolved until the climactic events at the end of Phase Three of the MCU.

Stark's long narrative arc comes to a close in *Endgame* when he fatally injures himself while defeating Thanos and saving the universe, not long after he invents time travel and makes possible the reappearance of half the life of the universe that Thanos had previously disintegrated. This time, he lays down the sacrifice play for good, and dies surrounded by his wife Pepper, best friend Rhodes, and surrogate son Peter Parker, or Spider-Man. In one sense Stark's death is a stereotypical superhero resolution—the traumatic loss of millions of people is literally undone with the snap of some superhero fingers (first Bruce Banner's, and then Stark's), and Stark is able to die with closure, surrounded by people he loves. His actions bring back a number of characters that we knew couldn't really be lost forever—Nick Fury, Peter Parker, Stephen Strange (Benedict Cumberbatch), Sam Wilson, T'Challa (Chadwick Boseman), and Bucky Barnes among them. It is the kind of anti-revelation that Scorsese would rail against, fantastical problems addressed with science fiction and perfectly timed lines of dialogue.

But surprisingly, trauma becomes even more of a focus in the MCU after this point. This resolution brings about happy reunions that have been much anticipated, like that of Clint Barton (Jeremy Renner) with his family, or Bucky Barnes with Steve Rogers. But the MCU suggests that you can't really put things back again. Sometimes this point is made as a light joke, as when *Shang-Chi and the Legend of the Ten Rings* (2021) makes passing reference to "Post-Blip Anxiety" and a National Blip Support Hotline. ("The Blip" refers to the disappearance and then the restoration of all those people.) The television series *The Falcon and the Winter Soldier* reveals that after everyone reappeared after five years, so many of them had been displaced from their homes in the interim that the UN created something called the Global Repatriation Council. In *WandaVision* (2021), Monica Rambeau (Teyonah Parris) is bereft when she discovers that her mother died of cancer during the five years that she disappeared. How does one mourn an illness and a death that happened in what felt to you like no time at all?

WandaVision focuses more prominently on Wanda Maximoff and her war-induced trauma. Her beloved partner Vision (Paul Bettany) was killed in the war, one of several deaths that, like Stark's, were irreversible. Though she tries, she simply cannot handle the devastation of her grief, and magically creates an artificial, comforting world where she can live with Vision and two children. It's a lie that also ensnares other innocent people, but she won't let it go without a fight. The fight eventually ends in *WandaVision* but then continues in *Doctor Strange in the Multiverse of Madness*, about which more below.

Despite the triumphant and operatic closure of *Endgame*, the conflict as well as the trauma continues. Part of the reason for all that trauma, in fact, is that war is never over, even given cumulative acts of superhero bravery. "Nothing lasts forever," Black Widow comments to Nick Fury at the end of *Avengers: Age of Ultron* (2015), and he corrects her. "Trouble, Ms. Romanoff. No matter who wins or loses, trouble still comes around." Although the suggestively titled *Infinity War* is followed by the more definitively titled *Endgame*, there are always new battles and enemies to fight—newer Marvel projects are titled *Secret Wars* and *Armor Wars*, and at this writing the MCU is entering Phase Five of its story cycle. Star Wars, too, expands conflict to different parts of the universe and in different temporal directions in spinoff films and television series. The first Star Wars film, *A New Hope*, was released in 1977, and at the end of *The Last Jedi* in 2017, a grizzled Luke Skywalker insists that "the war is just beginning." Forty years of war—and that's just the beginning. Perpetual, infinite war has become as ingrained in our fantasy storytelling as in our contemporary national history.

Fantasy, War, and Fragmentation

Recent MCU films and television series have introduced the idea of the multiverse—an idea borrowed from physics and explored in different literatures that there might exist multiple or even an infinite number of parallel universes, worlds in which reality is different from the way it is in the world we live in. It is a fun concept, ripe for storytelling, especially if characters can see or visit alternate worlds—exploring roads not taken, contemplating the ripples of cause and effect both historical and personal, or playing with different laws of physics. But fractured storylines have darker implications, as we have seen with both American and Iraqi literature about contemporary war. This is often what happens, those authors suggest, when violence ruptures a life or many lives, or when the consequences of the use of force get wildly out of control. Although the affect is different, the loss of boundaries between realities and ensuing narrative fragmentation in superhero stories has many of the same implications.

In 1961, DC Comics first introduced the idea of the multiverse in *The Flash* #123, "Flash of Two Worlds!" In it, the Flash suddenly disappears from his regular life and reappears on an alternate Earth, an Earth in a parallel universe, where he encounters an older, different version of himself. Those two Earths, and crossovers between them, featured in a number of Justice League comics, ultimately leading to a 1985 series called "Crisis on Infinite Earths," a storyline that allowed DC writers to simplify a constellation of multiple versions of characters and world that they felt had become too complicated for readers to follow. Marvel Comics introduced the idea in 1962 with *Strange Tales* #103, in which one of the Fantastic Four visits an alternative universe. The planet he ends up on is later termed Earth-1612, and the Earth we're familiar with becomes Earth-616. The comics took off with the idea as the 1960s progressed, with the characters visiting places like Sub-Atomica, Other-Earth, the Dark Dimension, and the Negative Zone. In 1977, Marvel launched the series *What If . . . ?*, specifically devoted to imagining different character identities and plot outcomes. A 2014 series called *Secret*

Wars cleaned house in something like the same way that DC Comic's "Crisis on Infinite Earths" had, but the comics quickly reinstated the multiverse and its accompanying complications (Marston).

The MCU first takes up the notion of the multiverse in *Doctor Strange* (2016), in which the title character learns about the existence of alternate dimensions and how to navigate them. The idea resurfaces in *Endgame*, when Bruce Banner notes that if the Avengers time in travel to defeat Thanos, any changes they make will not change the present—rather, they will create alternate realities. Those alternate realities become central, rather than peripheral, to the plot in the television series *Loki* (2021), in which Loki (Tom Hiddleston) meets and interacts with several versions of himself from alternate universes. The multiverse is also the central premise of the series *What If . . . ?* (2021) and the 2022 film *Doctor Strange in the Multiverse of Madness*. The MCU is now so enmeshed in the concept that its Phases Four, Five, and Six, beginning with *Black Widow* in 2021 and running through films planned for 2024, 2025, and 2026, is known as the Multiverse Saga.[2]

And all of this is, of course, inextricably bound up in war. In *Doctor Strange*, Stephen Strange travels to Kathmandu in search of someone he thinks could help heal his disability—hands that were severely damaged in a car accident. He finds The Ancient One (Tilda Swinton), who appreciates his persistence but also recognizes his arrogance. She only agrees to take him in and teach him about the multiverse because he might prove to be an asset in the conflict with Kaecilius (Mads Mikkelson) and the evil entity Dormammu—because he could be another warrior. She further explains that their power derives from harnessing energy "drawn from other dimensions of the multiverse" and that they use this power to fight.

The multiverse doesn't just provide power for combat. It is also a battleground itself, a vast, all-reaching one. In the television series *Loki*, the title character is apprehended by the Time Variance Authority, or TVA, because he is a variant—a person who has done something at odds with the "Sacred Timeline," and created an alternate reality and an alternate version of himself as a result. In the course of the series, he meets other Loki variants (including a woman, a child, and an alligator) and learns that the TVA was created to keep these kinds of things in order and ultimately to avoid war. "Long ago there was a vast multiversal war," an informational video tells him, "with countless timelines battling each other for supremacy, resulting in the total destruction of, well, everything" ("Glorious Purpose"). Eventually everything was organized into a single timeline, which the TVA polices. But by the end of Season 1, those controls have been loosed, and a multiversal war looms once again.

More combat across the multiverse takes place in *Spider-Man: No Way Home* (2021). But perhaps the most telling use of the multiverse as battlefield and storytelling space takes place in *Doctor Strange in the Multiverse of Madness* (2022), in which Strange meets America Chavez (Xochitl Gomez), a young girl who can travel between the different universes. Wanda Maximoff wants to take that power from her—which would likely kill her in the process—in order to travel to the universe that she dreams about, where her two children are alive, happy, and safe. Directed by Sam Raimi, the film is imaginative and fast-moving, featuring touches befitting the *Evil Dead* director, like a zombie version of Strange and some clever cameos. But despite the often-rollicking tone, Wanda's character is a serious one. Her motivation isn't profit, like all those Iron Man baddies, or world domination, or even "balancing the universe," as Thanos claimed was his goal. It is finding a world where she doesn't have to suffer the loss of her beloved partner and children. The multiverse, then, is the way to alleviate her grief. "Everything I lost can be mine again," she tells Strange. Strange questions her further, and her response is precise: "I am going to leave this reality. And go to one where I can be with my children." Strange objects, telling her that her children "aren't real," that she created them using magic. "That's what every mother does," Wanda counters.

Wanda is so set on finding them that she is willing to sacrifice America to do it, saying that it would be "for the greater good," which Strange likens to "the kind of justification our enemies use." Wanda questions him about his decision to give Thanos the time stone (which he does in *Infinity War*, an action that forces Wanda to watch Vision die twice). Strange is clear: "That was war," he says, "and I did what I had to do." In war, he implies, sacrifices must be made. But Wanda's war is still ongoing. "You break the rules and become a hero. I do it and become the enemy. That doesn't seem fair," she notes, and the battle lines have been drawn.

Wanda can see this other story, the one she so desperately wants for herself: a life without loss, or at least a life where the loss of her partner is alleviated somewhat by the presence of their children. And she even gets there, when America opens a portal for her near the end of the film. But it doesn't work—she doesn't belong in that story. The children scream and run from her in fear, leading her to ultimately give up and retreat. There might be an infinite number of stories, but she must live with her own. Likewise, Strange has to leave a world in which his great love Christine hasn't married another, one where she might love him in return. They both must live in awareness of those other narratives, the temptation of other worlds where loved ones are more than ghosts and dreams; instead, they have to continue to face the painful consequences of those losses. It is not exactly an archive of colloquies, like Wadood's in Antoon's *Fihris*, but like those colloquies, the multiverse is woven from expansive narrative possibilities as well as losses caused by violence and war. And although there are different mythologies about how the multiverse came to be, one story holds that there was once only a single universe called the First Firmament, which was shattered into pieces by a war between the Aspirants and the Celestials. Thus, the MCU's multiverse is not just a set piece for war and its devastation but the very product of that violence ("Multiverse").

Fantasy War, Real Leaders

As I noted earlier, it has taken the MCU a while to make superhero representation more equitable. *Black Panther* has been widely praised for its portrayal of Black identities and communities, and Black Widow and Captain Marvel now both have solo films to their name. "Black Widow's role commanding an intergalactic Avengers task force and Captain Marvel's (Brie Larson) demonstrations of incredible power in *Endgame* indicate that the hierarchy's higher levels are becoming available to women," writes James Taylor. However, in *Endgame*, the MCU's biggest set piece to date, "Tony's sacrifice also leaves the universe indebted to the white male American entrepreneur who proved its savior" (Taylor 156). Marvel gained more ground with its 2022 television series *Ms. Marvel*, which follows Kamala Khan (Iman Vellani), a 16-year-old Pakistani American who is the MCU's first Muslim superhero. Kamala Khan also features in 2023's *The Marvels* alongside Captain Marvel and Monica Rambeau.

Star Wars, however, has been working longer and more assiduously on issues of representation, and particularly gender representation in stories about war and military leadership. These narratives aren't exemplars of the second wave of twenty-first-century war stories in the same ways as most of the others in this study. While they do feature ongoing, all-consuming conflict that transcends delineations of time and space, it doesn't lead to psychological or temporal fragmentation of the same kind that we see in Ben Fountain or Kevin Powers, for example, or to the narrative splintering that occurs in the MCU's multiverse. Instead, the notable feature of these stories is their focus on female soldiers, female leaders, and a rejection of styles of leadership traditionally coded as masculine. As with the war stories and authors I covered in chapter 2, Star Wars is challenging the standard model of the war story and doing so in ways that are particularly relevant to the contemporary moment, even if the characters tend to maintain their sense of personal delineation and wholeness.

In *Rogue One*, Jyn is a military leader whose gender is largely unremarkable in the story itself but notable for audiences. When she was sixteen and training with Saw Gerrera (Forrest Whitaker), he insists that she was already "the best soldier in my guard." In his original story pitch for *Rogue One*, John Knoll of Industrial Light & Magic (who also served as an executive producer on the film and as its visual effects supervisor) described Jyn Erso: She is "team leader, female, spartan tough, battle worn, a little cynical and jaded from everything she's been through. She's seen it all, and maybe that makes her seem a little callous to those who don't know her" ("Bonus Features"). This makes *Rogue One* an outlier in the history of war films, certainly, though interestingly not among other recent Star Wars stories— which feature the female heroes Rey and Ahsoka Tano—or considered alongside the changing demographics of the American military. Since 2013, women have served in units that experience direct combat, and in 2016, all combat jobs were open to women; Captain Kristen M. Griest became the Army's first female infantry officer that same year. In 2020, a woman met the rigorous qualifications needed to become the first female Green Beret, which led to news stories about Kate Wilder, who successfully completed the Special Forces Officer Course in 1980 but was prevented from formally graduating because of her gender (Ismay).

In film, women have been gaining ground in the action genre since the 1970s: Ripley was the "last man standing" in *Alien* (1979), Sarah Connor showed off both her skill with weapons and her biceps in *Terminator 2: Judgment Day* (1991), and Lara Croft made for a very lucrative *Tomb Raider* (2001). Writing in 2001, Stephanie Mencimer noted the trend of female action heroes beating the bad guys and—as in the *Charlie's Angels* film from the year before—looking good doing it. But, she added, "Women are still only allowed to be violent within certain parameters largely proscribed by what men are willing to tolerate": that they display pure motives, that they don't get too messy, and that they stop short of "being so threatening that men would be afraid to sleep with the leading lady." If these women are action figures, they must be action figures that are "a cross between Gidget and Bruce Lee." In succeeding years, those action heroes arguably got more serious: Beatrix fought her way through two volumes of *Kill Bill* (2003 and 2004), Letty Ortiz led the pack in eight *Fast & Furious* films (2001–2023), and Furiosa (who is also disabled) crusaded against sexual slavery in *Mad Max: Fury Road* (2015). But films that show women in the military have typically focused the entire plot on that exceptional status, like *Courage under Fire* (1996), *G.I Jane* (1997), or even the Goldie Hawn comedy *Private Benjamin* (1980), and these have been few and far between.[3]

Not so in the recent Star Wars films. These female characters fight battles and wars, their work firmly focused on that larger cause, and the films as a whole make broader points about what female military leadership looks like and why it is often more effective than leadership strategies traditionally coded as masculine. This is a defiance of traditional gender delineation that is productive both narratively and culturally—though because these are war stories, the characters aren't immune to injury, devastation, and death. These include both minor characters like Resistance fighter pilots and First Order captains as well as major ones, like Jedi-turned-Force-sensitive warrior Ahsoka Tano (Ashley Eckstein and Rosario Dawson) and Leia Organa (Carrie Fisher), the all-important Resistance General and inspiration for the movement itself. Most important of all is Rey (Daisy Ridley), the hero of the sequel trilogy—*The Force Awakens* (2015), *The Last Jedi* (2017), and *The Rise of Skywalker* (2019). While Rey's gender provokes mild surprise at the story's outset, it quickly becomes unremarkable, in the best sense.

Rey is a lot like Jyn—tough, capable, a bit cynical and wary of others but ready to rise as a leader when the time comes. Also like Jyn, she is an orphan, unsure what happened to her parents. In *The Force Awakens*, she is introduced under wraps, outfitted in protective goggles and a full balaclava, stripping parts from the innards of an abandoned spacecraft. When she drinks from her canteen, she lowers the wrap to reveal a female face— the shot is a quiet assertion that the new Star Wars films will operate with a different set of assumptions, much like the shot in the scene immediately preceding it when a Storm Trooper takes off his helmet and turns out to be a Black character. That character, Finn (John Boyega), has to shake off his own outdated associations when he meets Rey on the planet Jakku. When they are both targeted by the Empire, they have to flee, and she repeatedly refuses his gestures of protection: "I know how to run without you holding my hand!" They head for the Millennium Falcon, and Finn protests: "We need a pilot!" "We've got one," she responds, and still, he's surprised. "You?" When Han Solo and Chewbacca later board the Falcon, Han has the same question: "Where's the pilot?" Rey identifies herself, and he says the same thing. "You?" But her bona fides are obvious—she can maneuver the ship like an ace and understands it mechanically as well, commenting with Han's agreement that installing a compressor on the ignition line puts too much stress on the hyperdrive. It doesn't take long for Han to be convinced. He offers her a blaster, to which Rey responds, "I think I can handle myself." "I know you do," he replies. "That's why I'm giving it to you." It's an acknowledgment that she does, in fact, handle herself well, but that the stakes are high and she'll need to be prepared for the fights that are coming.

As her newfound friends stop being surprised at her abilities, Rey saves those surprises for her enemies and, to some degree, herself. When Kylo Ren (Adam Driver), the primary antagonist of the trilogy, captures and restrains her, and then tries to psychically extract the image of a map from her mind, he's confident in his own superior power. "You know I can take whatever I want," he tells her, an unsettling statement with a distinct undercurrent of sexual violence. "I'm not giving you anything," she responds, and after a mental struggle, she's the one who penetrates his mind rather than the other way around—she sees that Ren is afraid, that he doubts his ability to live up to the strength of his grandfather, Darth Vader. "The scene, in fact, is one of the greatest 'no-means-no' moments in recent cinema," notes Glen Robert Gill. "When she later uses this ability again to free herself from captivity, we realize that we are in the presence of a potential Jedi knight" (10).

That potential is on its way to being realized by the end of *The Force Awakens*, when she locates Luke Skywalker (Mark Hamill) on a remote planet and offers him his old lightsaber, an invitation to return to the war. The next film in the trilogy, *The Last Jedi*, follows Rey as she pushes against Luke's reluctance and seeks a deeper understanding of the Force, of Kylo Ren, of the nature of the war, and of her own identity. Rey's competence and toughness no longer elicit surprise in the other characters, though a different lesson in female military leadership plays out over the course of the film, one focused primarily on Poe Dameron (Oscar Isaac) as well as the audience for the film itself.

As the story begins, Resistance fighters are evacuating the planet D'Qar while under fire from First Order ships. Poe, a pilot, targets one of the dreadnaughts, but Leia orders him to disengage, because the evacuees have all made it onto the transport ship. Poe refuses: "No, General, we can do this! We have a chance to take out a dreadnaught!" He hits his target and cheers, but a number of other Resistance ships are shot down. When Leia sees Poe again, she slaps him and tells him he's demoted. He protests, celebrating the downing of the massive enemy ship and insisting that if "you start an attack, you follow it through." Leia reprimands him in clearly gendered terms: "Get your head out of your cockpit," she spits. "There are things you cannot solve by jumping in an X-Wing and blowing something up. I need you to learn that." Poe insists that "there were heroes on that mission"—that heroism is *action*, and immediate, spectacular results. "Dead heroes," Leia corrects him. "No leaders."

Poe clearly respects Leia deeply even as he disagrees with her. Not so much Vice Admiral Holdo (Laura Dern), who assumes command after Leia is gravely injured in an attack led by Kylo Ren. As she speaks, reaction shots of Poe make his skepticism clear. "Four hundred of us on three ships," Holdo says. "We're the very last of the Resistance. But we're not alone. In every corner of the galaxy, the downtrodden and oppressed know our symbol and they put their hope in it. We are the spark that will light the fire that will restore the Republic. That spark, this Resistance, must survive. That is our mission." Poe makes clear that Holdo is "not what I expected" and is quick to insert himself into her strategizing. "So what's our plan?" he asks impatiently. "I just want to know what's going on." Holdo speaks to him with undisguised condescension, like Leia calling out his masculine need to charge ahead without thinking—what Poe thinks of as heroism. "I've dealt with plenty of trigger-happy flyboys like you. You're impulsive, dangerous—and the last thing we need right now. So stick to your post, and follow my orders."

But he doesn't. First he sends Finn and Rose (Kellie Marie Tran), a mechanic, on a secret mission to find and disable the First Order's tracking system, in hopes that will enable the Resistance to escape. In most adventure films featuring a cocky male character like Poe in the lead role, a scheme like this would prove successful, but this one fails as Finn and Rose are betrayed and captured. Later, when Poe sees that transport ships are being fueled up, his skepticism at Holdo's leadership boils over into outrage. He can't believe that they are abandoning the large cruiser and taking a chance on unarmed and unshielded smaller ships. He tells her to "Cut it, lady," throws a chair across the room, and calls her both a coward and a traitor. When Holdo refuses to endorse his own plan to defeat the First Order and escape, he leads a mutiny, relieving her of her command "for the survival of this ship, its crew, and the Resistance." But his takeover doesn't last long—Holdo kicks open a steam vent and grabs a weapon. Leia enters and shoots Poe, stunning rather than killing him. As Leia and Holdo watch Poe being loaded onto a transport, their tenderness toward him is surprising. "That one's a troublemaker," Holdo says to Leia, as if he's a child who's still learning. "I like him."

When Poe comes to, he finally absorbs the lesson Leia urged on him when Holdo's full strategy is revealed. The First Order isn't tracking the transport ships, and so Holdo alone stayed on the cruiser to pilot it as a distraction. "She was more interested in protecting the light than she was in seeming like a hero," Leia explains. And when the transport ships are discovered and fired upon, Holdo's commitment to the cause is shown to be even more complete, as she maneuvers the cruiser and prepares to jump to light speed. "She's running away," someone comments, and Poe corrects them. He knows now: "No she isn't." Instead, Holdo aims her ship at the First Order flagship and bisects it when she jumps to light speed, sacrificing herself in the process.

Poe puts his new wisdom in action in the film's climactic sequence, as the First Order bears down on the last few fighters of the Resistance, huddled in a fortress on the planet Crait. As Luke Skywalker emerges to face Kylo Ren, Poe watches the impending showdown, and Finn urges them to make a last stand with him, to fight. "No—no! We are the spark that will light the fire

Figure 6. Admiral Holdo (Laura Dern) speaks with General Leia Organa (Carrie Fischer) as Holdo prepares to make her sacrifice play in *The Last Jedi*. (Walt Disney Studios, 2017)

that will burn the First Order down," Poe says, echoing Holdo. And instead of fighting impulsively, trying to blow something up, they run—deep into the cave, to an exit blocked by boulders that Rey moves using the power of the Force. As Rey does that, Luke says in voice-over that "the Rebellion is reborn today. The war is just beginning. And I will not be the last Jedi." Rey is ready to take up that mantle, and Poe is ready to lend support rather than look for opportunities to prove his own worth. When the two finally meet, his admiration for her is clear. "I'm Rey," she says. "I know," he responds.

Poe learns his lesson well, but for some audiences it was a harder sell because most of Hollywood history has taught that heroism is precisely what Poe initially thinks it is. Even positive reviews, like Manohla Dargis's in the *New York Times*, noted how the central standoff between ships feels like "a slow-moving game of space chess." Viewers complained about various aspects of the film, from its female hero and diverse cast to what they saw as untenable changes to Star Wars mythology, resulting in a surprising divide on Rotten Tomatoes—the website reports a 43 percent audience approval rating compared with a 91 percent rating from film critics ("Star Wars: The Last Jedi").

The authenticity of that audience rating, however, was itself the target of speculation, with some claiming that *The Last Jedi* had been "review-bombed" on Rotten Tomatoes or inundated with negative reviews generated in part by bots. Many of those negative reviews call out the film "for its inclusion of 'SJW' [Social Justice Warrior] concepts, criticizing the movie for its forced inclusion of race and powerful female figures" (Alexander).[4] In that sense, some people didn't just dislike the movie but actively worked against its success because they just couldn't stomach a story without a white male at center stage—because they wanted one that celebrated a traditionally masculine portrait of heroism and military leadership.

The trilogy ends with *The Rise of Skywalker*, which reclaimed widespread audience appreciation, rated at 86 percent on Rotten Tomatoes and protected from trolling by that website's new "verified audience" tool ("Star Wars: The Rise of Skywalker," Lee). Rey's status in this final installment remains clear, and she is second only to Leia as the most significant figure in the Resistance. "You're the best fighter we have," Poe tells her early on, protesting that she has spent time on Jedi training rather than going out on missions. As the film builds toward a final standoff between Rey and the Emperor Palpatine— revealed to be her grandfather—it repeatedly emphasizes that leadership is most powerful when shared rather than a mechanism for individualized self-aggrandizement. When Rey insists that she go in search of Palpatine alone, Finn responds, "Alone, with friends. We go together." Poe's old flame Zorii (Keri Russell) repeats a commonly held idea about their enemy: "They win by making you think you're alone."

For his part, Poe has absorbed the lesson and no longer forges ahead as an isolated hero, sure that his convictions will prevail. After Leia dies in the effort to save both Rey and, effectively, her son Kylo Ren/Ben Solo, Poe sits beside her body and doubts his ability to live up to her: "I don't really know how to do this. What you did—I'm not ready." Lando Calrissian (Billy Dee Williams) enters to set him straight: "Neither were we. Luke, Han, Leia, me—who's ever ready? . . . We had each other. That's how we won." Poe, acting general in the wake of Leia's death, then realizes that Finn should share the title and the responsibilities with him. "I can't do this alone," he tells Finn. "I need you in command with me." Now, the advantages of community are more important to him than the traditionally masculinist glory of the rugged individual. And so when Poe speaks to his fellow pilots, rousing them for their last battle, he does it in Leia's name: "Leia never gave up, and neither will we. . . . Today we make one last stand for Leia, for the galaxy."

As Poe and the others fight an army of Final Order ships, Rey faces Palpatine, and the symbolism of their standoff reemphasizes the same point about leadership and power. Palpatine urges Rey to strike him down, and thus transfer his being into her, the ultimate consolidation of power. "You will be Empress. We will be one." When Kylo Ren, who has now rejected the Dark Side and rediscovered his identity as Ben Solo, arrives to help Rey, their combined power as a "Force dyad" is considerable, but Palpatine incapacitates them and harnesses the power for himself. "The power of two restores the one true Emperor," he intones. In Palpatine's vision of power, everything is about that singularity, the oneness that consolidates and, in consequence, annihilates anything else. "You are nothing," he tells Rey. But her response, after Ben has seemingly been killed and she lies defeated, is to invoke others, to seek community rather than oneness. "Be with me," she says, and they are—she hears a number of Jedi voices urging her to rise. The moment features voice cameos from actors playing both male and female Jedi in the Star Wars universe, most recognizably Frank Oz as Yoda, Ewan McGregor as Obi-Wan Kenobi, and finally Mark Hamill as Luke. When Palpatine tells her that "I am all the Sith"—a faceless horde serving only his own primacy—Rey is able to respond, "And I am all the Jedi." By using both Luke and Leia's lightsabers together, she deflects his attack and destroys him.

In the final scene of the film, Rey visits Luke's childhood home on Tatooine and is asked by an old woman who she is, what her name is. She answers, choosing her last name for herself: Skywalker. The title of the film thus turns out to emphasize her two greatest achievements: that she determines her own identity and knows who she is and that she does so drawing on not only her own strength but also the strength of others. In the decisive moment against Palpatine, she quite literally rises in the face of overwhelming odds and does so through the acceptance of others rather than their rejection. As the trilogy ends, Rey is a whole person who has definitively delineated her own identity and her own story. She's not Billy Lynn from Fountain's novel, trying and failing to understand his war and himself. She's not John Bartle in *The Yellow Birds*, giving up on putting all the pieces back together. And she's not Kate Brady in *Sand Queen*, haunted, scarred, and broken beyond repair. (Unlike Kate, it should be noted, Rey staves off even the hint of sexual violence that Kylo Ren threatens—that's a problem of the real-life military that Star Wars doesn't consider.) But Rey's status as a female leader and the trilogy's emphasis on varieties of female leadership take her story beyond simplistic fantasy, even if many of the story's other characteristics don't hew to the model of blurred boundaries and ensuing fragmentation that this study is focused on.

Considerations of Rey and Jyn Erso encourage a rereading of Leia, whose own story is extended into the sequel trilogy, and other characters in the Star Wars universe. The roots of Leia's iconic status in these more recent films reach back to the original trilogy, in which she is referred to primarily as "Princess Leia." As Steve Ellerhoff notes, however, "The character inhabits many other roles: she is an Imperial Senator until the Senate is dissolved by the Emperor; she is the biological daughter of a queen-turned-senator (Padme Amidala) and a slave-turned-Jedi-turned-Sith-Lord (Anakin Skywalker/Darth Vader); she is twin sister to Luke Skywalker; she is the adopted daughter of the Queen of Alderaan (Breha Organa) and senator-turned-Rebellion cofounder (Bail Organa); she is an undercover dissident, courier, and leader at the heart of the Rebel Alliance; and [in later films] she is a mother and a general of the Resistance" (228). While Fisher-as-Leia has famously been gawked at in the gold bikini she wears as Jabba the Hutt's captive, she also famously responded to that objectification and captivity with efficient and deadly rage. Fisher laid out how to explain such a sexualized image of Leia to, for example, one's daughter, who might well have discovered a version of it as an "action figure" available for purchase. "Tell them that a giant slug captured me and forced me to wear that stupid outfit," she said, "and then I killed him because I didn't like it. And then I took it off. Backstage" (Calia). Ellerhoff celebrates that very agency—of a princess who challenged the conventional conceptions of that title long before Disney adapted to changing attitudes with figures like Merida (in *Brave*, 2012) or Moana (2016). As he writes, Leia "gives audiences a woman who will not be trapped in a role and a galaxy—that is, a metaphorical setting for real-life possibilities—where someone as stitched into the establishment as a princess can lead a rebellion against tyranny" (238).

It is an fitting tribute, although Will Brooker notes that Leia's agency and confidence stem in part from her aristocratic background; in other words, she may be formidable because of her title rather than despite it. She and C-3PO "belong to the culture of the old Republic—a world of moneyed elegance, poise and etiquette—rather than the rougher world of Tatooine homesteads and Corellian pirates" (24). It is why, Brooker writes, Leia "is undaunted by Tarkin and Vader, exchanging cold insults with her enemies, and even in prison, fits the clean white interior of the Imperial environment" (25). Luke and Han Solo, on the other hand, match the aesthetic of the Rebels—technology that is pieced together and dust-battered, outfits that are a collage of materials, a "make-do-and-mend" approach of "dirt, trash, scuffs, scratches" (23). Leia, then, can code-switch with ease, both gliding through the sleek halls of the Empire and also blasting a hole in one of those walls and leading her friends into a trash compactor by way of escape.

Rey, on the other hand, starts with trash and must work her way up. She is introduced as a scavenger making a hardscrabble, barely sustainable living, and as an orphan has only the advantages she cultivates in herself and develops with her newfound friendships. The only way for her to be in the world is the one she works out for herself. Leia uses her privilege on her own terms and arguably to the most admirable of ends, but that privilege is recognizable nonetheless, especially when compared with Rey. In that sense, the character of Leia absolutely broke new ground in the 1977, 1980, and 1983 films, but Rey and Jyn go further, in the centrality of their roles, their unapologetically heroic status, and the ways these films focus on their identities and their leadership. Jyn's story in particular shows that despite that hard-won heroism, war is tragic rather than merely a stage for self-aggrandizement—it's an all-encompassing, overwhelming force that takes her under in the end.

Ahsoka Tano is another prominent female leader whose story has been explored in the animated television series *The Clone Wars* (2008–2020) and *Rebels* (2014–2018), and who is one of the Jedi who impel Rey to rise at the end of *The Rise of Skywalker*. Voiced in the film and the series by Ashley Eckstein, she also makes an appearance as a live action character in *The Mandalorian* (2019–), played there by Rosario Dawson. Ahsoka is introduced in a 2008 *Clone Wars* film that kicked off the television series—there, she's the new Padawan, or Jedi apprentice, to Anakin Skywalker. Initial reactions to Ahsoka were mixed—Roger Ebert dismissed her in the *Clone Wars* film as simply "annoying," a character who "offers suggestions that invariably prove her right and her teacher wrong." But as she developed as a complex hero and a leader in the war against the Empire, her stature grew both literally and figuratively. "It's no exaggeration to say that the Empire never would have been defeated without Ahsoka's help," Jesse Schedeen noted in an article about Ahsoka's appearance in *The Mandalorian*. The final shot of the film foreshadows her importance—she is in the center of the frame, flanked by R2-D2 and Anakin on the left and Obi-Wan and Yoda on the right, and the iris-in that ends the film hones in on her.

Ahsoka's arc as a young Jedi is remarkably nuanced, with episodes that feature her struggling with questions about when to use violence, in what ways, and to what purposes, episodes that often showcase her dynamic lightsaber technique. She is also reacting to Anakin's development and the shadow that grows over his character. In Season 5, she is accused of murder, and the Jedi effectively abandon her. Anakin tracks down the real killer, who blames the Jedi for the course that the ongoing war has taken. When Ahsoka is exonerated and invited back into the Jedi fold, she refuses, newly skeptical of the order that claims moral intuition and righteous action but too often seems to fall short of those ideals. "I have to sort this out on my own," she insists to Anakin. "Without the council, and without you." Anakin understands, and the gravity of the moment is twofold: "More than you realize, I understand wanting to walk away from the order," he tells her ("The Wrong Jedi"). By the final episode of the *Clone Wars* series, they have both changed dramatically. Ahsoka has left the Jedi and faked her death, and when Anakin appears in the last scene, it is as Darth Vader, contemplating a lightsaber that she left behind. Both characters have faced the challenges of war, of military identity and leadership, and of the ethical conundrums of the use of force, but in the end, Ahsoka—much like both Captain America and Captain Marvel—is the one determined to make the most moral sense of it that she can, without recourse to dogma, a military hierarchy, or blind faith in power.

In Season 2 of the later series *Rebels*, Ahsoka fights Vader, a confrontation that has all the epic drama and complex backstory of Vader's face-offs with Obi-Wan Kenobi and Luke Skywalker in the earlier films *A New Hope* (1977) and *The Empire Strikes Back* (1980). "Anakin Skywalker was weak," Vader tells Ahsoka. "I killed him." "Then I will revenge his death," she vows. "Revenge is not the Jedi way," Vader taunts her. "I am no Jedi," she responds—a statement that is a threat, a declaration of identity, and a soldier's credo all at once ("Twilight of the Apprentice"). When Ahsoka appears as a live-action character in Season 2 of *The Mandalorian*, it is a moment of surprise, satisfaction, and gravitas for fans who have followed her character's long arc. Played by Rosario Dawson, Ahsoka advises the title character on his care of the "baby Yoda," whom she senses is named Grogu. The Mandalorian wants Ahsoka to train Grogu as a Jedi, but Ahsoka remains suspicious of what that could entail. "His attachment to you makes him vulnerable to his fears, his anger," she tells the Mandalorian. "I've seen what such feelings can do to a fully trained Jedi knight. To the best of us," she says—alluding, obviously, to Anakin. "I will not start this child down that path" ("Chapter 13"). Writer and director Dave Filoni, who has been responsible for much of the development of Ahsoka's character, notes the layers of her history: "We saw her basically hit the scene as a Padawan: young, and naïve, and brash, and aggressive. Then, in *Rebels*, she's more of a traditional knight, trying to figure out how to fight a war. . . . When you see this version of the character, she's world-weary from everything that she's experienced and lived through. She's seen so much happen in her time" (Breznican). Now, Ahsoka isn't just a young soldier, but an experienced leader whose advice people like the Mandalorian seek out and take seriously.

In that sense Ahsoka's arc is comparable to Leia's, in that audiences have seen her grow and change over decades instead of the shorter windows of time that *Rogue One* and the recent trilogy have opened on Jyn and Rey, respectively. But Ahsoka also stands out because, unlike the other three female leaders, she reads as non-white. Her character is Togruta, an alien race with orange skin, white markings, and large head tails called Lekku. While this is obviously not the same as being a human woman of color, when she stands next to characters like Anakin and Obi-Wan—as she does in that final shot of the *Clone Wars* film—it is clear that Star Wars is showcasing a hero that is not a white man. And that, too, makes a difference.

This gender progressiveness in particular is reflected in Lucasfilm's executive team—Kathleen Kennedy has been president since 2012, and on the company's "Leadership" website, nineteen out of the forty-one positions listed are staffed by women at the time of this writing. Disney, however, which purchased Lucasfilm in 2012, has lagged further behind, and of course has a longer history of relegating women to the role of helpless damsel or otherwise subordinate status. When *The Force Awakens* was first released in 2015, fans were excited about the first Star Wars movie in ten years, and, as Star Wars has always been known for its extensive merchandizing, many were eager to snap up toys and other representations of this new slate of characters. When they headed to the stores, however, they could find action figures of Poe and Finn—but not Rey. #wheresRey began trending, and fans were baffled. Rey is clearly the hero of the new trilogy, and so what accounts for her absence? It's pretty simple, writes Jeffrey Brown: "The disjuncture between *The Force Awakens'* presentation of Rey as a strong female protagonist and the character's extremely limited presence in the merchandising reveals persistent and institutionalized gender discrimination" (336). Undaunted, fans took up the task themselves, making their own Rey costumes to wear to parties and premieres and even constructing their own action figures, and that, of course, is when Disney execs took notice. "When criticisms of discriminatory merchandising become intertwined with alternative ways to celebrate the progressive character of Rey without Disney deriving any profits," explains Brown, "*that* is something any executive will listen to" (345). After that, Rey became more visible in the toy aisle.

These twenty-first-century Star Wars films and series, then, are notable not just for featuring female protagonists, or featuring female protagonists who are strong and capable, but also for challenging norms about what constitutes leadership, and particularly military leadership. Both female and male characters build their command out of partnership rather than braggadocio or self-aggrandizement, showing audiences that it is not only about who's leading but how they're doing it. And if that rubbed some viewers the wrong way, it was to the great delight of others. At the end of the documentary featurette that accompanied *Rogue One* on its release to DVD and streaming, cast and crew are seen celebrating at the film's premiere, and both filmmakers and some of the fans in attendance comment on what the film means to them. A mother says of her daughter, "I raised her on it—her nursery was Star Wars," and the daughter adds, "When I was a kid I actually wrote to George Lucas and said, 'I want to see more strong females in Star Wars'" ("Bonus Features").

War stories are powerful, and representation of female leadership is both positive and influential. That doesn't discount these films' portrayal of war's devastation—Admiral Holdo's "sacrifice play" is less discussed in media culture than Tony Stark's, for instance, but is no less consequential. And at the conclusion of *Rogue One*, Jyn and all her fellow soldiers are dead, killed one by one fighting the Empire, until finally all that's left is for Jyn and

Figure 7. Cassian Andor (Diego Luna) and Jyn Erso (Felicity Jones) embrace in the face of their oncoming death in *Rogue One*. (Walt Disney Studios, 2016)

Cassian to embrace in the face of an enveloping blast from the Death Star, the ultimate weapon of mass destruction.

Both the MCU and Star Wars tell war stories that bring together a remarkable array of perspectives on conflict, with characters who differ in their backgrounds and skill sets as well as their motivations for, reasoning about, and reactions to combat. Star Wars does this with its representations of who fights, who leads, and what those leadership practices look like. In the MCU, the multiverse takes that idea of inclusion into multiplicity, an exponential sense of identities that have their own stories and their own value. For me, this resonates with a notable characteristic of many contemporary films about actual war. In 2014, I wrote about Iraq War films use of "digital verité," or the inclusion of images and videos that appear within the frame of the larger narrative—soldiers' digital videos in *Stop-Loss* (2008) and *In the Valley of Elah* (2007), Iraqi-produced videos in *The Battle for Hadita* (2007), or the news videos, security camera feed, and video blogs that eventually take over the entire narrative frame of *Redacted* (2007). The use of multiple lenses in such films suggests that "in order to tell a contemporary war story, one must look through more and various lenses while always considering the motives of the framer and the restrictions of the frame itself" ("Lenses into War" 151). That provides what is often literally a broader overall view of war, built from the specificities of differing individual views. To some extent, these expanding crowds of warriors, leaders, and superheroes are functioning as differing lenses or frames into war, with implications for both personal psychology and political response. In fact, what narrative networks such as the MCU accomplish may be something like the "multiplicity of the collective" that Frederic Jameson calls for in war stories, a way of bridging those stories' tendency to focus either on the abstraction of strategy and tactics or the "sense-datum" of the existential experience of war. War is a collective reality, Jameson writes, "a manifold of consciousness as unimaginable as it is real" (1547).

And differing perspectives are literally what keep a cinematic universe going. I have argued that collective imagination is what keeps the story going in works by Iraqi authors like Saadawi, Blasim, and Antoon, and although the devastation is far less, and less affecting, in the MCU and Star Wars than that depicted by these authors writing about their home country and their personal losses, the response to war and loss is somewhat similar. Stories fracture, proliferate, nest within one another, move backward and forward in time, write and rewrite life, injury, and death, while creators build on one another's ideas to keep the story going. The war is never over, but neither is the tale, which is anything but singular.

Conclusion

Drones and the Illusion of Clarity

In the first *Iron Man*, Colonel James Rhodes leads a group of Air Force pilots through a hangar and muses to them about what lies ahead for their branch of the military. "The future of air combat," he asks, "Is it manned, or unmanned?" Although some unmanned aerial vehicles, or UAVs, had been used in the twentieth century, it wasn't until after 9/11 that the US military began slowly and then dramatically increasing their use of combat drones. Now, the drone has become emblematic of this new age of warfare—as much, Jonathan Marcus writes, as the longbow did at Agincourt or the tanks in World War II. But Rhodes is unmoved by the promise of the UAV. "I tell you, in my experience, no unmanned aerial vehicle will ever trump the pilot's instinct, his insight—that ability to look into a situation beyond the obvious and discern its outcome—or a pilot's judgment." The all-male group of pilots facing him would seem to agree. Although Tony Stark walks up and disrupts Rhodes's line of thought —instead of a plane without a pilot, how about "a pilot without a plane?" he asks, referring, the audience knows, to his Iron Man suit—Rhodes's reluctance to embrace the military's newest technology is clear. And why would he want to, when a highly trained, skilled, and courageous pilot can be celebrated for his instinct, insight, and judgment? The pilot can "look into a situation beyond the obvious," beyond what could be just displayed on a screen, perhaps. The pilot can *see*, and thus know both what's happening and what's going to happen.

In Rhodes's words, the pilot's gifts of surveilling sight, probing insight, and use of force combine to make him a formidable warrior, a good guy who won't make the wrong move—a good guy who'll win. It is a sentiment echoed in 2022's *Top Gun: Maverick*, in which Maverick's (Tom Cruise) hypersonic jet program is in danger of being shut down and replaced by drones. That's not, of course, what the audience came to see, and Maverick fights against it. "The end is inevitable, Maverick," Rear Admiral Chester Cain (Ed Harris) tells him. "Your kind is headed for extinction." "Maybe so, sir," Maverick replies. "But not today." And certainly in both the superhero and Star Wars worlds, the soaring flights of Iron Man, Superman, or Luke Skywalker—or Captain Marvel, either with or without her fighter jet—can be a cinematic wonder and an adrenaline-pumping thing to see.

The pilot and the idea of flight have been celebrated not only as central to this kind of heroic narrative but also in terms of military strategy. As Kimberly Dougherty has argued, air warfare has often been considered "cleaner," "because its key elements, quickness and precision, would actually save lives that might otherwise be lost" (2). It was an idea that was particularly seductive given the extensive damage caused by wars in the twentieth century. In fact, however, after aircraft were first used in combat in Libya in 1911, military strategists realized that the opposite was also true. "The imminent power of the airplane," Dougherty writes, "was its ability to attack the industrialized base of a modern nation well beyond the front lines. These ideas were significant because they meant that non-combatants, for the first time, would be systematically targeted in war" (1). Airpower, then, might make war a more targeted exercise—but paradoxically, it also makes war more totalizing.

What happens, then, when you separate not only the soldier from the target, but the soldier from the weapon, and from the entire sphere of battle? It keeps the soldier safe, but, as Thomas Bjerre has argued, it denies the historical association of the male body with "power, strength, and risk-taking." What makes a hero, Bjerre asks, "when war is waged with a joystick by someone thousands of miles out of harm's way?" (2). Hence Rhodes's glib rejection of this new technology, and *Top Gun*'s celebration of pilots with skin in the game. But other war stories aren't so dismissive, especially given drones' increasingly ubiquitous use in violent conflict.

Often, these drone stories have been mass market thrillers like Mike Maden's "Troy Pearce" series, featuring Pearce, the CEO of a private security firm specializing in drones. The title of Dan Fesperman's novel *Unmanned* (2014) indicates more of the issues at play when former F-16 fighter pilot Darwin Cole pivots to drone operation, moving him halfway around the world from his targets but oddly intimate with them, as he watches the heat signatures of his victims react to the strikes—victims that are both intentional and unintentional. As the story develops, he also becomes aware, not to say paranoid, of the military and private organizations using drones and other technologies to follow his every move. "What must it be like," he wonders, "to become an image lodged in the memory of some secret database, your digital signature retrievable by anyone with the proper clearance? More than ever before in his life, Cole now notices all the cameras that seem to be mounted almost everywhere he looks" (8). It's not paranoia, as the saying goes, if they're really watching you, and Cole's experience as well as the novel as a whole highlights technology's role in expanding the battlespaces of contemporary war.

Figure 8. Colonel Katherine Powell (Helen Mirren) confers with a risk assessment officer (Babou Ceesay) about the risk of civilian deaths from a drone strike in *Eye in the Sky*. (Entertainment One, 2016)

Fesperman's novel reads like a thriller, but it touches on some of the ethical considerations specific to drone warfare as well as the psychological effects on the drone pilot—effects noted by stories like NPR's "The Warfare May Be Remote but the Trauma Is Real" (McCammon) from 2017 and the *New York Times*' "The Wounds of the Drone Warrior" (Press) from 2018. The 2015 film *Eye in the Sky* extends the portrayal of the moral quandaries of drone strikes from the pilot up the chain of command, as a British Army Colonel Katherine Powell (Helen Mirren) must deal with the murder of an undercover agent by the militant jihadist group Al-Shabaab. Leaders of the group are meeting in Nairobi and arming two suicide bombers for an attack on civilians. Powell communicates with a drone pilot working out of Creech Air Force Base in Nevada, Second Lieutenant Steve Watts (Aaron Paul), and tells him to prepare a missile strike—but in the meantime, she confers with British Army legal counsel, who advises she track down the UK Foreign Secretary. That leads to the involvement of the US Secretary of State, other lawyers, politicians, and intelligence officers, as well as a risk assessment officer tasked with determining the likelihood of collateral damage. The conversations bounce between people in the UK, Kenya, Nevada, Hawaii, Singapore, and Beijing, highlighting what Susan Carruthers has called "a fascination with the remapped spatial and emotional coordinates in the digital age" (21).

The drone strike is ready to go, but Watts can see a young girl near the target selling bread. Attempts are made to get her to leave the area while the clock ticks down and the suicide bombers are readying their weapons. The risk assessment officer (Babou Ceesay) tells Powell that the risk of civilian deaths—namely, the girl—is 45–65 percent, but Powell tells him that

"I need that calculation to be below 50 percent . . . Sergeant, we need to make this work. Do you understand? We are locked into this kill chain. We have to make a decision. There are many lives at risk." The officer slightly adjusts the parameters of the strike, coming up with a 45 percent chance of collateral damage, and the strike order is then approved by the Minister of State for Foreign Affairs (Jeremy Northam). The faces of everyone involved register the solemnity of the decision, and the strike is executed, resulting in the girl's death. It's an outcome that is tragic but that, *Eye in the Sky* implies, is also necessary. All the complexity of global political and military interplay comes down to a relatively simple equation—the girl's life lost, the bombers' victims saved. In the end, Carruthers argues, this presents all the players in a generally positive rather than negative light. We can be rest assured, she writes, "that our civil and military leaders agonize strenuously over the business of killing" and that "technology has equipped the custodians of our safety with miraculous powers of omniscience" (23). The teams use drone cameras, facial recognition programs, and even a tiny, insect-shaped surveillance drone to literally be a "fly on the wall" of the terrorists. The outcome is sad, but clear—although it's a clarity that real-life drone warfare often lacks, as I discuss below.

Other works offer a sharper critique of the use of drones. Andrew Niccol's film *Good Kill*, released the same year at *Eye in the Sky*, focuses on Major Thomas Egan (Ethan Hawke), a former pilot who now operates drones at Creech Air Force Base near Las Vegas. Similarly, George Brant's play *Grounded*, which premiered in 2013 and has been widely performed in twenty-four different countries, consists of the monologue of The Pilot, whose unexpected pregnancy results in her being reassigned to operate drones, also at Creech. Both protagonists desperately miss being in the sky. Egan hopes that his skills at drone operation will enable him to fly again. His commanding officer, Lieutenant Colonel Jack Johns (Bruce Greenwood), is sympathetic, but as he tells a group of new recruits, drones are here to stay. "We get a lot of shit from the public," he acknowledges. "I've heard all the bleeding-heart arguments, read all the bumper stickers, about how the Air Force is the 'Chair Force' waging a 'Wii war.'" It doesn't matter, he says. "It's all a waste of breath, because the United States Air Force is ordering more drones than jets—excuse me, remotely piloted aircraft—you can call them whatever you want. Drones aren't going anywhere. In fact, they're going everywhere." The drones do indeed go everywhere, while Egan sits in a container unit, watching as the missile strikes kill the figures he targets. On his way home after his shift, when a convenience store clerk asks about his day, he answers in a way that's both glib and devastating: "Blew away six Taliban in

Afghanistan today," he says. "Now I'm going home to barbeque." The clerk, understandably, is nonplussed.

The Pilot in Brant's play is similarly frustrated by the new assignment. She misses "the blue," being alone up in a jet, and though she marries the man who fathered her child and loves both him and her daughter fiercely, she can hardly bear the loss: "I love her and him I do I ignore the tight ball-bearing in my sternum I do for years three years but it grows it grows I'll scream if I don't get out and up I was born for this but I was born for that too I don't can't can't not be there be up alone alone in my sky" (17). She dreams of blue, but all she sees all day at her job is grey—the grey screen, the grey shapes. "A month of grey / Of nothing / Of camera eye searching searching" (38). For Egan and The Pilot, it is both too much and not enough. They miss the risk and the thrill of being up in the air, but they also see too much on their screens. Egan has a wife and kids at home, but he can't relate to them anymore—he barely speaks, drinks too much, won't sleep with his wife, and eventually becomes violent. Paradoxically, coming home safe to their loved ones at the end of the day makes things worse. As The Pilot says,

> Hard to go home tonight
>
> The desert isn't long enough
>
> Still have bodies in my head
>
> I orbit our block a few times
>
> Hope Eric isn't looking out the window
>
> Then I pull up and the door opens and the happy family greets their hero home from the war
>
> Every day
>
> Every day
>
> Every day they greet me home from the war
>
> It would be a different book
>
> *The Odyssey*
>
> If Odysseus came home every day
>
> Every single day
>
> A very different book (42)

The erosion of distinction between home front and war zone is too much to bear. Carruthers argues that in this sense, *Good Kill* makes clear what *American Sniper* elides—that contemporary war continues to increase the distance between soldier and on-the-ground effects of war while paradoxically rendering those two spaces all too similar. Chris Kyle's work as a long-range sniper takes him off the streets and out of house-to-house searches—where, the film suggests, he actually wants to be—while drones extend that distance to thousands of miles. "New technologies that facilitate long-range communication, surveillance, and lethal destruction seem to collapse physical distance while exaggerating psychological detachment," comments Carruthers. "Boundaries between here and there, home and front, civilian and solider have become blurred." In *Good Kill*, there is no "over here" and "over there" anymore. Not only is there no front line anymore, but "home isn't what it used to be either. . . . Not really at war, Egan's not really at home either" (21). Thomas Bjerre notes that the film suggests this blurring from the outset, as aerial shots of the Las Vegas suburb where Egan lives with his family visually resemble the desert landscapes and grids of homes that he scans on the screen, "[eroding] the already unstable battlefront/home front binary further" (12).

In the end, both Egan and The Pilot refuse to obey orders to take a shot—and in doing so, they effectively blow up their own lives. After Egan has been repeatedly ordered to strike targets whose enemy status is unverified, in places like Yemen and Somalia rather than Iraq or Afghanistan, and in situations where women and children become collateral damage, he allows a group of civilians to escape a strike. Egan is then punished by being reassigned to a surveillance-only role, but in what Carruthers rightly calls the film's "murky last act," he happens upon a man that he had earlier observed raping a woman in Afghanistan and manages to ensure that a missile strike kills him (22). He then leaves the base, presumably for good. (As Carruthers notes, ending with Egan's successful vigilante action complicates the clear critique of the drone program that the film advances until that point.) In *Grounded*, The Pilot locks her sights on a target known as The Prophet, but when a small girl runs up to him, The Pilot sees that girl as her daughter, Sam. "It's not his daughter it's mine / It's Sam," she says (60). She pulls violently up on the stick and sends the drone skyward instead of making the shot. But her commander has noticed her erratic behavior and has sent another drone on the mission, which then fires, killing the man and the girl. The Pilot screams in horror. "There is only grey now," she says, "Only the grey" (63). She is apparently court-martialed and institutionalized, and the play ends with her biblically inflected warning:

Know That You Can Keep Me Here Forever You Can Bury Me in a
Bunker of Grey But That Does Not Protect You for One Day it Will
Be Your Turn Your Child's Turn and Yea Though You Mark Each
and Every Door with Blood None of the Guilty Will Be Spared

None

None

None. (64)

As both these works make clear, drones blur distinctions between civilians and combatants as well as those between the home front and the war zone. Grace Miller notes that in *Good Kill*, "Noncombatants such as women and children often run into the frame just before or after Egan has fired a missile he is now powerless to stop. . . . And, troublingly, as the camera and the capability to strike become synonymous, the body and the camera begin to intersect, further blurring the lines between war and domesticity, between combatant and noncombatant" (11). In *Grounded*, when The Pilot "begins to see her home merge with the desert home of the adversary," Kimberly Dougherty writes that this is often read as evidence of her mental breakdown. She argues, however, "that reading this phenomenon through the trope of home shows Brant's concern with the ubiquity of surveillance, the rapid proliferation of drones, and the possibility that this technology will rebound back onto its users" (179).

Despite *Good Kill*'s ending with an episode of drone-enabled violent justice, both that film and *Grounded* critique the implications of drone warfare for everyone involved. As Lieutenant Colonel Johns says, they are indeed "going everywhere." That combination of vision, distance, and lethal power is destructive for the soldiers and certainly for the civilians who wander into a targeted area. *Good Kill* makes much of the fact that Egan knows some of his targets are merely suspected enemy, that some are obviously civilian, and that he can even recognize a particular rapist when he sees him in a different context. In this sense, despite the film's differences in tone and ideology from *American Sniper*, they share the premise that the one who targets can *see*, and see with precision and detail. Isabelle Freda writes that *American Sniper* "repeatedly situates the spectator alongside the line of sight of the sniper, using not only point-of-view editing but also the subjective shot, as when we are given a shot of the view through the rifle scope's cross-hairs. Again and again we are aligned with this look through the telescopic sighting device, the extraordinary visual prosthesis," a prosthesis that allows Kyle to make the seemingly impossible 2,100-yard shot that kills his nemesis Mustafa—and to see and *know* that this is the person that he's killing (234). In these films, as well as in *Eye in the Sky*, to see through the rifle scope, or on the drone screen, is to see clearly, whether you believe the killing you're doing is right or wrong.

The end of *Grounded*, however, calls this certainty into question. The Pilot knows the girl on the screen is her daughter and refers to her as having been "slaughtered" when she's in the institution (63). This may indeed be a mental breakdown, but it is also Brant's commentary on the consequences of all that grey. How much can drone operators really see? Not as much as films like *Good Kill* suggest, as it turns out. Carruthers refers to Sonia Kennebeck's 2016 documentary *National Bird*, which features comments from former drone operators about how grainy and indistinct the UAV video feed can be. Heather Linebaugh, who worked in Air Force intelligence, finds statements made by politicians or the military about "precision" or "surgical" drone strikes "completely ridiculous . . . completely ludicrous." She shows an example of video that's about the best quality you can get, and as a number of blurry figures move in the distance, she says, "I'd say there are at least two possible . . . possible children." It's that hard to tell. In an essay for *The Guardian* in 2013, she writes that

> What the public needs to understand is that the video provided by a drone is not usually clear enough to detect someone carrying a weapon, even on a crystal-clear day with limited cloud and perfect light. This makes it incredibly difficult for the best analysts to identify if someone has weapons for sure. One example comes to mind: "The feed is so pixelated, what if it's a shovel, and not a weapon?" I felt this confusion constantly, as did my fellow UAV analysts. We always wonder if we killed the right people, if we endangered the wrong people, if we destroyed an innocent civilian's life all because of a bad image or angle.

The end of *National Bird* focuses on the victims of drone strikes in Afghanistan, including a mother who lost a husband and two children, and another son who lost a leg, in a strike that took place on February 21, 2010, and hit a caravan of families traveling home from a funeral, ultimately killing twenty-three. "We often hear that drones can see everything by day and by night," one of the men says, who lost a leg in the attack. "That's what pains me. You can see the difference between a needle and an ant, but not people?" Later, the camera lingers on shelves of patient records at a medical facility, files for hundreds of male amputees.

Lisa Ling was a technical sergeant and worked on something called the DCGS, the Distributed Common Ground System, which the Air Force describes like this: "The Air Force Distributed Common Ground System

(AF DCGS), also referred to as the AN/GSQ-272 SENTINEL weapon system, is the Air Force's primary intelligence, surveillance and reconnaissance (ISR) planning and direction, collection, processing and exploitation, analysis and dissemination (PCPAD) weapon system. The weapon system employs a global communications architecture that connects multiple intelligence platforms and sensors. Airmen assigned to AF DCGS produce actionable intelligence from data collected by a variety of sensors on the U-2, RQ-4 Global Hawk, MQ-1 Predator, MQ-9 Reaper and other ISR platforms." Ling marvels at what this all means. "This is global," she emphasizes. "This is getting information anywhere, at any time, shooting people from anywhere, at any time. And it's not just one person sitting there with a little remote control, a little joystick, moving around a plane that's halfway across the world. That's not all it is. It's like borders don't matter anymore." The lethal power is immense, but as *National Bird* argues, attacks are often undertaken with hazy visual information at best and guesses about what indistinct figures are likely to do rather than clear evidence about what they have done—rather like the "Project Insight" that Steve Rogers objects to in *Captain America: The Winter Soldier*.

Phil Klay followed *Redeployment*, his collection of short stories, with a novel titled *Missionaries* (2020) that similarly emphasizes globalized warfare, permeable national borders, and the real-life illegibility of violence and its many vectors. It is a portrait of "endless, invisible war," as the subtitle of his 2022 collection of essays puts it, and the novel goes beyond *Redeployment*'s grouping of varied, individual portraits as well as what Jennifer Haytock has called the "multivoiced novels" of the wars, in which authors present "at least two (if not more) first-person narrators from opposing sides of the conflicts" ("Reframing" 338). Haytock is thinking of books like Benedict's *Sand Queen*, Joydeep Roy-Bhattacharya's *The Watch* (2012), and Michael Pitre's *Fives and Twenty-Fives* (2014), all of which include points of view from both American and Iraqi or Afghan characters. But as Brian Williams has noted, such an approach still maintains a focus on nationhood and often a "soldier-Other" binary, while the "Global War on Terror" and contemporary globalized conflict and militarization demand a more complex narrative structure ("War's Implications").

The narrative structure of *Missionaries* certainly is complex, so much so that the plot is difficult to summarize. Williams notes that global novels generally focus on convergences and networks of influence, the play of contingency and complicity, more so than deep-dive portraits of individuals, and mentions scholars' work on novelists such as David Mitchell and Zadie Smith. "Rather than simply including non-American perspectives," Williams argues, "these works recognize that that addressing the Global War on Terror demands narratives that not only decenter the American experience but destabilize the very idea of nations and national belonging. These new war texts focus on spillage, the transnational consequences of national acts, and the ways that local populaces outside the immediate war zone or American home front both are shaped by American interventions and in turn shape them to fit local conditions" (82). These global or systems novels are necessarily very different in their emphases, and to some degree in affect, than the deep dives into a single character's war experience, like those by Kyle, Powers, or Fountain that I have covered in this book, though in Klay's case the focus on war as a system that is both globalized and contingent makes it a significant work to consider.

Missionaries centers primarily on the Colombian civil war, and the attempt in 2016 to move toward a peace agreement between the government, far-right paramilitary groups, and far-left guerilla groups. ("Klay's understanding of Colombia, the main theater of war in 'Missionaries,' is the chief source of admiration for this reviewer," noted Juan Gabriel Vásquez in the *New York Times*. "There are no simple wars, of course, but the Colombian conflict is as intricate as they come.") The novel toggles between different places and times, and four different first-person narrators: Abel, a Colombian boy who becomes a paramilitary lieutenant; Lisette, an American war correspondent who is mistaken for CIA and kidnapped while in Colombia; Juan Pablo, an officer in the Colombian special forces; and Mason, an American Special Forces operative with a variety of military experience. Even as the characters' orbits begin to draw together, it is not with the satisfying click of puzzle pieces that one might find in, say, a murder mystery or detective novel. Instead, as Williams puts it, "Multiplicity, chaos, and contingency rather than causality are intrinsic to understanding any specific events, and at best we can argue that Klay has crafted a narrative in which every player is implicated, even if no one person is to blame" (89). The complexity and contingency are perhaps exemplified by a complicated plot development: Juan Pablo's daughter Valencia and her friend Sara listen to a woman named Alma describe a brutal rape that occurred on the orders of Jefferson, a paramilitary leader. They mistakenly believe Jefferson to be responsible for Lisette's kidnapping (though she was actually kidnapped by Jefferson's enemies). In response, they tweet out an image of Jefferson with accusations of the kidnapping and other crimes. Although Jefferson had already secured Lisette's release from the kidnappers, the tweet causes the Colombian military to target him. He dies—as does Alma, when Jefferson's organization seeks reprisal for her testimony.

Klay's portrait of violence is vast and intricately woven, but impossible for any one character to parse—no one person knows exactly what's happening or why. Lisette, who makes her living as a journalist sifting through bits of information to craft a story, can't do it with her own story. "I don't know what happened to me," she says. "So what did she have that she could write about? Some shitty things that happened to her. But shitty things happened to people all the time. It doesn't make a story" (384). Williams writes that this realization is at the heart of Klay's project: "She sees her own agency as a causal factor in a much larger story: one whose discovery demands embrace of of the unknown as a catalyst for a new type of pluralist narrative; one where the struggle to understand is grounded in the recognition that such understanding is forever beyond our perspectives, that contingency and chance escape the narratives we attempt to craft yet we must struggle with such contingencies as a recognition of our culpability within the world systems that continue warfare in all its guises" (94).

In this sense, Klay's latest work not only expands the scope of the contemporary war novel, but also shows how globalized war exemplifies this lack of delineation and its devastating effects—and is a confusion and a fragmentation that can occur on an even greater scale in addition to the personal and national levels. It is a level of realism that is often not found in popular treatments of war, because it lacks the narrative satisfaction that comes from a combination of clarity and the use of force. Isabelle Freda highlights that distinction between clarity and realism when she contrasts *American Sniper*'s representation of clear—but limited—weaponized vision with the complex, intersecting vectors of vision and information in *The Hurt Locker*. Bigelow, she points out, avoids Eastwood's repeated use of classical "line of sight" shots and instead makes use of a number of other strategies: "working with Super-16mm film to render a grainy realism to the footage; shooting on location in Jordan and using Iraqis as extras; utilizing a unique sound and editing design and, finally, the strategic, and effective, use of hand-held camera and multiple camera set-ups.... Bigelow places the spectator alongside her protagonist in the midst of a *mise-en-scene* which is confusing and in which sightlines are anything but clear" (233). In the Introduction, I talked about the visual and narrative fragmentation of *The Hurt Locker* as reflective of Sergeant James's rewired temporal rhythms, his sense of personal fragmentation and disassociation. But as with many of the works I have addressed, fragmentation is multivalent, and the visual fragmentation evident in the film is also a denial of the more simplified clarity of *American Sniper*. As Freda writes about Chris Kyle and compares him with James of *The Hurt Locker*, "One is precise, the other complex and variegated; one targets, the other must think. One is a clear confrontation solved by the narrowing of sightline and the other is complex, unclear, operating in a space that is lacking in legibility" (234). James takes in a great deal of information each time he refuses to use a remotely operated bomb disposal robot and instead walks into the field himself. He makes mistakes, but they are "born of his own intelligence, and his own character—and character flaws." Chris Kyle is instead "trapped in an apparatus of precision, like his drone counterparts" (236).

The Hurt Locker isn't the only contemporary war story to embrace complicated lines of sight, whether literally or figuratively. With their emphases on all kinds of blurred boundaries and fragmentation, the works I have covered in this book become layered, complex, and, as these observations about drones suggest, more reflective of the lack of clarity endemic to the use of force. Any fan of horror movies would tell you that it's not what you can see, it's what you can't. Saadawi ends *Frankenstein in Baghdad* with the "specter of an unknown man" moving quietly in a ruined hotel room, petting an aging cat (280). Is this the *shesma*, the Whatsitsname, the reanimated collection of body parts stitched together by Hadi but operated like a drone, as it were, by the soul of a dead man? Or is the creature a fiction, also stitched together by Hadi as he tells his story to others, and sent out in the world to do as it will? It depends on where you're looking and on who you ask. Brian Turner ends *My Life as a Foreign Country* with Sgt. Turner, who is dead, and who sometimes walks the streets of Mosul but tonight is sitting in a connex, "each hand gripping the controls, his thumb on the safety, index finger over the trigger, with a bank of monitors arrayed before him, streams of remote data computed and digitized into analytics an air force officer considers while drinking from a twenty-ounce bottle of Mountain Dew at the desk behind him" (199). Coded targets are listed on the dry erase board, and he lowers the nose of the Predator drone as it approaches its objective—a house in Florida, where Turner and his wife sleep. The dead Sgt. Turner maintains a standoff distance from the living Turner but continues to monitor, collect data, change angles, and keep his hand on the trigger. Which one is the "real" Turner, and who is haunting whom? It depends on what you think Turner makes of his life and his war experience, and which of the many stories in the memoir that you respond to with the most acuity.

In the earliest works about the Iraq War, soldiers often compared this new war to older ones—the things that made the Iraq War similar or different from the Vietnam War, or at least the movies they had seen about the Vietnam War. Colby Buzzell, who wrote one of the first blogs about the Iraq War when he was in the field, remembers returning fire and yelling "*Get some!*" as he does so, "like they do in the movies," he adds (135). And he wants to put speakers on the Strykers and play loud music, like in "*Apocalypse Now*, when they had the speakers hooked up to the Air Cav helicopters" (208). Now, in this second wave of contemporary war stories, artists also contemplate what it means when war shows up in a new world—but this time, the world is your own, and it's yours whether you're soldier or civilian, American or Iraqi. Spatial or temporal distance becomes meaningless, and war lives with you. What happens next, then, is up to those who continue to tell the tale. War may be the oldest story in the book, but for those grappling with its implications and effects, there is always a new chapter.

Notes

Introduction

1. Aaron DeRosa and I discuss this event and its implications in more detail in "Enduring Operations: Narratives of the Contemporary Wars," our introduction to a 2017 special issue of *Modern Fiction Studies*.
2. The works I cover in *Welcome to the Suck* are all about the Iraq War. Even though the war in Afghanistan began a year and a half before the Iraq War, it inspired very few representations in the early years, leading Brian Castner to call the conflict "a stage without a play." Even now the Iraq War far outpaces Afghanistan in this regard.

Chapter 4: Imagining an Archive

1. In this chapter, Arabic titles, names, and terms are transliterated using the standards set by the *International Journal of Middle East Studies*. The exceptions are the names and titles associated with the three primary authors covered in this chapter: Ahmed Saadawi, Hassan Blasim, and Sinan Antoon. Because I am quoting from the published translations of these authors' works, all terms and names, including the authors' own, are rendered as they are in those publications.
2. This is a narrative characteristic that many Western readers might associate with *Alf laylah wa laylah*, or *One Thousand and One Nights*, sometimes known in English as the *Arabian Nights*, from the title of the first English-language edition. The collection of stories dates back to at least the early ninth century; in what exists now only as a fragment, Sheherazade is prompted to begin telling tales. In the frame story, Sheherazade tells tale after tale to her husband to keep him entertained and thus prevent him from killing her. The ensuing stories have a rich and varied ancestry. "Though the names of its chief characters are Iranian, the frame story is probably Indian, and the largest proportion of names is Arabic. The tales' variety and geographical range of origin—India, Iran, Iraq, Egypt, Turkey, and possible Greece—make single authorship unlikely" ("The Thousand and One Nights"). The particular stories that many Western readers associate with the book, however—Aladdin, Ali Baba, and Sinbad the Sailor—were added to the collection only in the eighteenth century, and only in European adaptations, and so are not Middle Eastern in origin.
3. It is not entirely clear why Wadood makes this slight clarification, or for that matter why Antoon titles the book *Fihris* rather than *Fihrist*. Some scholars have conjectured that al-Nadīm was Persian, which is not at all certain, but it is notable that he chooses the "rather rare Persian word *pehrest/fehrest/fehres/fahrasat*" for the title of his book on Arabic literature (Sellheim et al.). The "t" may give the word a more Persian connotation, and perhaps Wadood wishes to contradict that.

Chapter 5: The Fantasy of Endless War

1. Of course there is a robust body of scholarship about the original comics, which grappled with 9/11 in some pretty direct ways—Marvel's "Civil War" and

"Secret Invasion" sequences, DC Comic's "Final Crisis" and "Blackest Night"—though for my purposes here I will focus on the films.

2. The 2018 animated film *Into the Spider-Verse* focuses on Miles Morales, who becomes Spider-Man and also meets many other versions of Spider-Man from other dimensions—travel between them has been made possible by Wilson Fisk, who is trying to find a universe that will enable him to be with his late wife and son. *Spider-Man: No Way Home* (2021) does something similar, as Spider-Mans played by Tom Holland, Andrew Garfield, and Tobey Maguire all interact with each other when dimensional portals are opened. Although Spider-Man appears in many MCU films, these mentioned here are not considered part of the MCU, as they are distributed by Sony Pictures and the character is currently owned by Sony.

3. Paul Verhoeven's adaptation of Robert Heinlein's novel *Starship Troopers* (1997) is an interesting case, because both the novel and the film depict co-ed armed forces who seem to take little notice of gender difference in combat situations. The film includes a scene showing both male and female soldiers showering together without indications of sexual attraction or embarrassment. The film, however, can be understood as a satire of hypermilitarism and the fascistic tendencies of the military-industrial complex, and so it is hard to separate the gender dynamics from that larger context. That is, the film might suggest that such a smoothly integrated military is as much science fiction as fighting giant space bugs.

4. Rotten Tomatoes, for their part, defended the authenticity of their review scores and dismissed claims about bots manipulating the scores as "nonsense" (Cain). Such controversies, however, led the website to introduce a "verified audience" feature in 2019, designed to boost confidence in its numbers "at a time when some online trolls have tried to game the system, trashing movies they may have never seen" (Lee).

Works Cited

ACLU. *War Comes Home: The Excessive Militarization of American Policing*. New York: ACLU, 2014. https://www.aclu.org/report.

Air Force Distributed Common Ground System. U.S. Air Force, October 2015. https://www.af.mil/About-Us/Fact-Sheets/Display/Article/104525/.

Alexander, Julia. "Star Wars: The Last Jedi Is Being Review-Bombed on Rotten Tomatoes (Update)." Polygon.com, December 21, 2017. https://www.polygon.com/2017/12/18/16792184/.

Alkyam, Sami. "The Trauma of the Archive in Sinan Antoon's Novel *Fihris*." *Journal of Literature and Trauma Studies* 7, no. 1 (2018): 49–69.

Al-Masri, Khaled. "The Politics and Poetics of Madness in Hassan Blasim's *The Madman of Freedom Square*." *Journal of Arabic Literature* 49 (2018): 271–95.

American Sniper. Directed by Clint Eastwood, performances by Bradley Cooper and Sienna Miller. Warner Brothers, 2014.

Andreescu, Florentina. "War, Trauma, and the Militarized Body." *Subjectivity* 9, no. 2 (2016): 205–23.

Antoon, Sinan. "The Arabic Prose Poem." In *The Edinburgh Companion to the Prose Poem*, edited by Mary Ann Caws and Michel Delville, 281–94. Edinburgh: Edinburgh University Press, 2021.

Antoon, Sinan. *The Book of Collateral Damage*. Translated by Jonathan Wright. New Haven, CT: Yale University Press, 2019.

Antoon, Sinan. *The Corpse Washer*. Translated by Sinan Antoon. New Haven, CT: Yale University Press, 2014.

Apocalypse Now. Directed by Francis Ford Coppola, performances by Martin Sheen and Marlon Brando. Paramount, 1979.

Arkin, William M. "Why America Can't End Its 'Forever Wars.'" *Newsweek*, April 12, 2021. https://www.newsweek.com/.

Atia, Nadia. "The Figure of the Refugee in Hassan Blasim's 'The Reality and the Record.'" *The Journal of Commonwealth Literature* 54, no. 3 (2019): 319–33.

Auriemma, Alysa. "'I Can't Trust My Own Mind': How the Marvel Cinematic Universe Engages with Trauma." *TheMarySue*, June 28, 2016. https://www.themarysue.com/mcu-trauma/.

Avatar. Directed by James Cameron, performances by Sam Worthington and Zoe Saldaña. 20th Century Fox, 2009.

The Avengers. Directed by Joss Whedon, performances by Chris Evans, Robert Downey Jr., Scarlett Johannsen, and Tom Hiddleston. Marvel Studios, 2012.

The Avengers: Age of Ultron. Directed by Joss Whedon, performances by Robert Downey Jr., Chris Hemsworth, and Mark Ruffalo. Marvel Studios, 2015.

Baron, Reuben. "The MCU's Relationship with the Military, from *Iron Man* to *Captain Marvel*." *CBR*, March 16, 2019. https://www.cbr.com/.

Barrett, Alec. "Too Real for the Big Screen?" *Harvard Political Review*, May 25, 2010. https://harvardpolitics.com/.

Benedict, Helen. *Sand Queen*. New York: Soho Press, 2011.

Billy Lynn's Long Halftime Walk. Directed by Ang Lee, performances by Joe Alwyn, Kristen Stewart, and Vin Diesel. TriStar Pictures, 2016.

"Billy Lynn's Long Halftime Walk." *BoxOfficeMojo.* https://www.boxofficemojo.com/releasegroup/gr4043198981/.

Bjerre, Thomas Ærvold. "Unmanned? Military Masculinities in Filmic Representations of U.S. Drone Operators." *Men and Masculinities* 26, no. 1 (2022): 24–43. https://doi.org/10.1177/1097184X221139820.

Bradley, James, with Ron Powers. *Flags of Our Fathers.* New York: Bantam Books, 2000.

Blasim, Hassan. *The Corpse Exhibition and Other Stories of Iraq.* Translated by Jonathan Wright. New York: Penguin, 2014.

"Bonus Features." *Rogue One: A Star Wars Story,* directed by Glen Milner, Lucasfilm, 2016.

Bourne, Daniel. "A Conversation with Tim O'Brien." *Artful Dodge Magazine,* October 2, 1991. https://artfuldodge.spaces.wooster.edu/interviews/tim-obrien/.

Brant, George. *Grounded.* New York: Samuel French, 2014.

Bresnan, Mark. "'Bluffers and Blowhards': Speaking of Violence in Ben Fountain's *Billy Lynn's Long Halftime Walk.*" In *Violence in Literature,* edited by Stacey Peebles, 168–81. Hackensack, NJ: Salem Press, 2014.

Breznican, Anthony. "*The Mandalorian:* Rosario Dawson Tells All about Ahsoka Tano." *Vanity Fair,* November 30, 2020. https://www.vanityfair.com/hollywood/2020/11/.

Brooker, Will. *Star Wars* (BFI Film Classics). London: Palgrave, 2009.

Brown, Jeffrey. *The Modern Superhero in Film and Television.* New York: Routledge, 2017.

Brown, Jeffrey. "#wheresRey: Feminism, Protest, and Merchandising Sexism in *Star Wars: The Force Awakens.*" *Feminist Media Studies* 18, no. 3 (2018): 335–48.

Buchanan, David. *Going Scapegoat: Post-9/11 War Literature, Language and Culture.* Jefferson, NC: McFarland, 2016.

Buzzell, Colby. *My War: Killing Time in Iraq.* New York: Berkeley Caliber, 2006.

Cain, Rob. "Rotten Tomatoes Says Its 55% 'Star Wars: The Last Jedi' Audience Score Is Authentic." *Forbes,* December 20, 2017. https://www.forbes.com/sites/robcain/2017/12/20/.

Calia, Michael. "Carrie Fisher on Her Return to 'Star Wars.'" *The Wall Street Journal,* December 2, 2015. https://www.wsj.com/articles/.

Canavan, Gerry. "Wakanda Forever? On Ryan Coogler's *Black Panther* (2018)." In *Contemporary American Science Fiction Film,* edited by Terence McSweeney and Stuart Joy, 209–22. New York: Routledge, 2022.

Captain America: The First Avenger. Directed by Joe Johnston, performances by Chris Evans, Hayley Atwell, and Sebastian Stan. Marvel Studios, 2011.

Captain America: Civil War. Directed by Anthony Russo and Joe Russo, performances by Chris Evans, Robert Downey Jr., and Sebastian Stan. Marvel Studios, 2016.

Captain America: The Winter Soldier. Directed by Anthony Russo and Joe Russo, performances by Chris Evans, Sebastian Stan, and Scarlett Johannsen. Marvel Studios, 2014.

Captain Marvel. Directed by Anna Boden and Ryan Fleck, performances by Brie Larson and Samuel L. Jackson. Marvel Studios, 2019.

Caputo, Philip. *A Rumor of War*. New York: Holt, Rinehart and Winston, 1977.

Carruthers, Susan L. "Detached Retina: The New Cinema of Drone Warfare." *Cineaste* 41, no. 4 (2016): 20–25.

Castner, Brian. "Afghanistan: A Stage without a Play." *Los Angeles Review of Books*, October 2, 2014. https://lareviewofbooks.org/article/.

Castner, Brian. *The Long Walk: A Story of War and the Life That Follows*. New York: Anchor, 2012.

Cettl, Franciska. "Staying with the Paradox of *Avatar*: Decolonising Science/Fiction." *Science Fiction Film and Television* 12, no. 2 (2019): 225–40.

"Chapter 13: The Jedi." *The Mandalorian*, Season 2, episode 5, Golem Creations/ Lucasfilm, November 27, 2020.

Cheshire, Godfrey. "Billy Lynn's Long Halftime Walk." *RogerEbert.com*, November 11, 2016. https://www.rogerebert.com/reviews/.

Chivers, C. J. "An Iraq Veteran's Homecoming, with Arias." *New York Times Magazine*, July 10, 2015. https://www.nytimes.com/2015/07/10/magazine/.

Cleckley, Julia Jeter, with M. L. Doyle. *A Promise Fulfilled: My Life as a Wife and Mother, Soldier and General Officer*. CreateSpace Independent Publishing Platform, 2014.

Coming Home. Directed by Hal Ashby, performances by Jane Fonda, Jon Voight, and Bruce Dern. United Artists, 1978.

Crawford, Neta C. "The Iraq War Has Cost the U.S. Nearly \$2 Trillion." *MilitaryTimes*, February 6, 2020. https://www.militarytimes.com/opinion /commentary/2020/02/06/.

Creed, Barbara. *The Monstrous-Feminine: Film, Feminism, and Psychoanalysis*. New York: Routledge, 1993.

Da 5 Bloods. Directed by Spike Lee, performances by Delroy Lindo and Chadwick Boseman. Netflix, 2020.

Dances with Wolves. Directed by Kevin Costner, performances by Kevin Costner, Mary McDonnell, and Graham Greene. Orion Pictures, 1990

Darda, Joseph. "The Ethnicization of Veteran America: Larry Heinemann, Toni Morrison, and Military Whiteness after Vietnam." *Contemporary Literature* 57, no. 3 (2016): 410–40.

Darda, Joseph. "Military Whiteness." *Critical Inquiry* 45 (2018): 76–96.

Dargis, Manohla. "'Star Wars: The Last Jedi' Embraces the Magic and the Mystery." *New York Times*, December 12, 2017. https://www.nytimes.com/2017/12/12 /movies/.

Deer, Patrick. "Beyond Recovery: Representing History and Memory in Iraq War Writing." *Modern Fiction Studies* 63, no. 2 (2017): 312–35.

Deer, Patrick. "Mapping Contemporary American War Culture." *College Literature* 43, no. 1 (2016): 48–90.

The Deer Hunter. Directed by Michael Cimino, performances by Robert DeNiro and Christopher Walken. Universal Pictures, 1978.

Del Barco, Mandalit. "Movie Review: 'Andor.'" *NPR*, November 23, 2022. https:// www.npr.org/2022/11/23/1139078092/.

Devi, Sharmila. "Ahmed Saadawi on Being an Artist 'In Iraq's Chaotic Boiler Room.'" *The Arab Weekly*, September 9, 2018. https://thearabweekly.com/.

DeYoung, Karen, Dan Lamouthe, John Hudson, and Karoun Demirjian. "America's 20-Year War in Afghanistan Ends as Last U.S. Military Cargo Plane Lumbers

into the Sky over Kabul." *Washington Post*, August 30, 2021. https://www
.washingtonpost.com/national-security/us-afghanistan-longest-war-ends/2021
/08/30/.

Doctor Strange. Directed by Scott Derrickson, performances by Benedict Cumberbatch and Tilda Swinton. Marvel Studios, 2016.

Doctor Strange in the Multiverse of Madness. Directed by Sam Raimi, performances
by Benedict Cumberbatch, Elizabeth Olsen, and Xochitl Gomez. Marvel Studios, 2022.

Dougherty, Kimberly K. *Airpower in Literature: Interrogating the Clean War, 1915–2015.*
Lanham, MD: Lexington Books, 2022.

Dyer, Geoff. "America's Team." *New York Times*, May 18, 2012. https://www.nytimes
.com/2012/05/20/books/review/.

Ebert, Roger. "The Force Has Left the Building." *Rogerebert.com*, August 14, 2008.
https://www.rogerebert.com/reviews/.

Eisler, David F. *Writing Wars: Authorship and American War Fiction, WWI to Present.* Iowa City: University of Iowa Press, 2022.

El-Ariss, Tarek. "Majnun Strikes Back: Crossings of Madness and Homosexuality
in Contemporary Arabic Literature." *International Journal of Middle East Studies*
45 (2013): 293–312.

Ellerhoff, Steve Gronert. "Rebellion in Star Wars: Forty Years of Princess Leia and
the Rebel Alliance." In *Rebellion*, edited by Robert C. Evans, 223–40. Hackensack, NJ: Salem Press, 2017.

Erb, Cynthia. "A Spiritual Blockbuster: *Avatar*, Environmentalism, and the New
Religions." *Journal of Film and Video* 66, no. 3 (2014): 3–17.

Everett, Jim A., M. J. Crockett, and David A. Pizarro. "Inference of Trustworthiness
from Intuitive Moral Judgments." *Journal of Experimental Psychology* 145, no. 6
(2016): 722–87.

Eye in the Sky. Directed by Gavin Hood, performances by Helen Mirren and Aaron
Paul. Entertainment One, 2015.

Fallon, Siobhan. *The Confusion of Languages.* New York: Putnam's Sons, 2017.

Fallon, Siobhan. *You Know When the Men Are Gone.* New York: Henry Holt, 2011.

Fesperman, Dan. *Unmanned.* New York: Vintage, 2014.

Filkins, Dexter. *The Forever War.* New York: Knopf, 2008

Filkins, Dexter. "The Long Road Home." *New York Times*, March 6, 2014. https://
www.nytimes.com/2014/03/09/books/review/.

First Blood. Directed by Ted Kotcheff, performances by Sylvester Stallone and Brian
Dennehy. Orion Pictures, 1982.

Flags of Our Fathers. Directed by Clint Eastwood, performances by Ryan Phillippe
and Adam Beach. Paramount Pictures, 2006.

Fountain, Ben. *Billy Lynn's Long Halftime Walk.* New York: Ecco, 2012.

Fountain, Ben. "Soldiers on the Fault Line: War, Rhetoric, and Reality." *War, Literature, and the Arts* 25 (2013): 1–14.

Fox, Rachel. "Capturing Iraq: Optical Focalization in Contemporary War Cinematography." *Interventions* 20, no. 4 (2018): 470–87.

Freda, Isabelle. "Screening War: American Sniper, Hurt Locker, and Drone Vision."
International Journal of Contemporary Iraqi Studies 10, no. 3 (2017): 229–39.

Gallagher, Matt. "Where's the Great Novel about the War on Terror?" *The Atlantic*,
June 14, 2011. https://www.theatlantic.com/entertainment/archive/2011/06/.

Gaouette, Nicole, and Steve Visser. "Dallas Police Shooter a Reclusive Army Reservist." *CNN.com*, July 11, 2016. https://www.cnn.com/2016/07/08/us/.

The Gilder-Lehrman Institute of American History. "The Vietnam War: Military Statistics." https://www.gilderlehrman.org/.

Gill, Glen Robert. "Re-envisioning Myth in *Star Wars: Episode VII: The Force Awakens*." *The Journal of Religion and Popular Culture* 31, no. 1 (2019): 3–15.

Gilman, Owen W., Jr. *The Hell of War Comes Home: Imaginative Texts from the Conflicts in Afghanistan and Iraq*. Jackson: University Press of Mississippi, 2018.

"Glorious Purpose." *Loki*, Season 1, episode 1, directed by Kate Herron, performances by Tom Hiddleston and Owen Wilson. Marvel Studios, June 9, 2021.

Good Kill. Directed by Andrew Niccol, performances by Ethan Hawke and Bruce Greenwood. IFC Films, 2015.

Goodwin, Nicole. *Warcries*. CreateSpace Independent Publishing Platform, 2016.

Goolsby, Jesse. "A Group Conversation with Veteran Artists David Abrams, Jerri Bell, Brian Castner, and Colin Halloran." *War, Literature, and the Arts* 28 (2016): 1–16.

Gregory, Derek. "The Everywhere War." *The Geographical Journal* 177, no. 3 (2011): 238–50.

The Green Berets. Directed by John Wayne and Ray Kellogg, performances by John Wayne and David Janssen. Warner Brothers, 1968.

Hagley, Annika, and Michael Harrison. "Fighting the Battles We Never Could: The Avengers and Post-September 11 American Political Identities." *PS, Political Science & Politics* 47, no.1 (2014): 120–24.

Harrigan, Kathleen. "Author Spotlight: Siobhan Fallon Interviewed by Kathleen Harrigan." *War, Literature, and the Arts* 23 (2011): 175–86.

Haytock, Jennifer. "Reframing War Stories: Multivoiced Novels of the Wars in Iraq and Afghanistan." *Modern Fiction Studies* 63, no. 2 (2017): 336–54.

Haytock, Jennifer. "Women's/War Stories: The Female Gothic and Women's War Trauma in Helen Benedict's *Sand Queen*." *War, Literature, and the Arts* 27 (2015): 1–17.

Heath, Vicki. "Reporter Vicki Heath in Conversation with Hassan Blasim and Translator Jonathan Wright." *The Reading Group of Zesto*, February 9, 2018. https://zestoakoirakurletaldea-wordpress-com.translate.goog/2018/02/09/v.

Heberle, Mark. *A Trauma Artist: Tim O'Brien and the Fiction of Vietnam*. Iowa City: University of Iowa Press, 2001.

Hediger, Ryan. "Uncanny Homesickness and War: Loss of Affect, Loss of Place, and Reworlding in *Redeployment*." In *Affective Ecocriticism*, edited by Kyle Bladow and Jennifer Ladino, 155–74. Lincoln: University of Nebraska Press, 2018.

Heinemann, Larry. *Paco's Story*. London: Faber and Faber, 1987.

Heller, Joseph. *Catch-22*. New York: Scribner, 1955.

Hellmann, John. *American Myth and the Legacy of Vietnam*. New York: Columbia University Press, 1986.

Herr, Michael. *Dispatches*. New York: Knopf, 1977.

Holland, Jessica. "A Nightmare of Violence and Terror." *Guernica*, May 1, 2014. https://www.guernicamag.com/.

The Hurt Locker. Directed by Kathryn Bigelow, performances by Jeremy Renner, Anthony Mackie, and Brian Geraghty. Voltage Pictures, 2009.

Hynes, Samuel. *The Soldiers' Tale: Bearing Witness to Modern War*. New York: Penguin, 1997.

Iğsiz, Asil. "Interview with Sinan Antoon." *1508 [A Blog Where Poetry Lives]*. The University of Arizona Poetry Center, November 30, 2010. https://poetry.arizona .edu/blog/interview-sinan-antoon.

In the Valley of Elah. Directed by Paul Haggis, performances by Tommy Lee Jones, Charlize Theron, and Susan Sarandon. Warner Independent Pictures, 2007.

Iron Man. Directed by Jon Favreau, performances by Robert Downey Jr. and Jeff Bridges. Marvel Studios, 2008.

Iron Man 3. Directed by Shane Black, performances by Robert Downey Jr., Gwyneth Paltrow, and Don Cheadle. Marvel Studios, 2013.

Irwin, Robert, ed. *Night and Horses and the Desert: An Anthology of Classical Arabic Literature*. New York: Overlook Press, 1999.

Ismay, John. "The True Story of the First Woman to Finish Special Forces Training." *New York Times Magazine*, February 28, 2020. https://www.nytimes.com/2020 /02/28/magazine/.

Jameson, Frederic. "War and Representation." *PMLA* 124, no. 5 (2009): 1532–47.

Jammes, Lucie. "An Interview with Phil Klay." *Transatlantica* 1 (2017). https://doi.org /10.4000/transatlantica.8951.

Jeffords, Susan. *The Remasculinization of America: Gender and the Vietnam War*. Bloomington: Indiana University Press, 1989.

Johnson, Shoshana, with M. L. Doyle. *I'm Still Standing: From Captive U.S. Soldier to Free Citizen—My Journey Home*. New York: Touchstone, 2011.

Johnston, Carrie. "Postwar Reentry Narratives in Leslie Marmon Silko's *Ceremony* and Ben Fountain's *Billy Lynn's Long Halftime Walk*." *Studies in the Novel* 49, no. 3 (2017): 400–18.

Kaiserman, Adam. "Unreality in America: Reading *Billy Lynn's Long Halftime Walk* in a Post-Truth Age." *Critique: Studies in Contemporary American Fiction* 62, no. 5 (2021): 574–85.

Klay, Phil. *Missionaries*. New York: Penguin, 2020.

Klay, Phil. *Redeployment*. New York: Penguin, 2014.

Klay, Phil. *Uncertain Ground: Citizenship in an Age of Endless, Invisible War*. New York: Penguin, 2022.

Kristeva, Julia. *Powers of Horror: An Essay on Abjection*. Translated by Leon S. Roudiez. New York: Columbia University Press, 1982.

Kyle, Chris, with Scott McEwen and Jim DeFelice. *American Sniper: The Autobiography of the Most Lethal Sniper in U.S. Military History*. New York: Harper, 2012.

Kakutani, Michiko. "Human Costs of the Forever Wars, Enough to Fill a Bookshelf." *New York Times*, December 25, 2014. https://www.nytimes.com/2014/12/26 /books/.

Kaveney, Roz. *Superheroes! Capes and Crusaders in Comics and Films*. London: I. B. Tauris, 2008.

Komatsu, Matthew. "The Uncomfortable Whiteness of Contemporary War Literature." *TheMillions*, October 17, 2017. https://themillions.com/2017/10/.

Kyle, Chris, with Scott McEwen and Jim DeFelice. *American Sniper: The Autobiography of the Most Lethal Sniper in U.S. Military History*. New York: Harper, 2012.

Langley, Travis. "Freedom versus Security: The Basic Human Dilemma from 9/11 to Marvel's *Civil War*." In *Marvel Comics' Civil War and the Age of Terror: Critical Essays on the Comic Saga*, edited by Kevin Michael Scott, 69–76. Jefferson, NC: McFarland, 2015.

Lee, Wendy. "Rotten Tomatoes Fights Trolls with New Verified Audience Tool." *Los Angeles Times*, May 23, 2019. https://www.latimes.com/business/hollywood/.

Linebaugh, Heather. "I Worked on the US Drone Program. The Public Should Know What Really Goes On." *The Guardian*, December 29, 2013. https://www.theguardian.com/commentisfree/2013/dec/29/.

Luckhurst, Roger. "Iraq War Body Counts: Reportage, Photography, and Fiction." *Modern Fiction Studies* 63, no. 2 (2017): 355–72.

Luckhurst, Roger. *The Trauma Question*. London: Routledge, 2008.

Manhel, Ghyath. *American and Iraqi Prose Fiction of the Iraq War: Traumas of the Self, Traumas of the Nation*. PhD diss., University of Arkansas, Fayetteville, 2019. https://scholarworks.uark.edu/etd/3558/.

Marcus, Jonathan. "Combat Drones: We Are in a New Era of Warfare—Here's Why." *BBC*, February 4, 2022. https://www.bbc.com/news/world-60047328.

Marston, George. "How the Marvel Universe Became 'Earth-616' and Grew into an Entire Multiverse." *Gamesradar+*, May 10, 2022. https://www.gamesradar.com/marvel-multiverse-earth-616-mcu/.

Mary Shelley's Frankenstein. Directed by Kenneth Branaugh, performances by Kenneth Branaugh and Robert De Niro. TriStar Pictures, 1994.

Masmoudi, Ikram. *War and Occupation in Iraqi Fiction*. Edinburgh: Edinburgh University Press, 2015.

McCammon, Sarah. "The Warfare May Be Remote but the Trauma Is Real." *NPR*, April 24, 2017. https://www.npr.org/2017/04/24/525413427/.

McCann, Colum. "Foreword." In *Fire and Forget: Short Stories from the Long War*, edited by Roy Scranton and Matt Gallagher, vii–xii. Boston: Da Capo Press, 2013.

McSweeney, Terence. *The "War on Terror" and American Film: 9/11 Frames per Second*. Edinburgh: Edinburgh University Press, 2014.

Mann, Joelle. "Mapping Memory: Moving between Trauma and Terror in *The Yellow Birds*." *Critique: Studies in Contemporary Fiction* 5, no. 4 (2017): 340–50.

McGunnigle, Christopher. "The Difference between Heroes and Monsters: Marvel Monsters and Their Transition into the Superhero Genre." *University of Toronto Quarterly* 87, no. 1 (2018): 110–35.

Mendelson, Scott. "Five Years Ago, 'Avatar' Grossed $2.7 Billion but Left No Pop Culture Footprint." *Forbes*, December 18, 2014. https://www.forbes.com/sites/scottmendelson/2014/12/18/.

Mencimer, Stephanie. "Violent Femmes." *Washington Monthly*, September 1, 2001. https://washingtonmonthly.com/2001/09/01/.

Meyer, Sabine. "'Yes, *Avatar* Is *Dances with Wolves* in Space . . . Sorta': Repetitions and Shades of Difference in Two Blockbusters." In *Remakes and Remaking: Concepts, Media, Practices*, edited by Rudiger Heinze and Lucia Kramer, 153–70. Bielefeld, Germany: Transcript-Verlag, 2015.

Miller, Grace. "'Boom/[S]he Is Not': Drone Wars and the Vanishing Pilot." *War, Literature and the Arts* 29 (2017): 1–17.

Molin, Peter. "2011: The Year Contemporary War Fiction Became a Thing." *Time Now: The Wars in Iraq and Afghanistan in Art, Film, and Literature*. August 21, 2015. https://acolytesofwar.com/2015/08/21/.

Molin, Peter. "Black Voices in Contemporary War Writing." *Time Now: The Wars in Iraq and Afghanistan in Art, Film, and Literature*. July 4, 2020. https://acolytesofwar.com/2020/07/04/.

Molin, Peter. "No Thank You for Your Service: Helen Benedict's *Sand Queen*." *Time Now: The Wars in Iraq and Afghanistan in Art, Film, and Literature*. 20 May 2014. https://acolytesofwar.com/2014/05/20/.

Molin, Peter. "A 'Phrase Too Cute to Do Our Ugliness Justice': Portraying 'Wounded Warriors' in Contemporary War Fiction." *War, Literature, and the Arts* 27 (2015): 1–21.

Molin, Peter. "Wayward Warfaring: Black Voices in Contemporary War Writing." Paper presented at the 32nd American Literature Association Annual Conference, Boston, MA, July 2021.

Montogomery, Fielding. "*Rogue One*: A U.S. Imperialism Story." *Journal of Popular Film and Television* 48, no. 1 (2020): 27–37.

Mort, John. "The Booklist Interview: Tim O'Brien." *Booklist* 90 (1994): 1990–91.

Muller, Christine. "Post-9/11 Power and Responsibility in the Marvel Cinematic Universe." In *American Cinema in the Shadow of 9/11*, edited by Terence McSweeney, 269–90. Edinburgh: Edinburgh University Press, 2017.

"Multiverse." Marvel Database. *MarvelFandom*. https://marvel.fandom.com/wiki/.

Murphy, Sinéad. "*Frankenstein in Baghdad*: Human Conditions, or Conditions of Being Human." *Science Fiction Studies* 45, no. 2 (2018): 273–88.

Naaman, Mara. "Landscapes of Iraqi Poetry: Reconfiguring the Image of Iraq in the Arabic (and American) Lyric Canon." *Journal of Arabic Literature* 43 (2012): 336–71.

National Bird. Directed by Sonia Kennebeck, FilmRise, 2016.

Nowotny, Joanna, and Betina Jossen. "The Evil Foreigner: Marvel Villains and the American National Identity from World War II to the War on Terror." In *The Function of Evil across Disciplinary Contexts*, edited by Malcah Effron and Brian Johnson, 165–86. Latham, MD: Lexington Books, 2017.

O'Brien, Tim. *Going after Cacciato*. New York: Delacorte Press, 1978.

O'Brien, Tim. *The Things They Carried*. Boston: Houghton Mifflin, 1990.

O'Gorman, Daniel. "Refiguring Difference: Imaginative Geographies and 'Connective Dissonance' in Three Novels of the Iraq War." *Critique: Studies in Contemporary Fiction* 56, no. 5 (2015): 545–59.

Ondaatje, Michael. *The Conversations: Walter Murch and the Art of Editing Film*. New York: Knopf, 2002.

"One World, One People." *The Falcon and the Winter Soldier*, Season 1, episode 6, directed by Kari Skogland, performances by Anthony Mackie and Sebastian Stan. Disney Studios, April 23, 2021.

Packer, George. "Home Fires: How Soldiers Write Their Wars." *New Yorker*, March 31, 2014. https://www.newyorker.com/magazine/2014/04/07/.

Peebles, Stacey. "Lenses into War: Digital Verité in Iraq War Films." In *The Philosophy of War Films*, edited by David LaRocca, 133–54. Lexington: University Press of Kentucky, 2014.

Peebles, Stacey. *Welcome to the Suck: Narrating the American Soldier's Experience in Iraq*. Ithaca, NY: Cornell University Press, 2011.

Percy, Benjamin. "On the Ground." *New York Times*, October 4, 2012. https://www.nytimes.com/2012/10/07/books/review/.

Petrovic, Paul. "Beyond Appropriation: Arab, Coptic American, and Persian Subjectivities in Brian Turner's *Here, Bullet*, Phil Klay's *Redeployment*, and Elliot Ackerman's *Green on Blue*. *War, Literature, and the Arts* 30 (2018): 1–24.

Pitre, Michael. *Fives and Twenty-Fives*. Bloomsbury, 2014.

Platoon. Directed by Oliver Stone, performances by Charlie Sheen, Willem Dafoe, and Tom Berenger. Orion Pictures, 1986.

Powers, Kevin. *The Yellow Birds.* Boston: Little, Brown, 2012.

Press, Eyal. "The Wounds of the Drone Warrior." *New York Times,* June 13, 2018. https://www.nytimes.com/2018/06/13/magazine/.

Qutait, Tasnim. "Dislocation in Ahmad Saadawi's *Frankenstein in Baghdad* and Hassan Blasim's *The Madman of Freedom Square.*" In *Claiming Space: Locations and Orientations in World Literature,* edited by Bo G. Eklund, Adnan Mahmutovi, and Helena Wulff, 85–110. New York: Bloomsbury, 2022.

Rabin, Nathan. "*Avatar's* Rapid Rise, Sudden Downfall, and Endless *Billy Jack* Connections. *The Dissolve,* January 9, 2015. https://thedissolve.com/features /forgotbusters/.

Randell, Karen. "It Was Like a Movie, Take 2: *Age of Ultron* and a 9/11 Aesthetic." *Cinema Journal* 56, no. 1 (2016): 137–41.

Rihani, Ameen. *The Book of Khalid.* Dodd, Mead, and Company, 1911. https:// www.gutenberg.org/files/29257/.

Rogue One: A Star Wars Story. Directed by Gareth Edwards, performances by Felicity Jones and Diego Luna. Lucasfilm and Walt Disney Studios, 2016.

Saadawi, Ahmed. *Frankenstein in Baghdad.* Translated by Jonathan Wright. New York: Penguin, 2018.

Sanfilippo, Brenda. "Combat Prosthetics: Recovering the Literature of the Wounded Female Soldier in the War on Terror." *Modern Fiction Studies* 63, no. 2 (2017): 225–46.

Saving Private Ryan. Directed by Steven Spielberg, performances by Tom Hanks and Matt Damon. Dreamworks, 1998.

Schedeen, Jesse. "Rosario Dawson's Ahsoka Tano Explained: Who Is the Mandalorian's Jedi?" *IGN,* November 30, 2020. https://www.ign.com/articles/.

Scorsese, Martin. "Martin Scorsese: I Said Marvel Movies Aren't Cinema. Let Me Explain." *New York Times,* November 4, 2019. https://www.nytimes.com/2019 /11/04/opinion/.

Scranton, Roy. "The Trauma Hero: From Wilfred Owen to 'Redeployment' and 'American Sniper.'" *Los Angeles Review of Books,* January 25, 2015. https:// lareviewofbooks.org/article/.

Sellheim, Rudolph, Mohsen Zakeri, François de Blois, and Werner Sundermann. "Fehrest." *Encyclopædia Iranica,* December 15, 1999. https://www.iranicaonline .org/articles/.

Silko, Leslie Marmon. *Ceremony.* New York: Viking, 1977.

Star Wars: The Clone Wars. Directed by Dave Filoni, performances by Matt Lanter and Ashley Eckstein. Lucasfilm, 2008.

Star Wars: Episode III—Revenge of the Sith. Directed by George Lucas, performances by Ewan McGregor, Hayden Christensen, and Natalie Portman. 20th Century Fox, 2005.

Star Wars: The Force Awakens. Directed by J. J. Abrams, performances by Daisy Ridley, Harrison Ford, Adam Driver, and Carrie Fisher. Lucasfilm, 2015.

Star Wars: The Last Jedi. Directed by Rian Johnson, performances by Daisy Ridley, Adam Driver, Carrie Fisher, and Oscar Isaac. Lucasfilm, 2017.

"Star Wars: The Last Jedi." Critics Consensus. Rotten Tomatoes. Accessed 29 March 2020. https://www.rottentomatoes.com/.

Star Wars: The Rise of Skywalker. Directed by J. J. Abrams, performances by Daisy Ridley, Adam Driver, Carrie Fisher, and Mark Hamill. Lucasfilm, 2019.

"Star Wars: The Rise of Skywalker." Critics Consensus. Rotten Tomatoes. Accessed 29 March 2020. https://www.rottentomatoes.com/.

Stone, Robert. *Dog Soldiers.* New York: Houghton Mifflin, 1974.

Tankard, Alex. "Disruption and Disability Futures in *Captain America: The First Avenger* and *Captain America: The Winter Soldier.*" *Journal of Literary and Cultural Disability Studies* 16, no. 1 (2022): 41–57.

Taylor, Bron. "Prologue: *Avatar* as Rorschach." In *Avatar and Nature Spirituality,* edited by Bron Taylor, 3–12. Waterloo, Ontario, Canada: Wilfrid Laurier University Press, 2013.

Taylor, James C. "Reading the Marvel Cinematic Universe: *The Avengers'* Intertextual Aesthetic." *JCMS: Journal of Cinema and Media Studies* 60, no. 3 (2021): 129–56.

Thompson, Lucas. "'PsyOps Works Best When You Mean It': Literary Manipulation in Phil Klay's *Redeployment.*" *Critique: Studies in Contemporary Fiction* 60, no. 2 (2018): 191–204.

"The Thousand and One Nights." Britannica.com. https://www.britannica.com/topic/.

Turner, Brian. *The Dead Peasant's Handbook.* Farmington, ME: Alice James Books, 2023.

Turner, Brian. *Here, Bullet.* Farmington, ME: Alice James Books, 2005.

Turner, Brian. *My Life as a Foreign Country.* New York: W. W. Norton, 2014.

Turrentine, Jeff. "Review: 'Fives and Twenty-Fives,' by Michael Pitre, a Tale of Dangerous Duty in Iraq." *Washington Post,* August 25, 2014. https://www.washingtonpost.com/entertainment/books/.

"Twilight of the Apprentice" *Star Wars: Rebels,* Season 2, episodes 21–22, directed by Dave Filoni, performances by Ashley Eckstein, Matt Lanter, and James Earl Jones. Lucasfilm, March 30, 2016.

Vásquez, Juan Gabriel. "The Intricacies of Colombia's War, Stitched Together in a Novel." *New York Times,* October 6, 2020. https://www.nytimes.com/2020/10/06/books/review/.

Vernon, Alex. "Introduction: No Genre's Land." In *Arms and the Self: War, the Military, and Autobiographical Writing,* edited by Alex Vernon, 1–40. Kent, OH: Kent State University Press, 2005.

Vernon, Alex. "Spectator-Citizen-Soldier: History, Genre, and Gender in *The Hurt Locker.*" *Modern Fiction Studies* 63, no. 2 (2017): 373–96.

Warshow, Robert. "Movie Chronicle: The Westerner." In *Film Theory and Criticism,* 6th ed., edited by Leo Braudy and Marshall Cohen, 703–16. New York: Oxford University Press, 2004.

Watson Institute for International and Public Affairs. *Costs of War.* Providence, RI: Brown University. https://watson.brown.edu/costsofwar/.

Wexler, Joyce. "The New Heroism." *War, Literature, and the Arts: An International Journal of the Humanities* 27 (2015): 1–12.

Whipp, Glenn. "Is *Avatar* a Message Movie? Absolutely, Says James Cameron." *Los Angeles Times,* February 10, 2010. https://www.latimes.com/archives.

Whissel, Kristen. "The Digital Multitude." *Cinema Journal* 49, no. 4 (2010): 90–110.

Williams, Brian. "The Desert of Anatopism: War in the Age of Globalization." *American Literature* 87 no. 2 (2015): 359–85.

Williams, Brian. "The Soldier-Celebrity in *Billy Lynn's Long Halftime Walk*." *Texas Studies in Literature and Language* 59 no. 4 (2017): 524–47.

Williams, Brian. "War at the Home Front: Re-Gendered Trauma Tropes in *You Know When the Men Are Gone*." *Women's Studies: An Interdisciplinary Journal* 48 nos. 5–8 (2019): 510–30.

Williams, Brian. "War's Implications: *Missionaries* and the Global War Novel." *Studies in the Novel* 56 no. 1 (2024): 78-98.

Williams, John. "Writing Differently about the War, but Drawing from the Same Rich Vein." *New York Times*, November 13, 2012. https://www.nytimes.com /2012/11/13/books/.

Williams, Kayla. *Love My Rifle More Than You: Young and Female in the U.S. Army.* New York: W. W. Norton, 2005.

Williams, Kayla. *Plenty of Time When We Get Home: Love and Recovery in the Aftermath of War.* New York: W. W. Norton, 2014.

Wright, Geoffrey. "'A Kind of Misguided Archeology': The Iraq War and Post-modern Memory in Kevin Powers' *The Yellow Birds*." *South Atlantic Review* 84.1 (2019): 105–22.

"The Wrong Jedi." *Star Wars: The Clone Wars.* Season 5, episode 20, directed by Dave Filoni, performances by Matt Lanter and Ashley Eckstein. Lucasfilm, March 2, 2013.

The Yellow Birds. Directed by Alexandre Moors, performances by Alden Ehrenreich and Tye Sheridan. Cinelou Films and Echo Film, 2018.

"The Yellow Birds (2017)." *BoxOfficeMojo.* https://www.boxofficemojo.com/title /tt3739110/.